Dance as Educati
Towards a National Dar

D0321138

ss Library on Aesthetic Education

bbs, University of Sussex, UK

Setting the ran

LIVING POWERS:
The Arts in Education
Edited by Peter Abbs

A IS FOR AESTHETIC:
Essays on Creative and Aesthetic
Education
Peter Abbs

THE SYMBOLIC ORDER:
A Contemporary Reader on the
Arts Debate
Edited by Peter Abbs

THE RATIONALITY OF
FEELING:
Understanding the Arts in
Education
David Best

The Individual Studies

FILM AND TELEVISION IN
EDUCATION:
An Aesthetic Approach to the
Moving Image
Robert Watson

LITERATURE AND
EDUCATION:
Encounter and Experience
Edwin Webb

DANCE AS EDUCATION:
Towards a National Dance Culture
Peter Brinson

THE VISUAL ARTS IN
EDUCATION
Rod Taylor

MUSIC EDUCATION IN
THEORY AND PRACTICE
Charles Plummeridge

THE ARTS IN THE PRIMARY
SCHOOL
Glennis Andrews and Rod Taylor

EDUCATION IN DRAMA:
Casting the Dramatic Curriculum
David Hornbrook

Work of Reference

KEY CONCEPTS:
A Guide to Aesthetics, Criticism and the Arts in Education
Trevor Pateman

Dance as Education
Towards a National
Dance Culture

Peter Brinson

 The Falmer Press

(A member of the Taylor & Francis Group)
London • New York • Philadelphia

321347
792.807041
BRI
xx

GV1589.B75

UK   The Falmer Press, Rankine Road, Basingstoke, Hampshire RG24 0PR

USA   The Falmer Press, Taylor & Francis Inc., 1900 Frost Road, Suite 101, Bristol, PA 19007

© Peter Brinson 1991

All rights reserved. No part of this publication may be reproduced, stored in a retrieval system, or transmitted in any form or by any means, electronic, mechanical, photocopying, recording or otherwise, without permission in writing from the Publisher.

First published 1991   Reprinted 1993

British Library Cataloguing in Publication Data
Brinson, Peter
    Dance as education: towards a national dance culture.
    (Falmer Press library on aesthetic education).
    1. Great Britain. Education. Curriculum subjects: Dance
    I. Title
    792.807041

    ISBN 1-85000-716-0
    ISBN 1-85000-717-9 pbk

Library of Congress Cataloging-in-Publication Data available on request

Jacket design by Benedict Evans

Typeset in 11/12 pt Bembo by
Graphicraft Typesetters Ltd., Hong Kong

Printed in Great Britain by Burgess Science Press, Basingstoke on paper which has a specified pH value on final paper manufacture of not less than 7.5 and is therefore 'acid free'.

Contents

Contents

Dedicated
to the Unity of British Dance Culture —
all of it

List of Illustrations

Preface

There is a great need for a broad and vital understanding of dance in our society; of dance seen as an artistic form of expression crossing all cultures with a long variegated past and a rich present. Strangely such a broad understanding is absent not only among the populace at large, but also among most arts teachers, and, it must be said, even among a significant number of dance teachers and dance practicioners. This volume *Dance as Education* with its telling subtitle *Towards a National Dance Culture* sets out to provide the historical, political and structural elements necessary for such an understanding. It seeks to educate the reader not only about dance in the curriculum (though that is the major concern in two chapters of the book), but also about dance as an expressive and transformative energy throughout the whole of society. It is not a study made from a detached position; nor does it seek any kind of neutrality. It is an engaged study committed from the outset to the major premise that dance is a great art discipline which belongs to all people and should be made fully accessible to all people, a necessary element of the good society in the Athenian tradition, as defined by David Aspin in *The Symbolic Order*.

The need for such a volume is brought out by many of the facts and figures which Peter Brinson draws on. For example, from the Arts Council of Great Britain's total yearly budget of £200 million only £15 million are designated to dance. The bare figures alone dramatize an act of injustice. In our educational system, only 50 per cent of our schools actually offer dance to their pupils and in the majority of cases still exclude the male sex. But perhaps the most dramatic sign of gross misunderstanding in our times is the present Government's insistence that dance should be seen as a subordinate part of Physical Education. The only sustained references to dance in the National Curriculum documents are to be found in the HMI pamphlet *Physical Education from 5 to 16*. The absence of *dance* in that title is indicative of a gross act of intellectual suppression. For at least

the past two decades in education dance had been slowly but de-
finitively moving away from its uncomfortable position within PE.
As Anna Haynes made clear in her historical analysis of dance in
Living Powers, and as Peter Brinson further confirms in chapter 3 of
this volume, dance had come into its own in education through the
realization that it was an *aesthetic discipline belonging generically with the
other great arts disciplines.* The primary concern of dance is with the
expressive exploration and creation of moral meaning and spiritual
value through the medium of the body — and this in no way is a
central characteristic of PE. The attempt simply to amalgamate dance
and PE — making PE the dominant category — is therefore a sign
both of suppression and, more generally, of the problematic status of
dance in our culture. Certainly, until the confusion is confronted and
resolved with reference to the arguments proposed in this study there
can be no adequate realization of the power of dance in our state
schools.

Yet dance needs also a major expansion from within. In *Living
Powers* Anna Haynes called for a philosophical reformulation in
which dance reclaimed its past, delineated its diversity of forms, and
developed simultaneously a critical and scholarly dimension. It was
a question, she argued, of dance re-entering its own *aesthetic field,* of
making dynamic and structural contact with its whole grammar, its
diversity of styles and functions. Throughout this study Peter Brinson
amplifies and develops that call for a rich pluralism. Again and again,
he insists on a vision of dance which is inclusive; which can recognize
and relate to a diversity of expressive forms: from classical to contemporary, from folk dance to Asian dance, from jazz to reggae and
disco. Furthermore, he insists that mime is a necessary artistic and
historic element of the national dance culture he is advocating. Wherever the body is the prime means of expressive articulation there lies,
it might be said, the impulse that characterizes dance. Furthermore, in
relationship to critical studies and illuminative understanding, Peter
Brinson calls also for *a historical and political placing of expressive forms.*
What is meant by this is brought out well in the opening chapters
which provide a history of dance in our own culture over the last two
hundred years in relationship to social and industrial development.

Within this enlarged field of dance and dance education, a field
which radically breaks open protective coteries and class barriers, the
author would seem to be most critical of Post-Modernism. His de-
scription of Post-Modernism seems very close to what was designated
as Late Modernism in *Living Powers* and *A is for Aesthetic.* Different
definitions can be somewhat confusing, especially when they cross
over from one art form to another. Yet what Peter Brinson is questioning is precisely that essential emptiness of content attacked earlier
in the series which comes when all the artistic attention is given to the

structural elements of an art-form and nothing to its human significa-
tion. What we are strongly resisting is a kind of 'art for art's sake'
where no challenge is made on understanding, where there is no
engaged exploration of the human predicament. A pure, unremitting
and sustained formalism leaves both soul and society unprovoked and
undeveloped. In contrast, art engaged aesthetically with human
experience animates, develops, renews. In this crucial matter one great
example of the power of art lies daily under our noses, namely, the
revolution in eastern Europe; a revolution which was articulated and
largely lead by art-makers and intellectuals. Here we can discern the
power of the arts to represent freedom, solidarity and moral values
and to make those energies potent in the consciousness of society. It
is, therefore, no accident that one image that runs like a subterranean
current through this book is that of eastern Europe and, particularly,
of Czechoslovakia. A whole concept of a democratic Athenian aesthetic, a concept at the heart of the Aesthetic Education Library, is boldly
embodied there.

This book, then, is a broad, multi-faceted study of dance. It
considers not only the issues to which I have already drawn attention
but many others including: community arts, the politics of grant-
giving, dance and ecology, current movements in dance, the emerging global society, the narrowing power of comfortable audiences in
the consumer society, and the current reorganization of national funding for the arts. Readers are urged to consider closely the titles of the
chapters and the organization of the book. The first part is devoted to
an examination of dance culture within the theatre over the last two
hundred years; the second part to dance in education and the community. The dance practitioner, therefore, may well want to follow
the sequence of the book; but the dance teacher or the person committed to dance in the community may prefer to turn to the second half
first and then return to the opening two chapters. In brief, readers are
urged to read as their interests dictate but, nevertheless, as the aim of
the book is to engender a conception of a comprehensive dance culture, it is hoped that whatever segment is taken first, the whole
volume is eventually encompassed.

What matters, finally, is that the power of dance is fully recognized both in society at large and in all of our schools. Towards the
end of the book Peter Brinson confesses to one of his fantasies. He
writes:

> I imagine for myself a fantasy. It is of the forces of dance
> arrayed against the constraints of prejudice, hegemony, in-
> adequate aesthetic education, poverty of resources and internal
> division. The aim is to replace these constraints with alter-
> native values where prejudice and the rest will wither. The

battlefield extends beyond the United Kingdom to all the world where we have allies and into the airways of radio and television. We are assembled under the National Organization for Dance and Mime in a unity which has always been our hope.

This book will have served its purpose well if it begins to move its readers towards that vision and helps to secure the place of dance and mime in all our schools within a fully articulated arts education. There is much to fight for. This book gives dance practitioners and dance teachers their weapons.

Peter Abbs
Centre for Language, Literature and the Arts in Education
University of Sussex.
June 1990

Introduction

My personal philosophy holds that there is but one society on earth of humans, animals, fish and plants, interdependent, indivisible. They must live therefore together. The same is true of human cultures, material and non-material. This book deals with one aspect of non-material culture, the dance. In writing it, it became clear that dance cannot be separated from other aspects of culture — non-material like sport, education at all levels, and ideas of politics, economics, aesthetics; material like consumer society and dancers' pay and conditions. Like other cultures, too, dance is a paradox upheld by achievement and devotion on the one hand, threatened by prejudice and an hegemony of entrenched attitudes on the other hand.

All this I have tried to embrace helped by the fact that this book is part of the Falmer Press series on aesthetic education. For this series Peter Abbs has examined many of the broader aesthetic issues in *Living Powers, A is for Aesthetic* and *The Symbolic Order*, which constituted the first three volumes. I am indebted also to the UK Branch of the Calouste Gulbenkian Foundation not only for its seminal reports on *The Arts in Schools* (1982) and *Dance Education and Training in Britain* (1980), but also for later studies partly inspired by these reports like *Artists in Schools* (1990), Paul Willis' *Common Culture* and *Moving Culture* (both 1990) and the three-year Arts in Schools Project of the School Curriculum Development Committee under the National Curriculum Council (1990). These later works, appearing after my book had been drafted but reflecting research in greater depth than I could manage, caused me to re-write substantial sections, as did ministerial proposals to reorganize the Arts Council appearing at the same time. I am grateful for the patience of my editors during this re-write.

The book, therefore, considers dance from the point of view of aesthetic imagination, national culture and the sources of power which condition the uses of this culture. At the same time it is a personal document because dance is part of the fabric of my life. When I came

into dance a long time ago I was told that dance spoke of the unknown and was a gift of the gods. There is truth still in some of this
though the belief looks back to 1920s expressionism and to the sacred
dances of prehistory. Soon I learned what a hard world dance really is
— 'product' to theatre managers. To dancers, as Madame Rambert
used to say, it is 10 per cent art and 90 per cent perspiration. I learned
too how trusting and vulnerable is this world. It doesn't pay half
enough attention to the powers and politics which have sustained it,
or cast it down, throughout history. Nor does it project itself sufficiently into today's material society and argue cogently its point of
view and aesthetics. It becomes attached only belatedly to the mod-
ernisms, post-modernisms and other movements which have affected
so profoundly the painters, film-makers and writers. It trusts too
much.

This book is a result of such feelings, an argument that if dance
is to play its civilizing role, join the struggle against philistines, win
more and more people to understand its symbols and relationships, it
must establish its culture in a country whose imagination is not visual
but verbal and which, to be honest, is frightened of dance. British
people are frightened of their bodies, of physicality and the sins of the
body they learned at school. Dance in our culture has all this to fight
against. If it wins it will liberate in the process much of the guilt, the
snobberies and constrictions which plague modern society. We shall
be a more human and confident people if we can draw from dance
clearer images of ourselves, how things were and how they could be.

All this is a personal view. It is not common even in a dance
culture which has grown enormously over fifty years despite its
problems. I have sought help from many areas of this culture, their
friendships and antagonisms. As a result this is not a book specifically
about the art form nor about dance in education, community dance,
the dance cultures of south Asia, Africa and the Caribbean which are
enriching British dance culture. It is about all these things, acknow-
ledging too that social dance in commercial circumstances, recreational dance and folk dance traditions going back at least to the eighth
century are part of the same culture.

The book, therefore, is divided into three parts — In the Theatre,
Outside the Theatre, and a series of short pieces on specific aspects of
dance culture presented as appendices. The chapters are so arranged
that particular interests can be approached at once without reading the
whole book. Questions in the title of each chapter indicate the theme.
Thus teachers in schools might wish to turn at once to chapter 3;
workers in community dance to chapter 5. The errors they may find
will be mine, but for whatever is stimulating in the book my thanks
belong to scholars and friends who have helped me with advice and
generous time. They are too many to list in detail because I have

drawn on the experience of a life in dance — time with the Royal Ballet and other dance companies, large and small; time among community dancers across the country; time among teachers from primary schools to colleges, polytechnics and universities; time in the private sector of dance training, especially the Laban Centre for Movement and Dance, London Contemporary Dance School and the major bodies of classical ballet; time in very many theatres, dance spaces and dance situations throughout the United Kingdom; time outside the UK in Europe, Canada, Australia and Hong Kong; time among funding bodies and sponsors; time among critics, press officers and media representatives; time among scholars; time in conferences and committees; time among young people learning at the Weekend Arts College and dancing in discos and youth dance groups; time among the elderly and disabled.

There are, though, some I must thank specifically. First those who have read and commented on sections of the book — Dr North, Dr Bird and Chris Thomson of the Laban Centre; Jill Henderson, education officer of Birmingham Royal Ballet formerly with the Arts in Schools Project; Linda Jasper, Lucy Perman, Marie McCluskey and Janet Archer of the Community Dance and Mime Foundation. Second Peter Abbs and Werdon Anglin. Peter Abbs commissioned the book and proved to be a marvellously creative editor. Werdon Anglin was my essential aid, critic and administrator throughout what became a large project. Third the haematology department of St Thomas's Hospital, London, without whose skill and care there would have been no book.

Part 1
In the Theatre

Chapter 1

Is There a British Dance Culture

To talk about dance is to talk about you and you and me. Dancing, as I have said often before, is part of the history of human movement, part of the history of human culture and part of the history of human communication. Not for nothing were the English in Tudor times known throughout Europe as the dancing English. English men excelled especially in the leaps and athleticism of the galliard. Today the British are leaders still in dancing. They are the reference point in international ballroom dancing. Scottish dance is vibrant, not only in Scotland, but also in New Zealand, Canada and wherever Scottish people have settled. They dance still the sword dance in north-east England, the clog dance in Lancashire, and the Morris and other traditional dances in the Midlands, the south and in Cornwall. In the culture of our young people dance is linked closely with making and participating in popular music. Our youth dance companies and student companies are welcome visitors in Europe, south-east Asia and the USA. Our disabled and elderly are devising their own choreographic forms. We are embarked on the great adventure of exploring and learning the dance cultures of citizens from Asia and the Caribbean just as we have done over centuries with dance forms from Europe. As many tickets are sold each week for dance halls and discos as are sold for football matches and the cinema.

In dance halls and discos people are their own choreographers, varying rhythms and steps, well-known or new, the way their bodies and tastes dictate. Elsewhere in theatres, schools, private studios and community spaces other dances are choreographed and invented. Choreographers like Kenneth MacMillan, Christopher Bruce, Royston Maldoom, Lloyd Newson and Richard Alston are international figures in their art. Our companies like the Royal Ballet, London Contemporary Dance Theatre, Rambert Dance Company, DV8 and others rank high among the dance companies of the world. Our teachers and teaching methods in classical ballet and modern dance, ballroom and national dance are in demand across the world.

The commercial side of dance often is underrated but is important not only because of its recreational and social value. It extends people's dance horizons, allows them to dance on their own terms and to exercise personal creativity in incidental dance invention, their own choreography. It is a huge field which I would like to examine further some day alongside our folk dance legacy. It is the bedrock of our dance culture. The other side of our dance culture is what is explored and invented in schools, community situations, private dance studios and on stage. It too is a huge field with urgent problems of financial support, audience support and, above all, public communication. Nevertheless it is the element of our dance culture through which we make sense at many levels, and interpret in dance terms, our complex post-modern world of electronic revolution, global economy and growing global culture. This, therefore, is what I consider here always against the background of popular dance culture and dance interest.

Today's Theatre Dance

During a week in March 1990 the Royal Ballet was rehearsing in London after two weeks showing *La Bayadère* and MacMillan's new *The Prince of the Pagodas* in Birmingham and Manchester. Sadler's Wells Royal Ballet was in Christchurch, New Zealand, showing *Swan Lake*. Rambert Dance Company at Sadler's Wells Theatre, London, presented three programmes of post-modern dance which explored new ground and confirmed old prejudices. English National Ballet, seeking a new artistic director after dismissing Peter Schauffus, rehearsed in London while its smaller group, ENB2, took to Scunthorpe Civic Theatre, then Basildon's Towngate Theatre, a successful mix of works by Paul Taylor, Christopher Bruce, José Limon and August Bournonville — two American, one English and one Danish choreographer. At the Queen's Hall Arts Centre, Hexham, on England's Roman Wall against the Picts and Scots, London Contemporary Dance Theatre's programme revealed changing directions under its new American director/choreographer, Dan Wagoner. Like the green shoots of that year's early spring there were signs of a revival in the company's creative fortunes. Further north, at the Theatre Royal, Glasgow, Scottish Ballet explored American and Soviet styles through a triple bill of Balanchine's *Scotch Symphony* and *Who Cares?*, alongside a Soviet-produced, very classical *Paquita*. Still in the north, Northern Ballet Theatre finished showing its new *Giselle* to Sunderland before doing the same the following week in the Welsh capital, Cardiff. London City Ballet, meanwhile, took its new classical *La Traviata* to the Orchard Theatre, Dartford. Back in London, near Euston Station, the Place Theatre's annual *Spring Loaded* season reminded funding bodies that new or newish programmes of post-modern choreography can attract full houses of mostly young people.

In this sort of way London Contemporary Dance Trust at the Place and the Laban Centre with its Bonnie Bird Theatre in south-east London have become flagship organizations for a spreading audience conversion towards modern dance adventure and alternative dance forms from Britain's multi-racial society. Such developments are modifying not only the legacies of Martha Graham and Rudolf Laban but even classical ballet itself. As if to make the point, the annual Laban Centre Bonnie Bird Awards for new choreography were announced at the beginning of that week at the Royal Festival Hall on London's South Bank. In the Centre itself the showcase student company, Transitions, rehearsed its spring tour and London Contemporary Dance School's 4th Year Performance Group did much the same at the Place. These are part of a missionary movement for post-modern dance spreading across Britain. Pioneers of the movement like the Rosemary Butcher Dance Company appeared the same week at Nottingham University and at art galleries in Lincoln, Sheffield and Liverpool. The Welsh group, Diversions, was seen at the Marina Theatre, Lowestoft, and the black male Phoenix Dance Company appeared at Barnsley Civic Theatre. Shobana Jeyasingh's Dance Theatre appeared at the Wilde Theatre, Bracknell, in a programme of classical Indian dance styles and the African-inspired company Kokuma appeared at the Blackfriars Arts Centre, Boston — both symbols of dance forms now part of British dance culture and beginning to influence British choreography. Chisenhale Dance Space presented its Spring Collection 2 in London's East End. The all-women Cholmondeleys danced at the Gardner Centre, Brighton, and the all-male Featherstonehaughs at Warrington, Leigh and Crewe in England's north-west, both born of the Laban Centre. At the week's end there happened at the Baylis Theatre in London's Islington a remarkable range of choreography by a single artist, Royston Maldoom. Called *Across the Board* because its many dances embraced amateurs and future professionals, young and old, dance styles and themes from many races to many kinds of music, lighting, video, sound and design artists as well as dancers, this day of community dance symbolized a little of the future of Britain's dance culture.

Much else went on behind and on stage. Festivals like Dance Umbrella planned their seasons for later in the year; private funding bodies like Gulbenkian and Digital continued endless assessments of applications for help; the Arts Council's dance department pondered different ways to distribute inadequate government support for dance; so did Regional Arts Associations, all in turmoil from threatening plans to reorganize Arts Council procedures and priorities. Groups or choreographers like Second Stride and Siobhan Davies, Adventures in Motion Pictures and DV8, Kokuma and Gregory Nash prepared new programmes. Amici and Common Ground Theatre developed further the theatrical creativity of disabled people. Musical shows with dance either continued long runs in London, like *Cats* and *The Phantom of the Opera*, or toured these shows outside London, like *Show Boat* to Stratford's Royal Shakespeare Theatre or *42nd Street* to Southampton. The critics criticized and professional journals like *Dance and Dancers, Dance Theatre Journal* and *The Dancing Times* recorded, commented, advertised.

This was a week in the life of the performance side of British dance culture. It embraced many musicians, theatre technicians, administrators, secretaries, transport staff, writers, advertisers, designers, lighting artists, costume makers, wig makers, shoe makers, dieticians, medical specialists, physiotherapists, businesspeople, film crews, television teams, theatre staffs, travel agents, dance teachers, producers, audiences of many tastes — all relating to the 2,000 or so professional dancers who actually performed. Many thousands of people were involved and many millions of pounds were turned over, not counting the educational dance world, the community dance world, and popular social dancing.

The Modernist Impact

Every industrialized society has a theatrical dance culture of this kind, generated primarily in urban centres. Dance, after all, is a primitive response in each of us to the seen and unseen world in which we live. Our response in rhythmic movement is a fundamental expression of human nature, human emotion, human nurture and human communication, as primary as a primary colour. Therefore dance with music is the oldest of the arts. The questions we should really ask are not whether there is a British dance culture, but whose dance culture? Is it appropriate to the Britain we have today? What animates this culture? Who decides the taste which it displays? Why are the dances it dances like they are?

The days are gone when dance in Britain meant only classical ballet, Mecca dancing, folk dance, tea dances, or the charity balls of polite society. Dance means these things still, but it means also the many forms of contemporary or modern dance taking place in a single week of dance performance. It means community dance in inner cities; youth dance groups across the country; the dance forms of

Britain's many new racial communities; disco dance and other urban folk dance inventions by young people; and the visits of dance companies and styles from abroad. Especially it means dance in education at all levels from primary to higher and further education touching many disciplines like aesthetics, anatomy, anthropology, history, languages, philosophy, psychology, sociology, therapy and, of course, all the arts. At some point, briefly or always, dance touches everyone. The vigorous twentieth-century expansion of dance runs parallel with the expansion of industrial/electronic/nuclear technology, industry and manufacture, international trade, agriculture, transport and the consumer economy within which we live. To its traditional arts the century has added cinema, television and photography. Obviously there is a connection between dance and all these changes. The changes provide not only the social and economic context within which dance takes place today, but also the values which influence the creation of dance. Kenneth MacMillan's *Elite Syncopations* for the Royal Ballet and Christopher Bruce's *Ghost Dances* for the Rambert Dance Company illustrate this truism, but almost every work of dance art created since 1900 in every industrialized country in some way bears the mark of twentieth century technology. It follows that unless choreographers, teachers, dancers and dance students understand how life around them influences dance and for what they are creating dance, the art of dance will be marginal to urban society, lacking in influence, a minority concern within the rest of British culture.

This does not mean that dancers and dance teachers need at once to become students of politics, economics and international affairs. It does mean they should have acquired some understanding of these influences at school so that they can recognize the social forces in each period whose dances they dance and take account of outside influences in the creation of new work. For example, the dominant influence upon all theatrical dance in advanced industrialized countries this century comes from the modernist and post-modernist movements in art. These movements have shaped the dance we see in our theatres and much of the thinking behind the organization which brings this dance to audiences. Therefore, too, the movements have affected the taste and expectations of audiences partly through education and partly through the creative work of choreographers on stage and in films and television in reaction to the ways of thinking and the arguments which animate these movements. For this reason our first response to questions about dance culture must be to consider the images of dance art which choreographers create. Later we shall examine the interrelation of these images with the educational process and with many other aspects of British life.

Some historical parallels can illuminate the issues of modernism and post-modernism which have shaped the dance art within our dance culture. There are comparisons which can be made between the birth of romantic ballet in the 1830s and the birth of modernism in the arts in the early 1900s just as there are between the decay of romantic ballet at the end of the nineteenth century and post-modern dance in the 1960s and 1970s, especially in the USA. The fact that we involve the USA indicates another important parallel, a parallel between the globalization of culture since the second world war — that is, the merchandising of the arts on an international scale like pop music, cinema and fine art auctions through television, sound tapes, discs and other technologies — and the globalization of the economy in the same period. Two sides of the same dollar. The arts, of course, including dance, have been transnational for a very long time. Globalization through technological development is the latest step in an historial process. Because of this we must discuss Britain's dance culture today always with reference to other countries — the USA and USSR, France and central Europe, even Japan, the West Indies, India, South America and Africa.

There is, therefore, a deep connection between modernism in the arts and modernism in industry, life-style and public values worldwide. Similarly, of course, between post-modernism in the arts and the post-modern world of Vietnam, Nixon, Reagan and Thatcher. There may be now new departures in the arts after the events of 1989 in eastern Europe. For a long time the dance world in the theatre and in education has not paid much attention to the influence of political and economic change upon dance forms and dance content. The influence is acknowledged, of course, when one actually puts the question in a dressing room discussion or over a meal, but usually it is passed over quickly because changes in manufacturing methods, the growth of consumer society and what happens in Parliament seem rather remote, even contrary to 'art'. The treatment of dance in schools as a physical education subject, rather than an art like drama, reinforces this separation of dance from a common context with other arts. Dance in the curriculum is seen as adding a gloss of 'expression' to physical movement. It is useful, perhaps, in gymnastics but otherwise of little value in a games-centred syllabus. No wonder it becomes marginalized, a minority concern throughout the lives of most of those thus 'educated'.

History shows very clearly the error of this attitude. The romantic movement which gave us *La Sylphide* (1832), *Giselle* (1841) and the popular image of classical ballet today was born out of the huge social changes set in motion by the Industrial Revolution, starting in England at the end of the eighteenth century. This changed all the arts and revolutionized theatrical dancing in four important ways. First it altered the *status* of the art and its creators, confirming a development over the previous half century. Generally speaking, it replaced the patronage of court and nobility — never an ideal way to support the arts anyway — with a commodity status for the arts rather like the emphasis on market forces today. The Paris Opéra was turned into a private enterprise under Dr Véron from 1830. His entrepreneurial skills and clever publicity helped to personify romantic ballet in Marie Taglioni's *Sylphide* and in Fanny Elssler's passionate *Cachucha*. Similarly Her Majesty's Theatre, London, under Benjamin Lumley brought to England all the great ballerinas of the romantic era. From 1842 to 1848, thanks to the partnership of Lumley with Jules Perrot, romantic ballet's greatest choreographer, London became the creative centre of romantic ballet in Europe. In many ways, therefore, the introduction of new commercial practices at that time had positive results for the arts. The role and social impact of the arts were enhanced. Their communication reached to a broader public.

What communication? Véron and Lumley were successful because the ballets they presented caught a public mood in their themes and dance style. In its social appeal Romanticism reacted against the artificiality of themes from antiquity and the idealization of noble patrons in portraits which characterized the eighteenth century. Instead, the romantic endeavour looked to a future of imaginative truth overturning established custom. As Gautier observed at the time, young people wore their hair long and shocked their elders with strange clothes, new habits and different values. The romantic vision stirred artists the way revolutionary visions stirred new styles in 1917, 1968 and 1989. Then and since the artist stepped forward as social critic and rebel. William Blake proclaimed his new Jerusalem; Burns satirized convention and Shelley cocked a snook at establishment morals. For all of them the essential conflict lay between the world as it had become and the vision of a more generous alternative, between squalor and wealth, ugliness and 'beauty', reality and dreams of far away peoples in exotic lands, history become romance, a refuge in some supernatural world of unattainable love.

Such became the images of ballet from 1832 onwards. After the change in status, therefore, new themes were the second great change in theatrical dance stimulated by the new culture and values of industrialism. Of course the influence of this material culture was indirect and historically indeterminate. It was manifest first in England through poetry and the novel. Dance was last, a generation later. In between, painting, music, the drama all adopted the new themes and attitudes to life. The third change came naturally and ran in parallel. It was advances in *technique*. New techniques sought to realize better the new themes. In dance new methods of training explored the air to represent ethereality and mystery, to defy gravity by rising from the ground *sur la pointe* or fly above the ground in effortless jumps.

9

Techniques of the novel and poetry changed also to meet the new demands. So did the composition of music and the role of the actor and the format of dramatic presentation. The appurtenances of art were extended. Gaslight entered the theatre; the proscenium curtain separated stage and auditorium; a new style of dress was devised to represent the ethereal beings ruling the ballet stage. Today the romantic skirt influences still the feminine silhouette.

Dance was special in its refashioning of the instrument because the instrument is the human body. Change therefore became more than new sounds and conceptions through which Beethoven and Berlioz revolutionaized the orchestra. Being human, and communicating emotions through movement, the changed dance instrument emphasized also another aspect of reality at the time, the attitude of society to women and the female form. The nineteenth century displacement of men by women on the ballet stage was more than a triumph of physical achievement and artistry to create a different kind of focus for the new choreography. It reflected also sexual attitudes towards women and that total exploitation of women, the property of men, which was a nineteenth century characteristic. To make the point, entrepreneurs and public insisted more and more on feats of virtuoso display by women at the expense of exploring the themes which originally had brought the new middle-class audience into the ballet theatre.

Thus the romantic ballet became degraded. *Coppélia*, its last manifestation in 1870, showed the nature of change. On the one hand considerable development of choreographic skill in narrative dance, continuing brilliance in dance technique, especially in the adaptation of national dances from eastern Europe, and a major advance in ballet music through Delibes' use of leitmotif and the symphonic form. On the other hand the romantic formula of *La Sylphide* and *Giselle* in a setting of rural beauty was appropriate no longer to an urbanized, industrialized world. *Coppélia*'s theme reflected a new public interest in automata and other scientific experiments. The national dances in St Leon's well-crafted choreography and Delibes' brilliant score were in tune with Europe's rising national feelings. The male lead, Franz, was danced *en travestie* by a woman, confirming the sexual focus on women, while the male dancer was eliminated from all but character roles on all dance stages outside Russia, Denmark and some countries of eastern Europe. The elevation of Woman was complete and dance art was demeaned. Such were the aesthetic perceptions of the ballet stage on the eve of the modernist revolution.

In Russia the creation of *The Sleeping Beauty* and *Swan Lake* in 1890 and 1894-5 show similar contradictions but held other lessons in considering the modernist project. They demonstrated for example that the hegemony of a particular social order is not reproduced automatically in the arts of the day. Historically the arts do not move according to the bias of social and economic forces, except in very general terms. Nor do they all advance at an even pace, one with another as the laggard development of romantic ballet shows. In Russia at the end of nineteenth century there is the paradox of a decaying political order within which the creation of two ballets, *The Sleeping Beauty* and *Swan Lake*, together represent the highest achievement of a new classical style replacing the romantic style. *Swan Lake* in its second act (the lakeside scene by the choreographer Ivanov) signalled particularly the establishment of the Russian School of Classical Ballet as the fourth great school in Europe, drawing inspiration from the ideals of romantic ballet. At the same time their themes, especially of *The Sleeping Beauty* recalling the court of Louis XIV, marked them as the product of a regime frozen in an established imperial style. The style was characterized in the theatre by a narrow circle of balletomanes and supporters whose perceptions and prejudices derived from a worship of feminine dance technique within rigid social conventions. Nothwithstanding this regime the ballets survived because they were masterpieces of choreographic form through the genius of Petipa and Ivanov combined with the musical inspiration of Tchaikovsky.

Dance works, then, are a choreographic adaptation of dance heritage to the ideas and influences of the time in which they appear. The adaptation may confirm those ideas, as most new dance works do in England today, or challenge those ideas, as many theatre works did in eastern Europe during 1989. Whichever choice is made the result gives visual form to some part of current perceptual experience. This perception comprises what Peter Abbs in *Living Powers*[1] calls sensuous and imaginative impressions and feelings rather than any literal documentation of facts. There lies the power and longevity of art.

Whence come these sensuous and imaginative impressions? The development of modernism in the arts suggests that they come from the influence of material culture and material change — machines, commerce, trade — acting upon non-material culture of which dance, painting, music, drama, cinema are a part. This is not a view adopted by many dance writers, but consider the rise of the Diaghilev ballet. This gave expression to the criticisms of Fokine, its first choreographer, against the aesthetics and, as he saw it, the emptiness of Petipa's classicism in, say, *The Sleeping Beauty*. Fokine stood for the restoration of content to choreography, for an end to outdated conventions, for forms of movement appropriate to the subject matter and time and character of the music rather than clinging to fixed steps; for dance and mime to express a dramatic situation through the whole body used as a means of expression and thus for whole groups of dancers used for the same purpose. Finally he stood for the equality of dance with music and design to make the whole work greater than its parts. This was his aesthetic perception, the overture to modernism in dance. In reproducing Fokine today or Petipa or any choreographer of the past, including Ashton and Balanchine, it is the aesthetic perception one should seek to represent rather than some static reproduction of their period movement. One should ask what does the aesthetic perception of a time, as expounded in a dance work, have for people today. Thus one retains the romantic or classical perception as far as possible, but it will be modified by today's perceptions formed within the dominant cultural climate.

Fokine, and the young artists and composers with whom he worked, gave an early Russian response to the questioning of former stabilities in religion, politics, morality and social behaviour which began to affect the perceptions of his day throughout Europe. What had seemed fixed became fallible and changeable. Different perceptions of reality emerged from new knowledge of psychological states and new images based on the work of Freud and Jung, and the invention of photography. Therefore artists reached out to explore the collective mind and an extended sense of time embracing past, present and future all in one work. Here was 'inner' as well as 'outer' reality, the soul of Fokine's Petrouchka in his cell as well as everyday St Petersburg where the Showman displayed Petrouchka's outer form. In single works of art artists began thus to seek to reproduce the many-sidedness of new realities which science and technology were revealing. The world of the twentieth century was far more complex than had been supposed. The microscope discovered new, minute realities of shapes and colours. The aeroplane began Man's exploration of the huge realities of space. The structure of reality itself, of the material world, was investigated in ways which extended humanity's self-knowledge and therefore the styles, methods and visions of artists. This was the essence of literary and artistic modernism. It is the justification of my social approach to modernism in dance.

The seeds of this modernism were sown in impressionism by the advent of photography, the fleeting instant captured by the camera. Symbolist poetry of the same period stressed the absolute significance of words to clean the windows of perception.[2] Presently painters sought to emulate this approach by representing emotion directly on to canvas and choreographers, at all times communicating through symbols, absorbed from the symbolists a wider symbolic reference. Jointly impressionism and symbolism played John the Baptist for modernist forms to come. Of these the most influential in dance were cubism, futurism, constructivism, surrealism and expressionism. All have their origins before the first world war. All were modified in British dance culture by the parochial nature of this culture, its rigid class system and traditional attitudes engendered by the system.

Nevertheless, among all the arts the totality of modernist forms represents a new kind of culture, modernist culture, arising from technological advances, urbanization, the extending influence of international finance, imperialism and the values, or reaction to the values, of new forms of social organization and social life arising at the end of the nineteenth century to affect all Europe.

Since all theatrical dance and most choreography reflects this influence it is necessary to understand its consequence for the British dance scene. Cubism began among painters whose vision of the object world was as varied, multi-dimensional and ever-changing as human perceptions of it. Thereby a new modernist realism was postulated, constructed, rational, positive and based on an argued analysis. It reorganized reality on canvas (reconstructing, for example, the human form), developing the notion of constant change and alteration in the organization of society and its ideas; not evolution but revolution. Proclaiming such attitudes cubism influenced all other artists, including choreographers, as Nijinski showed in *L'Après-midi d'un Faune* and *Le Sacre du Printemps*. It became the progenitor of left-wing art movements, particularly in central Europe and Russia. It fuelled — even drew together — other movements in the general climate of artistic deconstruction and reconstruction before the first world war.

Futurism provided in some degree additional arguments for the attack on established art forms. Launched in 1909 with a manifesto by the Italian poet, Marinetti, it represented in extreme form reaction against the past and approval of the speed and technological potential of the twentieth century. Thus it argued the necessary breakdown of traditional forms of text in literature. Later the futurist movement condemned all that smacked of academicism in art and placed the portrayal of movement high among its aims. Painting and sensation, it argued, are inseparable; what must be rendered is dynamic sensation, painting of states of mind. Perhaps this is why the movement exerted an important influence on Diaghilev's artistic policy as his Ballets Russes changed from the Russian-rooted choreography of Fokine to the modernist choreography, music and, above all, design of its post-1914 years.[3] Certainly futurism influenced not only cubism and the Ballets Russes, but also dadaism, expressionism, surrealism, and both fascist and left-wing theories. It disappeared towards the end of the first world war or, rather, became taken up by constructivism.

Constructivism, therefore, could claim to be an extension both of cubism and futurism. It celebrated machines in much the same terms as the futurists, seeing them as models of human achievement and possibility. The celebration was carried out in the choreographic experiments of post-1917 Russian dancers until the late 1920s, especially choreography inspired by machines. It could be seen in the theatre and cinema of Meyerhold, Eisenstein, Dovchenko and others. In this way constructivism challenged the established practices of Stanislavski's Moscow Art Theatre, the traditional ballets of the Mariinsky in Petrograd and those of the Bolshoi in Moscow. It spilled over even into the British documentary film movement of the late 1920s and 1930s, thus strengthening the modernist influence in British performance art. In Germany as well as in Russia it saw little distinction between theatre and cinema as art and as education. The echoes of such a message were felt in the work of Unity Theatre in London, of the New Dance Group with Jane Dudley and other dancers in New York under the impulse of the New Deal and, later still, in the powerful influence of Brechtian theatre. But constructivism also was an extension of cubism in its challenge to conventional views of social reality and its confidence in the new world which humanity could construct for itself. It saw plenty for all and a new beauty in cheap mass production. It expressed this beauty in the creation and design of buildings and everyday articles, ending the distinction between art and craft in the philosophy of schools like the Bauhaus, and creative labour for all in a rearrangement of social priorities. We live still with the effects of this hopeful illusion.

Surrealism sought less to restructure reality than to liberate humanity's inner fantasy and subconscious life. Its ideas were expressed principally in painting but with an important influence also on sculpture, literature and some choreography, classical and modern. Two main trends are apparent. One explored the juxtaposition of unlikely objects, symbols, forms rarely related in everyday life. The result produced on canvas dreamlike sensations and fantasies. The other trend was influenced by the discoveries of Freud, entering the hallucinatory world of the subconscious. The logic of both trends derived from dreams, free associations and release from the constraints of the formal world. There was an obvious connection with earlier artists like Breughel and Bosch and, in our own time, with Chagall, Klee, Max Ernst, Miro, Magritte and Salvador Dali. Dali designed in dance not only for Massine (*Bacchanale, Labyrinth* and *Mad Tristan*) but also for Eglevsky, Argentinita and Bejart. There are influences from both trends in Ashton's *Apparitions* (1936) and de Valois' *Checkmate* (1937). The movement reached its full maturity in 1930–5 as a revolt against the increasingly abstract values of declining modernism. Its influence was important to the arts in its focus on the inner reality of human beings, today an area much explored by choreography.

The strongest modernist influence on dance, however, has been through expressionism. Reacting against impressionism at its strongest in Germany, Russia and Scandinavia, expressionism reflected much of the doubt and despair of the European turmoil between 1900 and the second world war. Concerned with the impact of changes in external reality upon the inner reality of individuals, it endeavoured to express inner subjective life and feelings, inner reality, to an extent that external reality became distorted, suppressed and even unrecognizable. This was true especially of the human form which expressionism distorted on canvas to extreme, even brutal, degrees (e.g. Max Beckmann's *Die Nacht* 1918–19) without the reconstruction or resynthesis cubism would have provided. Such an approach inspired much of the technique and many of the images of central European dance in the work of Laban, Jooss, Wigman, Kreutzberg and others. There was suffering and longing for the regeneration of society in much of the work of Laban with pleas for social harmony and brotherhood, the power and joy of community action against automation and the oppression of factory life. There was the dominance of emotional experience in the work of Wigman and Kreutzberg; the central influence of modern city life and values in the choreography of Jooss. City life, the masses, machines were natural sources of inspiration and protest treated in many ways as causes of loneliness, degradation, liberation, hope, pain, pessimism, erotic stimulation and community suffering. Types often were substituted for individual characters as in Jooss' *The Green Table* and *Big City*, later developed in psychological terms by Antony Tudor. Classical ballet also reflected the powerful influence of expressionism. Massine's *Les Présages* in 1933 depicted man's struggle with his destiny; and Ashton's *Dante Sonata* in 1940 showed a similar conflict between darkness and light, good and evil. There are many other examples not only in dance but also in cinema (*The Cabinet of Dr Caligari*), in literature (Kafka and James Joyce), in painting (Munch, Kandinsky, Kokoschka) and music (Schoenberg and Berg).

Thus did modernism introduce the extended perceptions of reality we take for granted today.[4] The extended perceptions derived from extended experiences which an ever-dominating urban society brought to people's lives and values. They sprang from changes in the real world across the world, in the USSR until the early 1930s as much as in capitalist Europe and America. Clearly, therefore, the modernist movement could have offered neither a unified vision nor a general code of aesthetic practice. It was as multi-faceted as the new realities it perceived and to which it responded. This opened enormous creative possibilites as Salman Rushdie pointed out in his 1990 Herbert Read memorial lecture. 'Change', said Rushdie, quoting Read, a leading British modernist, 'is the condition of art remaining art.' Therefore, argued Rushdie, following the principle, 'no aesthetic can be a constant, except an aesthetic based on the idea of . . . "perpetual revolution".'[5]

Pursuing these possibilities it was the climate of the new thinking from the West which influenced the young Russian artists around Diaghilev and other artists involved in the European convulsions of 1917–20. It was not so much the detail of what painters and poets actually were creating in Paris, so much as the climate of thinking and creativity which induced change. Part of the result was modern or 'free' dance. This had evolved since the beginning of the century in direct challenge to classical ballet and in direct response to the new thinking which stirred dancers and artists in central Europe[6] as much as in England.[7] Rudolf Laban, moving between central and western Europe, experienced personally what was happening in Paris and became a dadaist before he became a leading dance expressionist. In America Isadora Duncan felt the influence more remotely translating her rebellion at first into the recreation of Greek dance images. Only later in the work of successors like Humphries and Graham, perhaps Ruth St Denis, does one begin to see the interior exploration, the emphasis on dynamic sensation, the penetration into the subconscious and the crisis of confidence in the future with which we are familiar through modernist forms in Europe. Thus cubism and futurism influenced the transition of Diaghilev's Ballets Russes into the French-dominated world of Massine, Nijinska and Balanchine, Picasso, Stravinsky and Satie during the 1920s. Constructivism reshaped and extended dance in Russia after 1917 until experiment was suppressed by Stalin. Expressionism became the dominant influence in central European dance under Laban, Jooss and Wigman until the time of Hitler.

The strengths and positive influence of modernism lay in the new territories it discovered for the arts in every industrial society. Art — in this case choreography — is a mediator of the object-world, autonomous from immediate economics or politics while linked at the same time with these realities by questioning them and seeking to resolve the issues they pose in their ever-changing development. To fulfil this role required the construct of different symbols and images, alternative representations of time and particular concern for the mediation of content by form through a wide range of alternatives. Hence the extended use of symbolism by Ruth St Denis[8] and Loie Fuller; the 'rise of synchonous montage as an alternative to merely linear additive time'[9] in the work of Martha Graham and many others of her generation; techniques of 'de-familiarizing' the object world in, for example, *Relâche* by Jean Borlin for Les Ballets Suedois[10] (1924); the cultivation of paradox and ambiguity in Nijinska's *Les Biches*, also 1924, rather than present a single objective, usually narrative reality; and the continual exploration by many choreographers, then and since, of the fragmented experience of individuals in modern urban and industrial societies. Thus the range of artistic communication, including choreographic communication, was infinitely increased.

At the same time modernism does not necessarily require rejection of the romantic or classical past in order to embrace a different future. In England it assumed local forms modified by the conscious recreation in an English context of traditions from the French, Italian, Danish and Russian Schools of classical ballet plus the influence of British folk dance and music. These forms can be seen in all British classical choreography from Ashton and de Valois to Tudor, Gore and Andrée Howard to Cranko, MacMillan and Bintley. The emphasis on classical tradition, in fact, so schooled audience taste in France as well as in Britain that it delayed the establishment of modern dance movements until the 1960s and 1970s, a generation after modern theatrical dance had been developed in central Europe and the USA. The influence of Laban and Jooss from central Europe was little felt in British choreography when a Jooss–Leeder School opened at Dartington Hall in 1934 and British teachers and dancers, trained in Germany, began to filter into British colleges and schools. This was extended through the presence of Laban and Jooss in Dartington and Cambridge during the 1940s and the teaching of Sigurd Leeder in Cambridge and in Morley College, London, during the 1940s and 1950s. The influence of American modern dance was felt not at all until the 1960s when Robin Howard established the London Contemporary Dance School and Company based on the teaching of Martha Graham. There had been, certainly, home-grown forms of modern dance emerging in Britain about the time Rudolf Laban began his mission in central Europe. There was the Revived Greek Dance of Ruby Ginner, the Natural Movement of Madge Atkinson and, especially, Margaret Morris Movement. None developed as a theatrical force except Margaret Morris but all exerted considerable influence in education.

The modernist legacy thus was absorbed in British classical choreography through the prism of Diaghilev and his later choreographers. It enriched positively the classical tradition in the work of the first two generations of British choreographers up to and including Cranko and MacMillan. It was communicated through modern dance in Britain during the 1960s and 1970s at a time when the negative influence of post-modernism from the 1950s and 1960s had begun to assert itself. There are, therefore, three elements mingled in the birth of British modern dance, that of Laban–Jooss–Leeder felt mainly in schools, that of Graham deriving from American modernism and transmitted through London Contemporary Dance Theatre, and that of American post-modernism transmitted principally from Cunningham through Ballet Rambert, now called Rambert Dance Company, and through teachers in vocational schools.

Post-Modernist Lessons

Again one sees art forms developing at different times and in different directions within the same social milieu. We have entered the post-modern era of consumerism, global economy and global culture. It touches all the arts and is manifest most prominently in architecture. It is launched in painting through abstract expressionism in the 1950s. It is nourished in dance from the late 1950s onwards through choreographers and dancers at Judson Memorial Church, New York, and in dance workshops at other informal centres across America, especially San Francisco.[11] From America it came to Europe in the 1970s, proselytized in England at Dance Umbrella Festivals and by the Association of Dance and Mime Artists around the now departed magazine *New Dance*. Of this more later.

There is much in post-modernism which marks new excursions for each art, but much also to regret. In dance the principal regret is a retreat of the artist from responsibility for public communication. It seems to me that any piece of theatrical communication must seize the imagination and stir the mind of the spectator. Otherwise it fails as theatre art. The marks of this retreat in dance, as in other arts, can be found in attitudes which sanctify esoteric and private communication for oneself or for those within the narrow circle of the artist; a concentration on form or craft at the expense of content; therefore obscurantism and extreme limitation of communication; therefore alienation, or at least withdrawal of the artist from daily experience; intense exploration of particular elements of technique or uses of the body. Often these are presented as forms of short-lived revolt following current fashion, or to set a fashion. Or rejection by the dancer of recognized dance languages in favour of, say, no movement at all.

Any assessment of change mixes positive with negative. Post-modern dance shows many of the limitations of post-modern art in general but can be said also to be a pioneer in the way of romantic ballet. Romantic ballet introduced a new status for the dance art and artist through new themes emphasizing especially the conflict between the world as it had become and some misty alternative. To realize these themes it introduced new techniques and new attitudes to the body, the instrument of communication. All this is present in American post-modern dance during the late 1950s and 1960s.

I am thinking of Steve Paxton offering as a dance in the early 1960s the act of moving furniture from a studio office piece by piece, or *Words Words* by Paxton and Yvonne Rainer in 1963 when the same ten-minute movement piece was performed by a nude man, then a nude woman, then both together, so one might compare what? Gender? Physical structures? Movement quality? Temperaments? Or Twyla Tharp's *Tank Dive* in 1965 which was devoted to a diver's slow preparation for a dive; or a dancer sitting on a chair for long minutes, then leaving the stage, chair and all, which I watched in London at the Commonwealth Institute, or the separation of dancer from emotion contrasting gentle movement on stage with sounds of catastrophe and torture on the sound machine. Or the dumping of garbage on audiences in Carole Schneemann's 1964 *Meat Joy*. Such examples began to be repeated less sharply in Britain and Europe during the late 1960s and the 1970s.

What, therefore, lay behind these post-modernist stigmata in America and Britain? Some of it, at least, was political, a snook cocked at Lyndon Johnson's affluent society and Harold Wilson's complacency; a protest to shock, shake, shatter a society which could prosecute a Vietnam war; a wish to destroy the hegemony of societies which seemed to offer no future and no more positive philosophy than the atom bomb. Hence anti-elitism on the dance stage; hence attempts to destroy the separation of dancer and audience which possession of a dance technique can create; hence non-dance and a return to everyday movement; hence the use of dance spaces other than conventional theatres. The paradox is that the making of art more like life does not necessarily make the art more accessible any more than the exploitation of technique alone can communicate with more than those who appreciate technique.

The lesson seems to have been absorbed because I perceive now — in the repertory of Rambert Dance Company, for instance — a return to rigour, polish, virtuosity, spectacle, though still often an emptiness of communication beyond movement quality. Nowadays, in the work of Cunningham or Richard Alston one goes to see dance *qua* dance, as one goes to hear music *qua* music, not necessarily to receive anything other than the aesthetic experience. The most positive result of the post-modern experience is that the dancers have won the battle for dance to be seen as an autonomous art form not dependent on music or design or even on individual dancers. I am reminded of the thoughts, images, sometimes bizarre, irreverent and irrelevant which can come to mind while listening to a concert. Jerome Robbins made a comic ballet from such images in *The Concert*, but he needed good dancers to do it. So, too, if movement now is centre stage; if dance now is often no more than a choreographer's feelings about the movement potential in his dancers' bodies; if dance is liberated from music and design to go its own way calling on the experiences of the 1960s and 1970s to assert liberations from conventions, if all these now happen on the dance stage, the choreographers can ask, 'Why not?'

Why shouldn't artists be able to do their own thing, represent their own vision of the world in their own way without thinking too much of the public? Even if their own thing is, say, the emptiness of abstract expressionism or a claim that advertising techniques are, in fact, art. Audiences don't *have* to support such manifestations, though, as John Stuart Mill might have said, we support to the death an artist's right to create.

The issue, once more, is one of artistic responsibility and moral responsibility. Art's justification is that it lifts the human spirit outside the confines of material, physical existence and by doing so questions, challenges, enriches that existence. We know that in all the countries of eastern Europe and in all other repressive regimes art and artists have been the first to be placed in chains and the first to resist until finally there is the triumph symbolized today by Czechoslovakia. That triumph was not won by small-scale communication or the exploitation of this or that element of the art process to which post-modernists have accustomed us. In many ways, of course, the post-modernists have brought fresh air into a theatre dance in Britain stifled by convention and history. This is their positive contribution along-side new abilities for dance to speak for itself. Hurrah, then for Dance Umbrella and Riverside Studios and Chisenhale Dance Space and *New Dance* and the lamented Association of Dance and Mime Artists and the few other venturesome centres outside London like Arnolfini in Bristol. Without these we might not breathe fresh air. With them I can welcome the notion that dance is not just steps to music but can be all kinds of expressive movement. I can applaud the legacy of improvisation, everyday clothes, every day spaces, everyday gestures and uses of the body, the deconstruction of dance, the scepticism and questioning. I rebel with them against the poverty which the Estab-lishment decrees for us to limit our daring and our potency. Where I part company is over triviality, narrow interests, self-indulgence and the self-examination, examination of the navel, which characterize much post-modern choreography in the name of experiment.

As Jean-Paul Sartre pointed out in a lecture at the Sorbonne in 1960 part of our problem is the stultifying effect of bourgeois audi-ences. Sartre argued in Kenneth Tynan's summary.[12]

'The bourgeois, wants to see people like himself on stage, in order to identify his troubles with theirs, but he cannot stom-ach the kind of play in which he is surveyed with scientific objectivity. He likes dramatists whose concept of human nature conforms to his own ... it is "human" to cheat, to lie, to compromise, to envy. That is the condition of our species, and the bourgeois view is that we are stuck with it. But the fulcrum of all good drama is purposeful human action, and this often implies a desire for change ... It is here that the bourgeois calls a halt, since his picture of the world precludes the possibility of radical change.'

For 'drama' read 'dance'. For 'dance' read choreographers like Kenneth MacMillan or Lloyd Newson whose work often shows people as they *really* are, not as the bourgeois would like to see them. Hence the resistance to their work. It is this stultifying influence which makes the ballet programmes at Covent Garden so unadventurous and often boring. In the last decade or so seat prices at the Royal Opera House have risen to levels beyond the pockets of many in the sort of audience which attended regularly twenty or thirty years ago. In addition, substantial numbers of seats in the grand tier, stalls circle and elsewhere are bought up regularly by business concerns more interested in the social and commercial value of a lien on Covent Garden than in the ballets. To keep such wealthy custom the ballet must be 'safe' with star names more important than original work. Sartre's bourgeois — what Lord Drogheda called the plutocracy[13] — really have taken over.

The other part of the problem, where original work really does take place, lies in the discharge of the choreographer's responsibility. It is the reason why I said just now that any piece of theatrical communication must seize the imagination and stir the mind. There is nothing wrong with the display, technical daring and physical excitement one sees in the virtuoso dances of a classical ballet, even the Black Swan, Don Quixote and Corsaire *pas de deux* presented one after the other at English National Ballet's fortieth anniversary gala in March 1990. Such showpieces remain valid because audiences can wonder at and share kinaesthetically the achievement of human bodies, like watching a sports contest. Post-modern Soviet ballet, and much Balanchine choreography, have developed this athleticism to extremes. It is the equivalent of the overemphasis on form found in much post-modern contemporary dance the world over. Athleticism seizes sometimes the imagination but rarely stirs the mind. Being empty of content it fails in the choreographer's principal task to communicate understanding. I don't mean by this that dance works should be clear and simple narratives. Dance in our post-modern world speaks now for itself about things which cannot be expressed in words. It requires us, therefore, to understand its language. I am reminded how Beckett's *Waiting for Godot* was condemned as pretentious nonsense by many people when it appeared in Paris, London and New York. Such post-modern theatre has a meaning if one searches. The meaning disturbs. *Godot* is recognized today as a supreme statement of pessimism about the human condition in our time. It forced also a rethink of the rules of spoken theatre. So, too, with Stravinsky in his time and John Cage in our time and the rules of music; so with Cunningham and the Judson dancers and the rules of danced theatre. So with MacMillan and the three-act ballet. So with the young choreographers emerging now from the Laban Centre and London

Contemporary Dance School. We have to learn to understand the choreographic language — but the choreographer needs also to reach us. That reaching has to offer more than the human body moving wonderfully without illuminating the human condition enough to move the spirit. A bit of humour would do, some laughter, above all originality. Yet most dance routines on television are what they say, routine, while the special dance seasons on BBC2 and Channel 4 are too often complex, obscure and therefore narcoleptic.

The central issue in our theatre dance culture today, therefore, lies with the audience. Restating old beliefs in established classical ballets merely sustains a static if substantial audience while new works in classical or contemporary styles touch only declining audiences. It seems that British dance theatre is out of touch with the times. Too conservative and bourgeois on the one hand; not aligning itself enough with change and new times on the other hand in ways, as Sartre urged, which can effect change. We are stuck and stationary in this dilemma.

The post-modern dance forms which express this dilemma emerge from the most advanced industrial and urban societies of the 'free' world. How free are we in a world of market forces and globalized living controlled by transnational companies? If artists fail to fulfil their deeper spiritual responsibilities in this world, are they actually any freer than artists were in eastern Europe before 1989? All of us, it seems, have been questioning but without direction or purpose. The last 30–40 years of post-modern dance have been like a cell or cage with dancers and choreographers beating the walls to find a way out. A way out was opened in 1989, a reinvigoration which flows from demonstration of achieving a common vision expressed most strongly by artists in protest and now in leadership. This is to place the arts in their right role and right perspective. It is to be proclaiming, exploring, more resonant about the possibilities of human meaning and existence. It is to move forward again from small concerns of post-modernism to the bigger things of reaching and moving a larger audience about values and sincerities in a global, market-dominated world. It is the only way to increase today's dance audience in Britain beyond its 1 per cent of the population.

Notes and References

1 Abbs, Peter: *Living Powers*, London, Falmer Press, 1987, p. 26.
2 Lunn, Eugene: *Marxism and Modernism*, London, Verso, 1985, p. 42.
3 Garafola, Lynn: 'The making of ballet modernism', *Dance Research Journal* (New York), Winter 1989, pp. 23–32.
4 Lunn, *op. cit.* I am indebted to Lunn for many ideas in this chapter.

5 Rushdie, Salman: *Is Nothing Sacred?* Cambridge, Granta 1990, pp. 2, 5.

6 Preston–Dunlop, Valerie, 'Rudolf Laban — The Making of Modern Dance', *Dance Theatre Journal* (London), 1989, pp. 11–16.

7 See Calouste Gulbenkian Foundation, *Dance Education and Training in Britain*, London, 1980.

8 Jowitt, Deborah: *Time and the Dancing Image*, New York, William Morrow & Co. Inc., pp. 125ff.

9 *Ibid.*, pp. 155ff.

10 Beaumont, Cyril: *Complete Book of Ballets*, London, 1937, pp. 833ff.

11 I am indebted for some American examples to chapter 8 of Deborah Jowitt's remarkable book above.

12 Tynan, Kenneth: *Tynan Right and Left*, London, Longmans, 1967.

13 The Earl of Drogheda, former chairman of the Royal Opera House, in a conversation with Peter Brinson at Covent Garden, July 1989.

Chapter 2

Whose Post-Modernism in Britain?

Modernism, then, has been the most powerful contemporary influence upon twentieth century British dance culture permeating the theatre, education, youth and community dance and public consciousness. It has exerted less influence upon popular dance in commercial halls but even here attitudes to dance, dress for dance and some dance styles inevitably reflect attitudes which are dominant in modernist/post-modernist culture generally, especially popular music. The development of British dance culture, though, is influenced not only by the movements of twentieth century art, but also by attitudes and prejudices inherited from the past or from other aspects of British culture.

To judge properly the place of dance in our culture, we need to understand its historical development and set it against the current character of British society. The role of dance changed with the division of society into classes, passing through tribal, slave and feudal eras. In the prehistoric world, social control often came to be exercised through ceremonies extolling some ruling authority, religious or secular. In renaissance Europe *ballet de cour* magnified and deified the role of the monarch. From that time, too, dancing masters taught the manners of polite society through four hundred years until the early part of our own century. In that way merchants sought to acquire the appearance of aristocrats. This class element remains today. Classical ballet, for all its audience-drawing power, is regarded as an art of the state, expressing the ethos of ruling elites, whether monarchical, presidential or Soviet. Modern/contemporary dance arose as the art of an urban middle class troubled, protesting, struggling within the conflicting values of twentieth century industrial/commercial society. These tensions lie at the heart of modernism and post-modernism. But every ruling authority comes to be challenged by its opposite so that urban youth creates constantly its own styles, its own urban folk dance in generational and class distinction from polite society, whether 'modern' or 'classical'. Nevertheless what urban youth creates influences in time both the art form and the ballrooms and discos of the rich. Throughout history new dances and styles of movement have started usually in popular form among ordinary people. Innovation travels upwards from common experience to be refashioned and returned in new forms from the top down. The history of classical ballet and of individual dances like the waltz demonstrates this point. Such is the dialectic of dance.

The modernist and post-modernist movements illustrate also this dialectic. Life experience created both movements. High modernism arose from the technological, industrial and economic changes in capitalism of the late nineteenth, and early twentieth centuries in dialectical relationship with what had gone before — a modernism which includes, by the way, the socialist realism of Soviet state capitalism. Today's post-modernist movement in the arts is related similarly to the changes in social life, technological development and the new international economic order following the second world war. Specifically it is embodied in the everyday experience and organization of consumer society, the media society, the transnational emergence of a global economy and a parallel, still-emergent global culture. This is the face of late twentieth century urban–industrial life from whose beginning arose the modernist movement in art a century ago. The arts are the spiritual manifestation of material changes.

Not surprisingly, the post-modernist movement in dance and the arts generally began in the United States in the late 1940s and early 1950s. It developed differently at different speeds in different countries — France in the late 1950s, in Britain not until the 1970s. The arrival of contemporary dance in Britain in the mid 1960s was a *modernist* development, not post-modernist. The year 1968 marked the first, most critical and failed challenge to post-modernist philosophy, a moment when 'the new international order (neo-colonialism, the Green Revolution, computerization and elecronic information) is at one and the same time set in place and is swept and shaken by its own internal contradictions and by external resistance'.[1] One of the characteristics claimed for modernism and post-modernism is a repudiation of the past, a rejection of tradition in favour of new practices and theories, totally new departures. In post-modernism this rejection is carried to extremes in the elevation of the new for newness's sake and, in the paradox of pastiche. Peter Abbs remarks that Modernism alongside Progressivism in education 'worked to sever the individual from the great symbolic continuum of Western Culture'.[2] 'Modernism, in particular, erased the sense of tradition.'[3] The evidence of dance history does not bear out this blanket accusation. Some of the explorations of post-modernism, let alone modernism, are crucial to dance development as I show later in this chapter. The evolution of post-modern pastiche, nostalgia and simulation, on the other hand, is a negative movement tarnishing all the arts. It is as if 'technology and consumer culture have changed our understanding of nature; its simulation is now more familiar than any first hand experience'.[4] This is realism in reverse making modern man 'a rare tourist in the natural world'. It is true, therefore, that an ecology of the arts is needed today against the post-modernist wave of advertising culture, supermarket taste, television soaps, chat shows and the general philistinism of monetarist philosophy. Such are the wounds inflicted on the arts by post-modernist consumer society.

With modernism it is different. High modernism, by which I mean the culture of Picasso, Stravinsky, Laban, Graham and the departures they represent, was not a break. It was a development, albeit in many new directions, introducing new techniques supported by new theories having clear continuity with what had gone before, like its link with the impressionists. Dance demonstrates this continuity more than most arts. The essential continuity, of course, is the human body. Isadora Duncan may have rejected the classical inheritance in the uses of this body, but Rudolf Laban, her central European contemporary and more rational pioneer of modern dance, understood the importance of continuity. He acknowledged not only the value for modern dance of Noverre's theories of ballet in the eighteenth century[5] but also the relevance of Diaghilev's modernist modification of this inheritance in the twentieth century. Similarly post-modernism is a part-popular reaction to the way high modernism dominates now much teaching, most galleries and theatres, and almost all criticism to form a quite specific hegemony of general arts discourse around the entrenched attitudes of a privileged minority. The world changes and it is no task of artists to reproduce old ways and simulation, rather to learn from these ways. Emily Brontë, in *Wuthering Heights*, did not recreate the moral world of mid–Victorian England. She created her own version of that England with a different morality. Hence the novel was unpopular when it appeared. Ashley Page today could not be refashioning classical style in his ballets if there had been no Petipa, no Ashton and no MacMillan from whom to learn. There could be no Richard Alston and Rambert Dance Company, no Dance Umbrella, no innovative dance at The Place, no New Dance at Chisenhale, no Lea Anderson and other young choreographers from the Laban Centre, no Green Candle at Oxford House, if there was not the high modernism of Graham, Bird and Cohan and teachers in their style against which to react. The issue is the nature of this reaction.

Here other aspects of post-modernism become relevant. They are Vietnam, the first post-modernist war; the aspects of consumer society found in airport architecture and airport bookstalls; automobile culture and the kitsch of petrol stations; muzzak, whether you like it or not; the superficiality of Andy Warhol, Wogan and Eurovision song contests; the penetration of advertising and commercial values into every aspect of living; unemployment and underlying racism in social life; the hijack of everyday consciousness by what is seen, heard, read in the media; the submergence of individuality and local cultures in global cultural practices, called values, mostly emanating from America. This is one part of the resource for post-modern choreography. Not surprising that audiences are undernourished in sensibility, that some art work of young people reconstructs this reality and that the violence to human values in dominant social practice is reproduced on the streets and in much choreography. The other part of the resource is the Green Movement, community arts, Caribbean poets and spoken poetry, Prince Charles' reaction to modernist architecture, youth dance and young people making music, wall murals, Sportsaid, issue politics, the move for racial harmony and the leadership of artists in eastern Europe, especially Czechoslovakia. The post-modernist scene is as disparate as its modernist original. Moreover the human need to see everything in forms and models does not change. Nor does the need to break those forms and models to create new ones.

How will choreographers and dance managements use these resources? After all, their ideas and stimulus for creative work arise from life experience. Choreographers give back this experience to audiences in a different form shaped by their own perceptions and imagination. The significance of great artists, great choreographers, is that they are greater in imagination than we are, not that we have no imagination ourselves. An Ashton, a Graham, a Cunningham, a Lavrovsky, can open visions we have not opened, whether tragic or humorous. Thus our own vision of life is extended or changed in some way. There is, or should be, a sense of revelation whereby we leave the place of choreography different in our understanding from how we entered it. This is the measure of the choreographer's responsibility to create a work which can be received by more than by just a narrow circle. It should, as I said before, seize the imagination and stir the mind.

The choreographer also can demean and distort talent in the service of commercial interests, pornography, political propaganda. Managements can do so even more in their search for commercial sponsorship. Hence the need of choreographers and managements to comprehend *social* responsibility. Governments, too, when not guided by monetarist ideology. Hence the audience's need for aesthetic appreciation and understanding of the dance language. In the broadest sense this is an educational issue having to do with moral being, personal taste and the quality of life. Thus artists and audiences are confronted with the post-modernist choice, to follow the consequences of consumer society or to evolve a reaction to its vulgarities. The great mark of post-modernism is its blend of the high and the popular, its erosion of the line between art and commercial forms combined with a tendency to eliminate the past, to live only for now. All the more need for audiences to comprehend social responsibility in concert with the artists. All the more need for choreographers to work from meaning or purpose towards movement rather than from movement towards meaning, which is a post-modernist approach. Performance is a beginning, not an end.

To eliminate the past, though, is to eliminate the soul. When the people of Poland were confronted with their devastated capital after the Nazi defeat some people advised building a new capital elsewhere. Instead, they began to rebuild Warsaw by recreating the Old Town which had been its heart. I saw this old town in 1956. Bit by bit since then they have reconstructed its palaces, monuments and streets to recapture more of Poland's soul. We, too, must retain the soul of our dance endeavour. We cannot do this by dropping from the repertory everything which is more than a few years old. 'Perhaps preparing a new season', wrote Richard Alston, artistic director of Rambert Dance Company in 1990, 'is not entirely unlike re-hanging the Tate ... setting off new works by Rambert's present choreographers against contributions from other phases of the company's history'. Artists cannot be captive to tradition if they are to help find alternatives to established living. At the same time they depend upon tradition. In British choreography this has produced unexpected responses.

The Contemporary Response

The issue raised by the arrival of Graham contemporary dance in Britain in the mid-1960s was not rejection of the past so much as how to reimagine the present, and what part of the present. Dancers have to take this present as they find it with all its dissonance. Their field, the aesthetic field, has become a principal area in which human beings can draw together to examine alternatives across barriers created by class division, racial conflicts and market competition.[6] Eastern Europe shows the power and possibilities of this examination today. In the early 1970s a group of dancers in London gave particular expression to the dissatisfactions and feelings of revolt occasioned by the dance establishment of the day. These feelings, I remember, had begun to stir even in the late 1960s when the political events of 1968 penetrated the walls of dance studios and rehearsal rooms.

The feelings were given expression initially by five dancers drawn from different sections of the British dance and movement world. Two, Fergus Early and Jacky Lansley, came from the Royal Ballet; two, Emlyn Claid and Maidée Duprès, came from a London

Contemporary Dance background; one, Mary Prestidge, came from a mixture of competition gymnastics and Rambert. All, in other words, had experienced a traditional, highly structured training whether balletic, Graham or gymnastic. They wished to break out of this structure to reconsider and reuse their training in experimental work and situations under their own control. They wanted to choose, even to form, their own teachers and teaching methods, and their own models from which to evolve new directions for their dance. All had met at The Place, headquarters of London Contemporary Dance Theatre, teaching or studying and had learned there the importance of a space of their own away from the day-to-day pressures of company life. Their answer was to form X6 Dance Space, a bare functional area of floor and walls in Block X, Floor 6 of a former warehouse at Butler's Wharf near the Tower of London. Hence X6. The year was 1976.

Around X6 became grouped a growing number of dancers and dance students who felt as its founders felt — individuals doing their own thing through solo concerts which were the norm in the United States but rare in Britain; small groups, some promisingly original, others boringly self-indulgent; eccentrics, mavericks, prospectors for dance gold; occasionally the gleam of gold itself in marked creative talent. The philosophy was strongly democratic maintaining that everyone had a right to try and to fail. Visiting X6 reminded me of an experience I had at an open air pop concert in the early 1970s. In the middle of it, as the linkman was announcing the next band, a girl climbed on to the stage and took off all her clothes. 'Do your own thing, sister', cried the linkman unabashed. 'Do your own thing.' This was an attitude disastrously absent from British classical ballet at the time but very much within Robin Howard's policy as founder of The Place and of Bonnie Bird's principles as she began to reorganize choreographic studies at the Laban Centre in the same period.

X6 formed a number of key relationships. Of these the most important, probably, was with Dartington where Laban, Jooss and Leeder had found a home forty years before. Steve Paxton, Mary Fulkerson and Contact Improvisation were the new influences but to these, and to the creative impulses brought by teachers and choreographers imported by X6 mostly from abroad, were added useful home-grown traditions from British experience like the theatrical side of classical ballet, quite different from contemporary dance theatre, and traditions from English performance arts newly adapted for community theatre in the early 1970s. Thus X6 challenged established dance on almost every level and many of the challengers starved in doing so. They were British post-modernists, contradicting the modernist hegemony of which I spoke in the last chapter. To emphasize and extend the contradiction they launched their own magazine *New*

Dance, soon after opening the X–6 Space. The title gave the movement a name. Needing money the New Dance movement challenged also the funding bodies most of whom were dominated by established thinking. Gulbenkian responded with support for the magazine in its early years and also for the movement's organization, the Association of Dance and Mime Artists. It felt that if the new movement was to be most fruitful it needed a voice to put its point of view and a symbol around which those who heard the voice could rally. *New Dance* more than repaid this confidence.

The Arts Council's dance department had doubts about helping the dance practice of so new and uncomfortable a presence. What precisely was this movement after? It was the same question the Arts Council itself asked when faced with funding the Community Arts Movement of which, in a way, New Dance was a part. Help certainly came from several quarters but because of the doubts, the help always was hesitant and insufficient. The movement, therefore, always remained undernourished.

The demands of the Association of Dance and Mime Artists epitomized a dilemmma before all funding bodies. The organization had no commanding philosophy upon which a funding case could be made. The case was the liberation of time to experiment and to go one's own way. This is not very different from experiments in science but it was quite new on such a scale in the dance of 1970s Britain. The magazine and the movement, it seemed to funders, were a collection of individual opinions even though the magazine, in particular, set quite new standards in dance journalism. How could the opinions be otherwise, given the origins and purpose of the movement and the relatively unknown names of most of its members? Such is the nature of challenge to anyone funding experiment and new work. Risk has to be accepted along with the right to fail as much as to succeed. This implies acceptance of the need for continuing support to known people on the one hand, and on the other hand to small ventures where most experiment takes place. This is where business sponsorship of the arts and the Government's faith in it are questionable. Business sponsorship rarely funds experiment. Business people are less interested in the new than in the established and prestigious. To hope that business sponsorship will fund the new in art, as ADMA was advised to hope at least in part, is to condemn the arts to a thirsty death.

Nothing like the New Dance Movement has happened in Britain before or since. It was never a large movement yet its few years' existence changed the dance atmosphere and thinking of its time. Many of its dancers supplemented and built upon the notions of dance residencies and workshops introduced mostly by London Contemporary Dance Theatre in the mid–1970s, giving to these opportunities an important local slant. Its vigorous sympathy for dance forms from the Caribbean, south Asia and elsewhere pointed the need to support these forms as part of British dance culture. Its determination to explore new themes and content, a special quality of New Dance, expanded interest in dance and created conditions for more controversial subject matter to stir consciences, like Lloyd Newson's prize-winning *Dead Dreams of Monochrome Men* about homosexual oppression, for DV8 Physical Theatre. Individual artists emerged from its ranks like Julyen Hamilton from The Place and Laurie Booth from Dartington, both now with international reputations. The habit of small dance groups was developed to supplement larger companies, bringing new choreography to small venues, schools and colleges in the regions. These groups led the way, in fact, out of London and thus nourished Dance Umbrella, the Community Dance and Mime Movement and today's small company network round Britain. British dance assumed a less establishment face and the Community Dance and Mime Movement, especially is the New Dance memorial.

There is, of course, another form of memorial in the dancers and dance styles who have developed out of the New Dance movement and who are taking dance today still in new directions. Frequently these directions are personal and personally expressed rather than a disclosure arising out of the group relationships implied by community dance. Julyen Hamilton is a case in point. Educated in England and one of the most articulate and individual products of the New Dance liberation, he was trained at the London School of Contemporary Dance in modern dance, classical ballet and folk forms with subsequent influences from Contact Improvisation, the Alexander technique and the Japanese martial art form Ki-Aikido. He danced with London Contemporary Dance Theatre in 1976 but also with alternative modern dance companies such as Rosemary Butcher Dance Company and Richard Alston between 1975 and 1980. In 1980 he left England for the freer air and greater dance opportunities of the Netherlands while retaining still his links with Britain. He teaches regularly at Dartington College of Art in Devon as well as in Amsterdam and has a reputation for inventive workshops and new teaching styles conducted throughout Europe and the United States.

As a dance artist he won the Silver Award for best dance performer in the Netherlands in 1984 and, before that, had appeared to critical acclaim at the 1983 Dance Umbrella Festival in London in *Musk Red* with the percussionist Matthieu Keijser and the Laban-trained modern dancer, Kirstie Simson. This was the follow-up to *Musk*, and earlier collaboration with Keijser in 1982, and was seen throughout Europe and the United States, succeeded by other productions with Simson, also in Europe and the United States. 'An un-

Plate 1 Other ways to dance. Julyen Hamilton in *Friday*. Photograph by André Hoekzema.

documented part of the past years here and travelling through Europe and the States,' he wrote to me from Amsterdam in July 1990,

> is the abundant improvisations with a 'pool' of dancers and musicians who either live here or regularly pass through Amsterdam — Katie Duck, Tristan Honsinger, Sean Bergin, Kirstie Simson, Alessandro Certini, Charlotte Zerbey, Pauline de Grout, Steve Paxton, Nancy Stark Smith, Andrew Harwood, Danny Lepkov, Ishamel Houston-Jones — the tone of Amsterdam has allowed these meetings which I feel are responsible in great part for the development of a certain depth within the work, whether set or improvised. What has been shared is the sense that the performance can be finely tuned and highly cared for, however radical, ribald or rough a form it takes.

Hamilton thus provides a glimpse of an alternative world of dance which part of the New Dance movement has become, though the Dutch equivalent of new dance is much older in the Netherlands than it is in the UK. It is a world of dance values strikingly different from the world of big classical or contemporary companies, strongly international and with an approach to choreography which includes the use of improvisation alongside created work. This is a world of which Britain may see much more after the integration of Europe in 1992. Hamilton goes on to explain the influence of improvisation on his work.

> I feel now equally dedicated to both set and improvised modes, valuing them as complementary. Poor old Improv has received such a bad press, probably because its exponents have sometimes (often?) used it as an escape or preliminary stage of choreography, rather than as a 'perfect' form in its own right. I really take sides with the jazz musicians of quality in that respect; how they support the 'instant composition' as a highly sophisticated creative form. I think improvisation is a strict discipline and moreover a wondrous path between the music/ inspiration and the forms which the audience receives.

In the last few years Hamilton has concentrated on solo programmes, bringing one to the Purcell Room at London's South Bank Centre in May 1990 as part of the Centre's imaginative Moves Afoot series of New Dance works. *Friday*, his most recent full-length solo programme presented in 1989 (another is being prepared for 1990), was shown outdoors (see photograph on page 33) as well as indoors.

It received its British première outdoors at Coventry Arts Centre in April 1989 because the Arts Centre had just been gutted by fire, but the outdoor milieu is an area explored by Britain's New Dancers just as it was by the Judson dancers and their followers in New York. *Friday* refers to Robinson Crusoe's Man Friday who becomes, in Hamilton's words, 'the catalyst for Crusoe's change and is constantly being observed by him, causing Crusoe to become increasingly aware of "another island" of perceptions growing within himself'.

This kind of approach to choreography, using improvisation or combining improvisation with previously created choreography to explore interior worlds, was a strong element of the New Dance movement. 'I must say', continued Hamilton,

> I find much of the discourse between 'set choreography' versus 'improvisation' to be simply avoiding the further and more important issue which is 'does something actually happen on stage'? Is the imagination touched?, the cells of the onlooker joggled?, the spirit elevated?, the intellect stimulated? Rather these questions than the 'how' of how it arrived. As ever I am trying to balance demands from the product-oriented scheme of festivals and venues with my own constant need to air work which I feel is just as valid and viewable, but of a different dynamic ... I feel my patience grow, though, supported by my passion for dance and how it can communicate deeply. I feel this often with teaching which has been an area of great enjoyment and development for me. People/students always seem to trust the teaching risks which I take and at base there is this wordless communication which is constantly wanting to flower ... The photos are the result of a three-year-old collaboration with photographer André Hoekzema where we have tried to consider the roots of each of the solo performances (themes, intentions, viewpoints) and use photographs outside as a metaphor for the inside performance. Visual analogies? We've carefully structured the elements, trying to keep the dynamics of the body in movement and building the whole to a point where the imagination is stimulated in a manner parallel to the way in which the performance might be received ... in the pictures is a statement about the origins of my inspiration and hopefully to others they might open perceptions of how we view dance movement as it touches the under lying myths which permeate our daily lives.

The founding of a Graham School of contemporary dance at The Place in the late 1960s not only trained Britain's future contemporary dancers, but also stimulated some dancers and choreographers to reject the high modernism which Graham represented. New Dance was one form of rejection. Richard Alston, now director of Rambert Dance Company, was another. Alston drew much from the London School of Contemporary Dance and from Robert Cohan's commission to create works for London Contemporary Dance Theatre. His early work like *Tiger Balm* in 1972 reflected this semi-American schooling but showed also clear signs of early departure along his own path. Those were spring days of experiment at The Place, for choreographers and audience. The decisive period in Alston's career was the formation in London of his small experimental group Strider with Gulbenkian support in 1973. For this he created *Headlong* the same year, followed by *Soft Verges* in 1974 and an early version of *Rainbow Bandit* in 1975. These showed his growing interest in dance as dance, in unemotional movement and a Cunningham future rather than the Graham path.

An extended period in the United States to study with Cunningham and others consolidated the conversion on his return in 1977. His philosophy has developed, but not changed, since then, that 'dance is about dancing', that dance movement has its own ability to communicate through its own structures. 'You might say,' wrote Stephanie Jordan in a series of thumbnail sketches about each choreographer in Rambert's printed Sadler's Wells programme for its 1990 spring season, 'you might say that he is a "symphonic" choreographer, handling large as well as small forms and packing them tight with dance ideas, challenging the audience's eyes and intellect, but providing the solid foundations that make the outline of a work clear.' Jordan made a good point, too, about Alston's connection with the dance heritage. After all, he is the only choreographer with Eton and the classical Rambert School in his education as well as London Contemporary Dance School. Like Cunningham there is classical ballet in his choreography as well as popular dance styles, all reflected in the training of his dancers, who receive classical as well as Cunningham classes. Therefore Alston does not go along with the more lunatic post-modern concentration on NOW, rejecting even last year's new choreography. In dance, at least, this kind of approach is not on. Dance is about change, certainly, but this year's body came out of last year's body which grew out of the year before.

The repertory of Alston's Rambert season at Sadler's Wells Theatre from 6 to 24 March 1990 in fact showed the alternative post-modern response to question marks facing British dancers and choreographers in a Britain of increasing penury for the arts. It is an answer within the established dance structure, rather than a departure outside the structure, like New Dance. Therefore it will be helpful to consider the repertory and presentation of the season in detail. It is the clearest statement of British post-modern dance. To support its effort to overcome penury, for example, the company has become a front runner among dance enterprises for the finance it persuades from commercial and charitable sources. A range of trusts and traders underpinned its Gala for Young People on 6 March 1990 from the Ronson and Baring Trusts to Pizza Express, and from McDonalds Hamburgers to Our Price Music — twenty-seven sponsors no less! Similar effort, but from private donations and on a wider scale, lay behind the annual Frederick Ashton Memorial Commission in association with *The Daily Telegraph*, which went in 1990 to Ashley Page. The company itself received major sponsorship from Digital and won the 1989 Prudential Award for the Arts. Perhaps the name of Rambert helps in winning so much support. The name at least is traditional. Maybe the company has a continual flow of good ideas. Good ideas, as Richard Alston pointed out in a programme introduction, involve risks. 'Not only that, but when a programme feels balanced and is greeted as a success, it is time to move on to new ingredients, new combinations. Movement is about change . . .' Digital, particularly among sponsors, has shown itself willing to support change.

Rambert's name now is synonymous with change. The major change was in 1966 when Rambert's British classical modernism was jettisoned for an American modernist approach. Glen Tetley set the company then on its new choreographic road with Christopher Bruce emerging later as an exponent of dance modernism with a human face and a distinctively British style. Now Bruce rules no longer the Rambert repertory and a post-modern revolution under Alston has changed both the image and the dancers of the Company. The image is rooted clearly in the example of Merce Cunningham, the greatest exponent of post-modern dance. Cunningham provides the company's aesthetic, two of its dance works in the Sadler's Wells March season and the principles upon which dancers are chosen and trained. The dominant American influence over all British modern dance thus is sustained with Trisha Brown as well as Tetley represented in the Rambert repertory, with Siobhan Davies somewhat altered in style after her Fulbright Arts Fellowship to the United States two years ago, and with Dan Wagoner as the second American artistic director of London Contemporary Dance Theatre following Robert Cohan.

Is British post-modern dance, then, a dependency culture or is there an indigenous form growing from the American graft? Alston has not pursued very far Cunningham's juxtaposition of the ingredients of a dance work independently created so that chance becomes a factor in the performance. On the contrary, he has emphasized consistently the integration of dance, music and design, as Diaghilev did! Consequently the contribution of composers, designers and lighting designers was a controversial and exciting element of Rambert's Wells season. Alston's independence is clear. His dance language is his own, neither pastiche nor copy of Cunningham.

This dance language was very visible in the Sadler's Wells season alongside, as Alston put it, being 'rather like the curator of a private collection with the responsibility not only of making new acquisitions, but also of keeping existing works in good order, bringing them out, arranging and re-arranging them in new contexts'. He said 'existing works' not old works. There was only one really old work in the 1990 Rambert repertory, Glen Tetley's *Embrace Tiger and Return to Mountain*, which he created for the company when he was called in to help change its style in 1968. The other 'old' piece was Cunningham's *Septet* created for his company's first New York season in 1953. It too, as Alston said, 'represents something at the roots of the whole business'. It only entered the Rambert repertory, however, in 1987 with the help of a Digital Award. Everything else in the 1990 season was mounted on the company in 1987 or later up to the newest works belonging to the season itself — Alston's *Dealing with Shadows* to music by Mozart and Gary Lambert's *Longevity* to extracts from the Dream speech by Martin Luther King. To be 3 years old in a post-modern context is really to be OLD.

Cunningham's *Septet* is a sort of memory, looking back to his beginnings. It fits easily Rambert's current group of dancers who are trained in the Cunningham method. Therefore the opening of the season with Cunningham's *Doubles* appeared as a sort of gesture towards the Master. *Doubles* also was new in the repertory. Created by Cunningham in 1984 but mounted on Rambert only in January 1990 through the 1989 Prudential Award, it was the company's third Cunningham work and Rambert's consolidation of its Cunningham allegiance. The two works together reflect the dance philosophy which captured Alston's imagination nearly twenty years ago. It is a philosophy as antipathetic to many traditions of classical ballet as it is to the high modernism of Graham which Alston forsook. The Diaghilev ideal of three compatible arts in perfect complementary balance is called in question by Cunningham, not dependent but independent. Dance, he asserts, can be freed from music, even from music's rhythmic content, going beyond the plotless ballet of Balanchine to live its own independent performing existence. It is neither more nor less, dance — not concerned to tell stories, nor to convey Great Ideas nor, on the evidence, concerned much with emotions. To dance well is enough, but the 'well' is important. If chance is an element of the Cunningham choreography, it is the dancers who make choices in direction, space, energy and timing, they therefore who give the work its quality.

Cunningham's first work using chance methods, called today 'open form', was *Suite by Chance* in 1953, the year of *Septet*. *Septet* therefore descends from a landmark period. Both it and *Doubles* illustrate also how good and *responsible* Cunningham dancers have to be. Chance methods actually are very hard work creating, then making, choices between one possibility and another, taking into account dancers' abilities, rehearsal time, virtuosity, energy, sense of space. It takes *hours* of rehearsal, the choices and the chances arising more often in rehearsal than in performance. The result is to place total focus on dancers and dancing with a huge demand on their interpretation of complex material, their independence and individuality.

Alston chooses his dancers the way Cunningham does, for their differences. Thus a company becomes like an orchestra of different instruments combined successively by the choreographer into a series of creative works. The present Rambert company must be one of the best of recent times, challenged by the contrasting styles of the choreographers Alston has gathered round him — Trisha Brown from America, and the home-grown Siobhan Davies, Ashley Page and Gary Lambert.

Trisha Brown, for instance, retains in her work the iconoclasm of New York's Judson dancers in the 1960s. The general theme for all post-modern movers at that time was liberation of the body from dance convention. Therefore pedestrain movement, sports movement, everyday gesture, running, walking, lying, jumping, *any* form of physical activity was source material reproduced unembellished. Chance too played its part; not the managed chance of Cunningham, but the chance of an unmanaged happening. Today Brown's *Opal Loop*, created in 1980 but added to the Rambert repertory in 1989 through another Digital dance award, shows the same source materials very much embellished by virtuosity and the zany humour for which Brown is famous. She shows the world outside the theatre through a distorting mirror, but it remains a real, living world.

Alston's own challenge, of course, is the most decisive in the season because his is the company's dominant and most familiar style. Clear in *Hymnos* and *Strong Language*, two of his four works in the season from 1988 and 1987 respectively, the style looks back to Alston's first *Hymnos* in 1980 to the same Peter Maxwell Davies score. Then *Hymnos* was part of *Bell High*, Alston's first dance work for Rambert and the prelude to his appointment as resident choreographer in May of the same year. So it, too, recalls something of history. Similarly, the composition of *Strong Language* recalls the Cunningham approach to relationships with allied arts. Its episodic dances with sharp transitions from one dance form and dance rhythm to another were composed alongside the music with composer and choreographer working to a basic rhythmic unit, allowing themselves to syncopate freely. Both dance works use strong contrast between gentleness and fast attack, harsh outbursts and pianissimo murmurs.

They are densely packed in movement, as Alston's choreography usually is, because his approach hasn't changed much, only developed and developed as the new *Hymnos* shows. Nor has his concern for music, design, costumes and lighting changed much since the experience with Strider. All of high quality in themselves, they tend to be directed by the choreography to emphasize the dance as dance. In this season, though, the invariable rightness of Rambert's allied arts went wrong twice, both times with costumes, one of them being Alston's new work, *Dealing with Shadows*.

In memory of the late Biddy Espinosa, *Dealing with Shadows* opened almost symbolically with a single dancer on stage. She moved forward as if to address the audience. Then did so, in dance. It's what this choreography is about, plus the mystery for the audience of how to interpret the dance communication. The same mystery attaches, of course, to music, like Mozart's *Piano Sonata in A Major* to which the choreography is written. Although constructed cleverly, the movement stays somehow separate from the music without achieving Mozart's depth of communication nor matching the 'wonderful succinctness of form' which Alston rightly acknowledges in Mozart. Partly the fault lies with distracting costumes by English Eccentrics, 'a leading print design house' said the programme. Alas, they seemed to know little about designing for dancers. The shorts and other accessories the dancers assumed half-way through the work not only distorted their line but also the line and atmosphere of music and choreography. It was a rare mistake underlined by Alston's other work in the season, *Pulau Dewata* created for Rambert's Wells season in 1989. Its costumes, lighting, design and choreography combined with Claude Vivier's music to create an homage to 'the spirit of Bali ... a life that is simple and direct'. Simple, direct and welcome it was.

The other costume problem was also a new work in the season, Ashley Page's *Currulao* made possible by the Frederick Ashton Memorial Commission in association with *The Daily Telegraph*. It drew together a specially commissioned score by Orlando Gough, lighting by Peter Mumford and costumes by John Galliano, a talented fashion designer whose inspiration obviously derived from Colombia where the currulao is a courtship dance of mixed Spanish and African descent. Page rather overplayed the courtship in male–female and male–male encounters, but everything else also was overplayed. Galliano's black and white costumes were fussy with bits and pieces you might wear to look fashionable in daytime or evening but which concealed the movement and were, in fact, mostly discarded. The score was noisy, unsubtle, streetwise but not dancewise. Here, in fact, was a partnership which seemed never to gell. Page is one of the most interesting of the Royal Ballet's rising choreographers because of his wide vocabulary, visual taste in imagery and choice of designers, independence and sense of adventure, even courage, in what he attempts. He can be complex and obscure — in experiments for Dance Umbrella and at Chisenhale, for example — but rarely unsatisfying. *Currulao* had strong images but choreographically it appeared muddled and the conception as a whole was unclear. Still Page's unquestioned talent had been proclaimed earlier in the season by his striking version of Stravinsky's *L'Histoire du Soldat*, first presented in 1988. It suggested that Page's post-modernism relates as much to Rambert as it does to the classical Royal Ballet.

So, too, Siobhan Davies. Rambert seems to have become a point of reference for some British post-modern choreographers. They relate to the company while doing their own thing elsewhere, like Page in classical ballet and Davies in other, smaller groups, especially her own. I remember her as a singularly thoughtful, concerned artist when she danced with Ballet for All at the beginning of the 1970s. In particular she had a deep sense of responsibility for her art. These qualities underlie her choreography today. *Soundings* and *Embarque*, her two dance works in the Rambert season, illustrated vividly these qualities — abstract, yes, always dance about dance, but never impersonal, never bodies just dancing but danced relationships lit by an humanity which seems stronger since her return from the United States. *Embarque* especially was worthy of its nomination for a Laurence Olivier Award in April 1990.

There were times when an evident humanity and social concern figured strongly in most of Rambert's repertory through Christopher Bruce's influence. It is not so strong today, except perhaps if Gary Lambert fulfils the promise shown in *Longevity*. Newly created for this Rambert season and made possible by a Digital Award, *Longevity* seems to lift the curtain on post-modernism with a human face. Its dance language is very much in post-modern idiom, as one might expect from a Rambert dancer today, but interesting and personal in technique, mixing influences from Lambert's training at the Royal Ballet School before he joined Rambert in 1985. The 'score' is an extract from Martin Luther King's *I have a dream* ... speech, emphasized by a big blow-up of King's face on the back cloth. The dream is symbolized through the dancing of two men, one black, one white, sometimes in antagonism, more often in partnership. It is never overstressed — indeed the piece is too slight for its theme — but coming in the last programme of the season it was uplifting and promising not just for Lambert and the new kind of more aware dancer now entering the profession, but for another direction of Rambert's forward move and for a stronger kind of communication.

Dancers dance to communicate, so at the end of this season what had been communicated? In terms of Richard Alston's Tate Gallery idiom it was a good post-modern collection. Some foreign masters, some English masters, some new talents. There was even a mix between post-modern abstract and post-modern semi-narrative. We could have done, though, with more European examples, especially from France. Yet all the good lighting, the colour of costumes, the trained bodies in movement and stillness, the sounds on the ear, the environments created by each dance work, to what did it amount? Should we accept that dances need have no meaning for anyone but the choreographer as Carolyn Brown, a Cunningham dancer, once wrote of the Master's choreography — 'Certainly he has taken precautions to see that little of it is intelligible to an outsider, or for that matter to an insider.'[7] Or is the purpose to let the audience draw its own conclusions, create its own dreams as Jerome Robbins shows in *The Concert*?[8] Can a post-modern work by Alston, say, or Davies really have meaning only in the mind of the spectator where the work of choreographer, composer, designer, lighting designer and dancer might be synthesized as a whole? Is the vital rhythm, deriving so often from within the dancer rather than the orchestra pit, repeated in the spectator's breast? Is the meaning and value of each work finally created by the spectator?

Some post-modern choreographers say this is so. The problem, though, has to do with the artistic responsibility of company and choreographers. Are they not both responsible in some degree for aesthetic communication with the public which pays them, even for that public's aesthetic education? So what if the range of aesthetic experience on offer is so special that 'the discerning public', which Richard Alston identifies for Rambert, becomes too small for box-office viability? Compare, say Michelangelo's *David* where the public was called to admire and be moved by the outer form and inner emotions of the work, its grandeur, solemnity and physical beauty. Post-modern choreography offers often only a rather rarefied range of inner emotions to those who discern. Its conception is that of private experience. But dance is not a private experience; it needs to be shared. For those who do not understand there are, judging from the reaction of much of Rambert's Sadler's Wells audience, only what my philosophy tutor used to call 'ooh' feelings. A visitor who saw the Rambert programme at the Theatre Royal, York, just before the Wells season said its style was 'passionless'. Is this really enough, especially when the great majority of the British public won't touch modern dance with a bargepole? Therefore, I question the moment of post-modernism in the long journey of choreographic art. Something bigger is needed to touch communities from time to time in ways that seize the imagination and stir the mind with visions beyond the present. The best of post-modernism may acknowledge its debt to the past but does not look beyond humanity's questionable today.

Much of the answer lies in a broader choreographic vision. I

Plate 2 Other ways to dance. Ursula Hageli with Richard Slaughter (in the background) of Ballet Creations introduce classical partnering to students at a Manchester School through their schools programme. Photograph by Paul Herrmann.

talked with Alston about the problem. How to reach, interest and hold audiences for post-modern dance, especially outside London? 'You have to beguile people a bit', said Alston.

> Balanchine did it with music. I try to do it by presenting balanced programmes, good music and design. The important skill, if you see part of our job as aesthetic education, is to be ahead, but not too far ahead and *never* the mixture as before. What must also come across always, as Madame Rambert insisted, is the integrity and quality of what is offered.

We talked about this problem a lot because programme balance and repertory obviously have to be mingled with other things like more explanation. Rambert's excellent programme notes might be expanded. Some part lies in education and the work not only of Rambert's animators in schools, colleges, arts centres and elsewhere, but of all animators from the Royal Ballet, Sadler's Wells Royal Ballet, Contemporary, Laban, Central School and local authorities coordinated regionally and nationally. Denigrated as dance is in the national curriculum, underfunded by government, hugely at risk in the current Arts Council reorganization, the dance community has no option but to fight back to nourish and win the public in its own way on its own terms. The alternative is oblivion.[9]

The Classical Response

The dance profession's projection of itself must embrace, therefore, much more than a post-modernism characterized by the Cunningham style. This is dance divorced on the whole from a music the public recognizes as music, divorced from even that 'basic' idea or 'personal fount of emotion' which Frederick Ashton once argued should inform all dance works.[10] Often the mark of such post-modernism is a wide-ranging use of sound rather than music and an absence of theme other than dance itself. It begins from human bodies and builds on dance techniques. It can be satisfying and interesting on its own terms, as the Rambert paradigm shows. Tetley can vere between post-modern approaches and narrative uses of classical ballet. Paul Taylor, the modernist, draws always on founts of emotion inspired frequently by eighteenth century music.

There are other manifestations, such as experiments at The Place or Chisenhale Dance Space in London (successor to X6), and, of course, new productions of classical ballet in new styles. We have to be ready, as Brecht pointed out long ago, for 'experimental phases ... in which an almost unbearable narrowing of perspective occurs, one-sided or rather few-sided products emerge, and the applicability of results becomes problematic'.[11] Yet experiment remains essential so that the smaller centres of dance which present it, the university studios and the school spaces, need continuing, tolerant support. One can suffer often, in these spaces in the cause of artistic freedom, never knowing what will emerge. I recall an evening of new choreography by London Contemporary Dance Theatre at The Place Theatre during April 1990. Two of the three pieces were familiar in their obscurity but also repetitious, structurally muddled and uninteresting in movement qualities. Even the excellent dancers could not turn base metal into gold.

The classical reverse of such evenings, surely, is the endless appetite for *Swan Lake*. The public takes refuge in the melodies and fantasy of romanticism, in star names and in nostalgia. The Establishment follows suit. Responsible for the aesthetic education of the public, having the power and duty to take risks in the cause of dance's forward move, it too takes refuge in *Swan Lake*. The excuse is market forces and niggardly government subsidy. This last is true, but the lack of adventurous policies has characterized Covent Garden for a long time, even when money was more available. The real point is that *Swan Lake* is 'safe'. There will be no upsetting of applecarts or the box-office with disturbing new works. Consider the case of Kenneth McMillan's *Song of the Earth* created in 1965 to Mahler's *Das Lied von der Erde*. He offered the idea first to the Board of the Royal Opera House, Covent Garden. They resisted the idea partly on musical grounds, partly because they did not have confidence in the theme of death and renewal. MacMillan offered it, therefore, to John Cranko at Stuttgart. From Stuttgart there emerged on 6 November 1965 one of MacMillan's finest works and one of the great ballets of post-war Europe. The Board of Covent Garden, having lost the distinction of a world première, presented it a year later. Stuttgart was proved more stimulating as a home for creativity than London.

MacMillan, with Christopher Bruce of Rambert and English National Ballet, offers another alternative face to modernist and post-modernist dance. He is not of the Establishment, not a poet laureate of dance, as Ashton became. 'There is a class system', he said in an interview on BBC 2 on 4 April 1990, 'an old boy network to which I've never belonged and which I've always kicked against and I always will.' Appropriately the programme was called 'Out of Line'. Mac-Millan is controversial. He does not sit down easily with the powers that be nor with the bureaucratic nature of institutions like the Royal Opera House. He has never forgiven the Royal Ballet for insisting that the first performance of his *Romeo and Juliet* on 9 February 1965 should go to Fonteyn and Nureyev when it had been created for Lynn Seymour and Christopher Gable.

Coming from a poor and fraught background MacMillan's concern has been for people, especially people at odds with the world, persecuted people, innocent people who are betrayed as the young girl was in *The Invitation* in 1960. This was an early adventure into the *nouvelle vague* and the beginnings of British post-modern classicism, the first time sex and sexuality had been treated so openly in classical ballet. 'I am very interested in people . . . in portraying the dilemma of people living and working with each other. That was not a very popular approach to ballet in the 1950s.' It still isn't. When MacMillan succeeded Ashton as director of the Royal Ballet in 1970 he was greeted with hostility, not only within the Royal Ballet and by British audiences but also by American audiences in New York. They wanted only the Ashton they knew. Like the conservative ballet audience of late nineteenth century Russia the conservative ballet publics in Britain and the United States do not welcome change and new ideas. Not for nothing is classical ballet perceived as an art for the State and its Establishment. Consequently the taste of this public has stayed with the modernism of Diaghilev's later period which Ashton translated and developed on British physiques and temperaments. MacMillan has found it difficult to move his audience beyond this point into his own post-modernism, especially now that the long-standing conservative taste of Covent Garden is compounded by a dance-ignorant public brought into its more expensive seats through business sponsorship. A creative inertia blankets the Royal Ballet which is neither MacMillan's fault nor that of Anthony Dowell, the company's director. It derives directly from the cultural climate of business audiences and contrasts strongly with the more positive climate of Birmingham Royal Ballet appearing before a more popular audience.

From the beginning of his career as a dance artist MacMillan has been on a collision course with consumer society's lack of concern for the injustices around it, its preference for glitter and display and its taste which asks only that ballet should be 'beautiful' and romantic. He was bored as a dancer with the pyrotechnics of Petipa, though he could perform them with brilliance. 'I prefer to explore the human psyche . . . I try to make people sometimes feel uncomfortable in the theatre.' This means addressing reality head on. Not for him the Jungian unconscious of Martha Graham, nor the inner self and abstraction which preoccupy so much of post-modern contemporary choreography from the Judson dancers in New York to Dance Umbrella and The Place in London. His post-modernism is to confront classical ballet with today's reality, especially its deceit. Much of his inspiration comes from literary sources like his *Manon* based on Prévost's *Manon Lescaut*. He is rare, too, among today's choreographers in using a librettist as he did for *Mayerling* and for *Isadora* both about 'people at odds with the world'. 'I have always been drawn to the narrative, to real people and what they feel. I think ballet is limitless.' His major contribution to classical choreography, therefore, has been to redirect the art form primarily to portray real people, rather than fantasy. Hence *Mayerling*, his masterpiece, with its vivid image of the Archduke Rudolf and the corrupt Hapsburg court, and his *Gloria* 'about the waste and carnage of the first world war'. True, and real, though not the realism of the cinema, *Gloria* protests against the inhumanity of that conflict by showing the reality behind it in terms of human beings and their suffering. *Gloria* illustrates vividly MacMillan's significance in the post-modern choreographic scene.

Often it has been said — and MacMillan has argued it himself — that he is giving Petipa's full-length fantasy formulae like *The Sleeping Beauty* and *La Bayadère* a meaningful twentieth century substance. So he is, but the humanity behind his whole approach to classical ballet also has combined the art's post-modern technical achievements with an humanism which provides an alternative to the kind of dance concentration which characterizes Balanchine and Cunningham. MacMillan therefore offers an alternative post-modern direction for the art form. In doing so he challenges the hegemony of thinking which dominates the Royal Opera House, most of the traditional public image of classical ballet and ultimately the view of government, Arts Council and private sponsors of what ballet should be about. His sin, and the reason for resistance to him, is to seek to update the image enshrined in *Swan Lake*, Ashton's *Ondine* and Balanchine's plotless works. He questions a repertory and way of thinking previously unquestioned and, indeed, thought to be unquestionable.

Christopher Bruce's choreography has concerns similar to those of MacMillan though he uses a dance language less directly classical, mingling the disciplines of modern and classical movement. His *Swansong* about the interrogation of a (political?) prisoner, his *Ghost Dances* dedicated 'to the oppressed peoples of South America', his *Ancient Voices of Children* about unloved, unwanted children in an adult world, his *Cruel Garden* with Lindsay Kemp about the oppression of the poet Lorca by the society of his day — these and other works are the response of an artist to the material world as he perceives it. He, too, broadens the competence of classically based dance. Neither Bruce nor MacMillan is 'political' nor concerned to communicate manifestos. That is not the choreographic way. Rather they respond to a cultural climate which can never be separate from the material world and the events within it. For years we have lived with the despair of the Cold War, the barbarities of South America, South Africa, Northern Ireland, which have produced for us at home climates of bigotry and prejudice. These affect many sections of society and it is these which the humanist post-modernism of Bruce, MacMillan and some younger choreographers ask us to confront.

Post-modernism is a social situation as well as an historical period and choreographic style.

The realism they employ is neither the expressionism of modernist pioneers nor the surface naturalism of, say, socialist realism. It is what MacMillan's wife has called 'a universal realism', a critical realism digging down to the causes of things, often within people, exposing pretence and hypocrisy, offering some illumination for the future but accepting and commenting on the truth of our present moment. This truth can be expressed in many ways, through the humour of MacMillan's *Elite Syncopations* or Christopher Bruce's parable of working class life in *The Dream is Over*, but truth has to lie at its centre in a way that truth does not lie at the centre of consumerist society. The advertisements of this society on television often show a marvellous technical originality one might admire on stage but they are economical with the truth, sometimes a lie. This is the conflict between artists and post-modern society.

The approach to realism of both choreographers is reflected in their choice and use of dancers. Both have the ability to perceive in dancers possibilities the dancers did not think they had. Both extend the qualities they find in dancers. Bruce drew an extraordinary communication from Koen Onzia in the lead role of *Swansong*. MacMillan used the sensuality of Ashley Page's movements to make the King of the South by far the strongest character among the four suitors of his homage to Petipa in *The Prince of the Pagodas*. It is an homage with echoes of Lear — the old King, the fool, the Kingdom divided and the good and evil daughters — not much to do with sleeping beauties. MacMillan's way has been the humanist practice of a classical form in the circumstances of post-modern society. Bruce's is the unity of dance forms in the service of his own realism. Alston's is the use of dance to portray dance as itself, often with an underlying humanity in the disposition of his dancers, but with 'meaning' left equally often to the audience.

These are alternative directions in post-modern choreography. They signal a continuing struggle between traditional approaches, explorations of 'dance about dance' and new humanist directions. This is neither to argue a break with the past nor an end to experiments which present dance for itself. After all dance for itself is as old as the hills. Perrot's famous *Pas de Quatre* in 1845 was a presentation of different dance communications by four ballerinas in contrasting styles 'speaking' only through dance. There have been many similar communications before and since. Rather it is to entice all this experience, past and present, in positive directions for the 1990s and to break the hegemony of traditionalist taste. The choreographies of David Bintley and Ashley Page at Covent Garden illustrate problems and opportunities. Bintley's immense talent has led him to explore choreography in many different moulds although the dominant influence upon his work appears to come from Ashton and Balanchine. As resident choreographer to the Royal Ballet he must create, too, in styles which appeal to the traditionalist audience. Hence a plotless work like *Galanteries* to music from a Mozart divertimento and serenade. It is a series of dances drawing its fount of emotion from the music, an exercise in the formal beauty, classical balance and calm restraint of the traditional modernist style of the British School founded by Ashton, satisfying and well danced. Bintley, though, is himself a distinguished character performer so that many of his ballets like *'Still Life' at the Penguin Café* have about them an implicit drama, in this case mixing humour and pathos in remonstrance against thoughtless destruction of birds and animals by Man. This element is carried further in his full-length *Hobson's Choice*, created in 1989. Its humour and vivid characterization in a very English theatrical tradition was received rather coolly at the Royal Opera House and by traditionalist critics but was welcomed warmly by the audiences of Sadler's Wells Royal Ballet outside London for whom it was created.

Ashley Page's *Pursuit* in a programme alongside *Galanteries* during the Royal Ballet's spring season in 1990 was reminiscent of Cunningham's 'open form' approach to music, design and dance. Page described in a programme note how he set about its creation in 1987. He aimed at 'an highly energetic piece within the boundaries of a rigorous (and vigorous) classicism'. To realize this he chose 'a predominantly textural composition' by Colin Matthews whose principal qualities were 'seamlessness' and 'energy'. For design he chose Jack Smith, a designer who goes his own way in costumes and stage set with bright colours and stark shapes which 'explode across the back cloth as music and choreography collide occasionally, like punctuation of a long and fanciful sentence'. To a large extent, therefore, the three art forms tended to go their own way. The work was

> 'as much about the dancers and the way they move as it is about the integration of three interrelated art forms ... Jack Smith, Colin Matthews and I share a desire to express an idea through the language of our chosen medium — to say something which is entirely in itself (painting, music, movement) and exists purely through an expression of itself without subject or narrative'.

In the event audiences seemed to find most difficulty with the music which had few of the melodic forms and none of the regular rhythmic pulse expected for dance at Covent Garden. The main problem, however, was the general emptiness of the work as a whole. One could appreciate separately the three creations but that is not why one goes to see a ballet. The individual creations did not come together as a combined communication so that the result is emptiness, a passing moment, one hopes, in Page's choreographic journey.

Other journeys are being undertaken daily by other choreographers in small groups and small theatres struggling to live, at Dance Umbrella festivals, in studios and community sessions, wherever the slow extension of British dance culture takes place. Already the names of Lea Anderson, Rosemary Lee, Kim Brandstrup, Jonathan Burrows, Royston Maldoom, Darshan Singh Buller, Lloyd Newson among other talents mean something in communities away from large stages. The decisive advances may begin there. Postmodernism is not necessarily negative in its use of modernist legacies. The issue is the relationship of choreography to the events of our time and the climate of culture they create. Hope arises from the events of 1989 in Europe but the response in choreography will lie as much in schools and communities as with the professional stage and its audience. It is possible to see there the outlines of a struggle for the soul of choreography to be worked out on stage, in the studio and among the audience.

Notes and References

1 Jameson, Frederick: 'Postmodernism and consumer society', in Kaplan, Ann (Ed.) *Postmodernism and its Discontents*, London, Verso Edition, 1988.
2 Abbs, Peter: *The Symbolic Order*, London, Falmer Press, 1989, p. xiii.
3 Abbs, Peter: *Living Powers*, London, Falmer Press, 1987, p. 4.
4 Schlieke, Andrea: Introduction to *Decoy* at the Serpentine Gallery, London, the work of six young artists, and comment by Andrew Graham-Dixon in *The Independent*, 15 May 1990.
5 Laban, Rudolf: *Modern Educational Dance*, 3rd ed., London, Macdonald and Evans, 1975, p. 3.
6 This notion is developed particularly in Terry Eagleton, *The Ideology of the Aesthetic*, Oxford, Blackwell, 1990, reviewed by John Banville in *The Observer*, 4 March 1990.
7 Carolyn Brown in Klosty, James (Ed.) *Merce Cunningham*, New York, E.P. Dutton & Co Inc, 1975, p. 25.
8 Ballet in one act, ch. Robbins to music by Chopin, partly orchestrated by M. Kay, costumes by I. Sharaff, first produced 6 March 1956 on New York City Ballet. Revised Spoleto Festival 1958. Revived for Royal Ballet, London 1975. See Brinson, Peter, and Crisp, Clement: *Ballet and Dance*, Newton Abbot, David and Charles, 1980.
9 For further reference in this section see Brinson and Crisp, *op. cit.*, and also Brinson, Peter: 'To be ahead', *Dance and Dancers*, June 1990.

10 'The subject matter of ballet', Ballet Annual 13, London, 1959, p. 13. See also David Vaughan: *Frederick Ashton and His Ballets*, London, A. & C. Black, 1977.
11 'Brecht against Lukács', trans. Stuart Hood, in *Aesthetics and Politics*, London, 1977, p. 74.

51

Part 2
Outside the Theatre

Chapter 3

Education for What?

Dance, then, is a political as well as a social and aesthetic issue. So, too, is choreographic creation. The parameters of this unspoken struggle around the nature and aesthetic impact of choreography in British dance culture were extended recently by two small polemics against the Gulbenkian Report, *The Arts in Schools*.[1] Published in 1982 the report was reissued in 1989 because of widespread impact and response throughout the British education system. It is one of the basic texts in forming the Falmer Press series of which this volume is a part. Belatedly, and for reasons which are obscure, two respected members of the education profession, the philosopher David Best, and the educationalist, Malcolm Ross, decided to question the report's significance seven years late. Ross did so only in 1989[2] and Best later still at the beginning of 1990.[3] Ross' criticism was that the report was 'a piece of bureaucratic writing', had no pedagogues among its advisory committee and generally encouraged more than it could deliver. In fact, the report's advisory committee balanced members with teaching experience against those without, as the report's list of its committee makes clear, and the Foundation's planned follow-up to the report included meetings of teachers throughout the country, the launch of an arts magazine *Arts Express* and, ultimately, the Arts in Schools Project for the School Curriculum Development Committee of the National Curriculum Council. The SCDC reported early in 1990[4] and some of its conclusions are incorporated in this chapter.

Best's criticism was more fundamental. While supporting the general purpose and tenor of the report he attacked the conflation of 'two quite distinct but sometimes overlapping concepts — the aesthetic and the artistic'. In posing this 'fundamental misconception' he acknowledged that he was attacking also a view that the artistic can be defined in terms of the aesthetic 'as Louis Arnaud Reid and other philosophers seem to think'. In fact, the Gulbenkian Foundation went to much trouble to have its presentation verified by Louis Arnaud

Reid and other leading specialists in the field so that, as so often in his career, Best presents himself as the White Knight doing lonely battle against confusions and misconceptions raised by everyone else. Moreover he is plain wrong. There is a deep connection between the arts and the aesthetic. In the circumstances of the time and the report's purpose it was entirely reasonable for Gulbenkian to emphasize this since the arts contribute fundamentally to aesthetic education. The Gulbenkian intention was to drive home not only the case for the arts in schools but also the need for an approach to education, especially aesthetic education, alternative to the emerging educational policies of the newly elected Thatcher Government. Thus, as I made clear in my introduction to the report, its primary aim was political, a point missed by both Ross and Best from their different positions. It is crucial to a proper understanding of the way the report is written. The target of the report was those with power to make changes even though it may be unusual to see aesthetic matters argued as a political issue.

The same approach is warranted now in the struggle for the soul of choreography and the place of dance in education. What is the responsibility of choreographers to the public and to fellow artists? In which direction should they lead their art? A political dimension has been present always but is thrown into relief at this moment by government policies, the reorganization of the Arts Council and attenuated support for the arts in the Education Reform Act, 1988. No one is exempt from this political dimension because consumerist values touch us all from the supermarket to the television screen. A piece of choreography like *Pursuit* which 'exists purely through an expression of itself without subject or narrative' is hardly less political than the most 'committed' other work because to disclaim relationships with the outside world is itself a deeply political act. Yet there are many, many choreographers in different styles who maintain such an approach. Theirs is a post-modern version of art for art's sake, the idea that art is transcendent, something only for those with the gift to create and the gift to understand, not for everyone. Choreographers and teachers have the absolute right to work in this way, but they should understand the damage they do to the public image of dance and to students who might be future choreographers.

David Aspin, one of the principal influences on *The Arts in Schools* report, draws attention to two traditions of the arts descended from the classical world. In a chapter in *The Symbolic Order* he characterizes the 'Roman' tradition as one in which the artist is a separate, special person producing art which can be appreciated only by equally select people. It can be displayed to, but not appreciated by, the generality of ordinary people. This is the 'high art' view, the argument of 'excellence' underlying many funding policies today, including those of the Arts Council. On the other hand is the 'Athenian' tradition, a view that 'it is part of the greatness of man that he alone of all creatures can enrich his existence and the environment in which he lives by creating and furnishing it with works of Art, the constant exposure to and contemplation of which can evoke and be a vehicle for the expression of the sublime in every man and can thus give to all a vision of beauty that can be a source of pleasure and...an "everlasting" possession'.[5]

This 'Athenian' tradition is followed today by choreographers who seek to communicate significantly with a general audience and by those today who seek to offer the practice and appreciation of the arts to all students in schools and higher education institutions or who work to the same end in community situations. It affects aesthetic judgments and guides policies which argue that art and artists need informed, educated audiences as much as society needs the arts. Inevitably this implies that arts policies in education and the country at large have a growing political dimension. The present British government, by and large, takes a 'Roman' view. So do many principal institutions where choreography is presented. Hence a political dimension arises in dance and choreography which I explore further in chapter 6. The 'Roman' view of the arts is neither one which ought to prevail in a public education system genuinely intended to open opportunities for all, nor among choreographers who seek a wide reception for their art.

There are two further dimensions to this issue. 'Of all the failures of modern Britain,' wrote Ian Jack in *The Independent on Sunday*, 15 April 1990, 'perhaps the greatest is the failure of our imagination, of our ability to think ourselves into the lives of others ... a rift in our common humanity.' He was writing about conditions in Strangeways prison and the riot they provoked at that time, but one can find failure of imagination in most other aspects of modern Britain from social caring to housing to transport and funding for the arts. British life is dominated by convention and by lack of imagination, most specifically in the upbringing of future citizens. Barrack-like and dangerous estates, street violence, suburbs empty of positive recreational facilities, routine education for routine jobs, destruction of the environment, lack of colour or uplift in daily life except the colours of television, a self-regarding and greedy morality spreading outwards from Government to all levels of society, such is the experience of many young people. There are oases in this desert, especially in the informal culture which young people themselves create, but why should we expect caring, imaginative human beings to emerge from such oppressive backgrounds? A society gets the humanity it creates.

Yet, since the real wealth of a nation lies neither in its coal nor oil nor agriculture but in the imagination of its people,[6] we impoverish ourselves by present policies.

The second dimension in the political aesthetics of dance is the significance of dance practice and appreciation in evolving harmonious multi-racial relations. To this I return in chapter 5 and appendix D. Both dimensions comprise the case for dance in education and the case for an extended national dance culture. The case rests first on historical understanding of the development of dance in education; second, a distinction between dance and physical education; third, a comprehension of what dance and choreographic creativity actually can do for people; fourth an arts education properly formulated to realize the social, economic and educational value of the arts, including dance, in an 'Athenian' tradition. I address now these four issues.

Understanding through History

British dance culture has to contend today with a range of influences from the past. Principal among them are the Church, sport, the imperial ethic, commercial development, internal rivalries and attitudes towards the sexes. British national psychology remains burdened heavily, for example, by its Judaeo-Christian inheritance. Suspicious of the body, linking it to sin, the Church over the centuries either has condemned dance or incorporated it safely within religious ceremony. The medieval Catholic church veered between these alternatives. Protestant churches throughout Europe and North America similarly have questioned dance practices on moral grounds. Church of England priests in Victorian England protested against the introduction of the waltz to the ballroom because it brought male and female bodies into dangerous proximity. Much the same objections were raised by a vicar after the first world war. He compared the new 'up-to-date' dances with 'the morals of a pig-sty'. Letters to *The Times* declared the moral and physical dangers of the foxtrot, the tango and jazz dancing. Criticism of the Charleston, introduced to England in 1925, had a nastier ring. It was thought to be 'freakish, degenerate, negroid': the *Daily Mail* thought it 'reminiscent only of negro orgies!'[7] The mass of the people, though, rejected such attitudes, as they had done always. Social dancing between the wars became a national pastime rivalling the cinema with Britain leading the world in ballroom competitions. Thus the Church was never able to suppress a natural expression of human feeling, though its attitude helped to poison the social climate against dance. The taint of moral risk remains. Even in the 1930s, when British ballet was developing, it was thought still not quite proper for young ladies to make a career in dance.

The connection between industrialization, imperialism and sport also distorted attitudes to dance. To the late Victorians and to many people today, sport is a transmitter of ethical values, an expression of national psyche and a training ground, if no longer for Empire, at least for management, 'England has owed her sovereignty to her sports', declared the headmaster of Harrow in the 1890s.[8] Sport in the curriculum of public schools was held to produce the qualities of discipline, leadership, competition, determination to win, arrogance and conviction of national superiority on which the Empire was based.

Later, as industrialization created the necessity for physical recuperation among factory workers, sport was encouraged as a national pastime, a means of filling time released by reductions in working hours, a means to fitness. It was understood also (particularly by church/social workers) as a stimulus to social harmony, a training of young men in the qualities of discipline, self-control, good temper and cooperation with others which would make them good workers. These same young men were potential recruits to the armed forces but, brought up in poverty, were seen generally not to be good physical material. A physical training syllabus therefore was introduced to the English and Welsh elementary school curriculum in 1909, including dance within the concept of physical education for children.

Concern for the fitness of army recruits in the run-up to the first world war naturally was only one reason for the introduction of physical training into the curriculum, called *training* not *education*. Development towards such a movement in British education had mounted since the 1880s under Swedish influence. The channel for this influence was a Swedish physical educationalist, Martina Bergman Osterberg, bringing the ideas and methods of the Swedish physical education pioneer Peter Henrik Ling (1776–1839). Miss Osterberg opened the Bergman Osterberg Physical Training College in Hampstead, London, in 1880 with a curriculum which included the waltz and (mostly Swedish) national dancing. Its focus was entirely feminine 'to cultivate the true perception of gracefulness, to stimulate the aesthetic faculties and impart perfect control of muscles'.[9] This pioneer venture transferred to Dartford, Kent, in 1885 and was followed soon by other pioneers. Anstey College for Physical Training and Hygiene for Women Teachers (Ling's Swedish System), opened near Birmingham in 1896. Bedford College followed at the turn of the century. All three colleges included dance in their syllabi and experimented with kinaesthetics and eurhythmics. All three also, incidentally, were connected closely with the movement for feminine emancipation. Dance, in the climate of the time, was regarded as especially a female activity.

The influence of these ventures and their attitude to dance was reflected in the 1909 syllabus. The influence was extended further through the establishment of other colleges after the first world war and the introduction of other national syllabi for primary education in 1919, 1933 and 1937. The philosophy behind the syllabi agreed always on the value of folk dance mixed with national and social considerations. Therefore folk dance was extended to embrace the character and national dances of England, Scotland, Wales, Ireland and other European countries. Even some training in court dances was given, based on technique modified from classical ballet. Dance in physical training, however, did not go beyond primary level so that confusion arose between the notion of dance generally and the rather limited horizon of dance teaching in primary schools. On this basis, though, dance in British education acquired a more secure foothold than in most other industrialized countries. The way was prepared for an expansion of dance after the second world war. This is not to say that British development was unique. Ideas of movement education, including dance, took hold throughout Europe and the United States where the American Physical Education Association was founded in 1885. It could be said that a particular kind of dance culture, appropriate to new economic and social conditions, began to grow throughout the industrial world. This was pioneered in Europe during the early years of the twentieth century by Rudolf Laban and was carried in time into the British education system from the 1940s onwards. I return below to this phenomenon.

From an early date, therefore, dance became linked with physical education. It was a link in the minds of educators and administrators based on convenience and pragmatism rather than any principled consideration of dance as an art form. One of the most serious consequences was a separation of vocational and private dance teaching from dance in general education. A huge gulf developed between the philosophy and practice of the two sectors compounded by the commercial needs of private teachers and their organizations. These organizations followed the example of sport in their creation of national, then international structures. Just as British sport had been first to export its teaching and principles following Britain's lead in industrial revolution and imperial expansion, so British dance organization led the way impelled by the same forces. Partly under the need to regulate and develop standards, partly under the impulse of capitalist enterprise, British sport in the twentieth century, especially rugby, tennis, cricket and soccer, became mass spectator sport, part of a vast entertainment industry organized on capitalist enterprise lines rather than being guided by preferable philosophies of public education, social welfare or leisure service. This meant that many of the most prominent school teams became professional clubs, like Droop St School, London, which became Queen's Park Rangers. The rules of the sports and the organization of the enterprises were exported under the imperial ethic first to territories of the Empire then to other countries, then to form international organizations. Thus the International Association Football Federation was formed in 1904, the Imperial Cricket Conference in 1909 and the International Lawn Tennis Federation in 1913.[10]

Dance became a part of this entertainment industry bringing a much longer tradition. Part of the tradition was theatrical recalling knowledgeable audiences in the eighteenth century, the triumphs of romantic ballet in London in the 1840s and spectacular dance attractions at the Alhambra and Empire theatres, London, at the end of the century.[11] These were of mixed quality: on the one hand squadrons of female dancers dressed as soldiers and sailors presenting jingo imperialist themes, on the other hand some of the leading male and female classical dancers of the day, usually Italian, appearing with star billing. Part of this tradition of dance interest came from social dance. Its popularity stimulated a growing number of public dance halls in cities throughout Britain thus creating by the beginning of the twentieth century a new dance industry. Part, therefore, was educational since the activity in theatres and dance halls encouraged the growth of a vigorous network of teachers. These had their own traditions descended from the generations of private teachers who had guided the manners and steps of polite society since the renaissance. Many were well trained in the styles of classical ballet and social dancing which they taught. Some, attracted by the popularity of dance, had such little knowledge they were a danger to their students. Against this threat to standards, status and livelihoods, a group of teachers established in 1904 what is today the Imperial Society of Teachers of Dancing.

The Imperial Society embraced the social dances of the day, academic ballet and national and character dancing. It was followed presently by a range of other organizations forming one part of today's structure of British dance culture. The English Folk Dance and Song Society began in 1911, the Royal Academy of Dancing in 1920, the Cecchetti Society in 1922, the British Ballet Organization in 1930 and the International Dance Teachers' Association in 1967. There are other smaller organizations (too many) but these international bodies today comprise the main structure of dance teaching, teacher training and dance examination in Britain outside the state education system. They are international because all of them between the wars, with the exception of the EFDSS and IDTA, expanded rapidly into the Empire and since then into the Commonwealth and other countries, exporting British ideas and standards of dancing. Like the big sports bodies they became organized on business lines earning considerable sums from examination fees, the provision of courses, summer schools, teacher training, dance wear and other services.

These organizations protected the interests of their teacher members within the limits of their own disciplines, sustained standards of teaching and examination within the same limits and encouraged the development of their dance culture within and outside Britain. There is no doubt that without their activity, particularly the activity of the Royal Academy of Dancing and the Imperial Society, classical and other forms of Western dance would not be taught today at a generally good standard to the extent they are in South America, large parts of western Europe, Japan and south-east Asia as well as the British Commonwealth. The same can be said of aspects of British ballroom dancing in a different cultural context. On the other hand, the methods of teaching and syllabi reflect the pattern of Britain's intensely class-divided society impeding a broader development of dance. An equal impediment can be found in the conflicts and rivalries between the organizations, notwithstanding attempts at collaboration, and their concentration on income-earning examination syllabi at the expense of other approaches to dance. In the case of countries outside Britain the remoteness of the British headquarters and syllabi from the life conditions of the countries in which they are examined tend to specialize the appeal of dance to particular sections of society thus retarding its local growth. In particular these organizations serve that section of the community which can afford to pay for private dance classes for its children, notwithstanding the existence of a small number of scholarships for poorer children. Hence their existence reinforces the notion that dance itself is divided — dance in the private sector and dance in the public sector, dance for those who can afford it, less dance or no dance for those who cannot, rather than dance opportunities of all kinds for everyone. It has to be said that teachers in state schools in Britain often equally reject what the private teachers have to offer. The chasm of differences remains unbridged, but bridgeable. Slowly today the bridge is being built.

Because of these differences the voice of dance is much weakened at the power centres of national education policy. I remember leading a deputation to Shirley Williams, Secretary of State for Education, in February 1979. We argued for a larger share of resources for dance as an art form in public education, the need for mandatory in place of discretionary grants for dance students in vocational training and the possibility of treating dance as an art form in the syllabus rather than as a part of physical education. She was sympathetic but said she could do little to help us until the dance world got itself together and could speak with the voice of a united profession. Appreciating this need was a reason why the Calouste Gulbenkian Foundation established the Council for Dance Education and Training about the same time. It was to speak for the whole profession. The Council, however, speaks today mostly for the private sector. The public sector speaks through its own National Dance Teachers' Association formed as a response to the Education Reform Act of 1988. Both feature in the list of organization near the end of this book. There remains a need to reorganize all the various bodies of the dance teaching profession in line with current social change and politics so that dance enters the power struggle on better terms. It would help greatly to strengthen the authority and influence of the private sector of dance teaching if major organizations like the Royal Academy of Dancing, the Imperial Society and the British Ballet Organization could find some way to establish a cooperative or federal structure under an agreed central organization. I declare an interest in this objective because discussions to this end were initiated by me with Peter Pearson of the Imperial Society towards the end of 1968. They have continued in various ways ever since so that now it is time for an answer. Needed is an end not only to the excessive number of dance organizations and examining bodies of variable standard and size in the UK — eleven at a recent count — but also the wide range of competing examination syllabi which confuse parents and students and lower the professional standards of private dance education.

One of the factors affecting such a reorganization is a third contradiction in British dance to do with attitudes towards the sexes. We have seen that historically dance in the physical training curriculum developed mostly as appropriate for girls and young women. Children of both sexes joined in the folk dancing but the older boys' element increasingly became influenced by army physical training methods. The philosophy of sport as training for Empire and training for work remained strong leaving little place for the arts as part of general education, least of all practice of the arts. The public schools substituted postures, manners and skills based on military practice and imperial need in place of the eighteenth century ideal of dance as part of a preparation for life. If dance had an educational value it was for physical skills it might encourage in boys and the 'gracefulness... aesthetic faculties...and perfect control of muscles'[12] it might develop in girls rather than the imagination and personal creativity it might stimulate in both sexes. Thus were established not only the concepts which have inhibited dance in education since the nineteenth century but even a view of dance as an activity with different values and applications as between male and female. I have thought often that the continuation today of this nineteenth century discrimination provides a case to go before the Equal Opportunities Commission on behalf of boys!

Dance and Physical Education

Clearly, the present situation of dance in British education is a result of outdated historical forces combined with social prejudice. This has created an hegemony of thinking and attitude, discussed in chapter 6, which gives little consideration to the contribution dance would make to aesthetic education. The development of the art form since 1966 makes nonsense particularly of the separation of dance from other arts in the national curriculum. This means a separation also from all the issues posed by choreographers in British cultural life outlined in the last two chapters. It is a failure on the part of policy-makers to recognize fully the essential presence of the aesthetic realm in education and, paradoxically, a failure to recognize the importance of continuum between dance in education today and dance in British educational history before the distortion of imperial interest. Hence young people are short-changed educationally. The extent of this short-change was made clear in a powerful document of protest and argument in September 1989 against proposals which link dance to physical education in the national curriculum. Authors of the document were the Council for Dance Education and Training, the Dance Section of the National Association of Teachers in Further and Higher Education, the National Dance Teachers' Association and the Standing Conference on Dance in Higher Education. The actual document is reproduced in appendix A and is a rare example of the profession speaking with one voice. Perhaps if Shirley Williams still was secretary of state for education this would have been enough to persuade her to remove dance from the category of physical education and treat it as an art among other arts.

Quite why the DES should be so stuck in the past is difficult to determine. No cogent reasons ever have been offered for dance policies so plainly out of touch with developments. One can suppose two areas of disagreement or misunderstanding. First, tradition — it has always been so; second, the present. The traditional argument embraces two sub-areas, the historical background outlined above coupled with a misapplication in today's circumstances of the Laban teaching which dominated dance in schools from the war period until the 1970s. The second area, the present, appears to be an unwillingness to abandon established practice to come to terms with the advances achieved by dance in education during the last twenty years.

Historical tradition, of course, is always powerful in Britain even though the class society from which it derives is less and less relevant to today's circumstances and young people. It fuels, in particular, a powerful physical education lobby which continues to see dance as significant to physical education and which has the ear of the DES. Dance *is* significant to physical education so that it might retain its place in the PE syllabus provided the anomalies and misconceptions are removed and the art form is given *separate* recognition alongside other arts in the curriculum. The anomalies are listed in the document in appendix A, making it clear that dance should be part of arts grouping in schools with its own discrete programme of dance study.

Hindsight suggests now that it might have been preferable to recommend this solution for dance in the curriculum when the Gulbenkian Foundation considered the problem in 1980 in its report on *Dance Education and Training in Britain*. At the time it was felt that to remove dance totally from physical education in order to go it alone in schools might have deprived dance of the resources available then through physical education advisors. This turned out to be true only of a few local education authorities so that dance has not acquired in schools the extra support hoped for as a result of the report. The grip of the physical education lobby remains unbroken. Yet dance with physical education is not, and can never be, a proper education introduction to the art form. Therefore dance needs to be recognized in schools today as an art form in its own right. It should be taught in schools like drama, music or art and related to the art form on stage with all its changes and achievements. This is the only rational partnership through which the country can develop its dance culture and dance itself can play its full role in the aesthetic education of British people of all ages.

I outlined in chapters 1 and 2 the changes and achievements in the theatre which have developed today into forms of British modern dance. Modern dance emerged partly out of the expressionism which was an element of the modernist movement at the beginning of the century. Rudolf Laban was a supreme exponent of expressionist dance developing it in performance and applying it in community circumstances during the 1920s in Germany. He is one of the major dance thinkers of the century. Later, towards the end of his career, his philosophy of dance and movement was used to complement new philosophies in British education, especially the notion of child-centred education. We recognize now that the application of Laban's thinking in the educational context was interpreted too selectively by many of his followers though it achieved impressive results. During the last fifteen years, therefore, his philosophy has been re-examined and rethought by a group of scholars at the Laban Centre for Movement and Dance in London. Some results of this re-examination are discussed in appendix B. They show that the fundamental principles of Laban's philosophy remain valid and useful for today's society at all levels, but that they became a rigid form of teaching in many schools and teacher training colleges during the 1950s and 1960s, doing great damage to the concept of dance as an art form in education.

This rigidity tended especially to exclude from young people's experience some forms of dance, like classical ballet, jazz or tap, on grounds that the discipline of studying techniques might inhibit a child's natural creativity and musical response. In the late 1960s I went to see Ruth Foster, a strong supporter of Laban educational dance and at that time responsible for dance policy in London's schools. I wanted the Royal Ballet's Ballet for All group, which I directed, to be able to appear in London schools the same way Gerrard Bagley's Laban-based British Dance Drama Theatre was doing to great effect. I admired Bagley as a teacher and had written several articles about his work in *The Times Educational Supplement*. Nevertheless I argued that Ballet for All would help to extend young people's dance interest and perceptions of dance, especially the dance they might see in the theatre or on television which was not the same thing as the dance they learned in school. 'Never!', said Ruth Foster, and tried to explain how educationally confusing such an experience might be. Classical ballet had nothing for children, she said, and was contrary to everything they absorbed from school. We never did tour London schools but later Ruth Foster modified her views. Ballet for All was invited a number of times to Dartington, whither she had moved, and her book *Knowing in My Bones*, written in 1976, provided valuable encouragement for the new dance thinking which emerged in education during the 1970s.[14] It has to be said that the Laban rigidity was matched by an equal rigidity from many teachers of classical ballet, especially in the Royal Academy of Dancing. The lesson to draw from this history is the need for pluralism in dance education. Some dance forms attract some children, other forms other children. It follows there is a need also to relate more closely with the variety of dance art forms available in the theatre, especially where these forms can be communicated through educational units from individual companies or supported by special school performances.

To suggest this is to introduce the second area of disagreement or misunderstanding which appears to lie behind current DES dance policies. The unwillingness to depart from tradition induces a failure to take sufficient account of theatrical and non-theatrical dance achievements over the last twenty years. These achievements have elevated the status of dance in society generally within and beyond education, rendering outdated the continued marginalization of the subject in schools and in teacher training. The marginalization is illustrated in a booklet, *Physical Education 5–16*, from the DES.[15] This is the only HMI document, we are told, which addresses dance. The address is limited to references which are all part of longer lists of desirable objectives and qualities seen to be part of physical education as a whole:

> the capacity to express ideas in dance forms ... appreciate, and respond to, contrasting sounds in music, percussion and words and to be able to react to simple rhythms ... respond physically to rhythms, moods, qualities in music, words and sounds ... develop and repeat phrases of movement in dance ... invent and improvise sequences ... choreograph dances.

Such objectives, of course, would form part of any independent dance curriculum in education, though not the whole part. Here their potential is subsumed under different physical education objectives, in brief paragraphs of explanation which cover only three pages in a booklet of twenty-two pages! This kind of cursory treatment is inadequate because it ignores the nature of developments in the art form during the last fifteen years. Therefore children never are offered the unique contribution which dance could make to their education at all levels, given the subject status to allow this contribution. At present dance takes place only in about 50 per cent of secondary schools, mostly excluding boys.

One of the most significant changes of the last few years has been the development of a career structure in dance starting in school. Unlike classical ballet the modern dance now offered increasingly in schools can be continued vocationally after 16 at institutions like the Laban Centre for Movement and Dance and the London and Northern Schools of Contemporary Dance. Such vocational studies can lead to a performance career or a career in dance administration or further studies in high education, apart from the possibility of teacher training studies. This important development alters significantly the status of dance as a school subject and as a career prospect for young people who discover an interest in that direction. In the interests of dance in schools and of young people, therefore, it follows that the dance teaching profession needs to build on whatever opportunities lie within the national curriculum and even within the limited conceptions of the HMI document. These opportunities are considerable. Dance, after all, must be taught by schools because it lies within a statutory subject. It must be taught, moreover, as an art form, even within PE because this is the only sensible way to teach it. The snag is that many PE teachers are not trained adequately in this approach. There is, too, considerable flexibility within the new curriculum leaving schools still free to timetable subjects how they wish. Schools are neither constrained in their methodology of teaching nor in their curriculum development, as the Arts in Schools Project demonstrates. Many new performance arts courses, including dance, are being established in schools with governors, head teachers and staff looking afresh at the opportunities. There is a realization that dance, drama, music and other arts subjects can be developed as a faculty with valuable relationships across the rest of the curriculum, such as relationships with science subjects. The national curriculum, in fact, offers opportunities for the interdisciplinary nature of dance to be emphasized rather than be tracked only within PE. Schools should seize these opportunities. The dance profession and dance teachers generally need to respond by listing all schools which teach dance creatively to form a national network of mutual support to which professional dance animators and company education units can offer also their services, thus linking schools with the whole dance profession.

Related to the development of a career structure, often supplemented by youth dance activities out of school hours, has been a dramatic change in teaching content and methods. Until the late 1960s/early 1970s it was accepted that dance teaching should adopt a child-centred approach, stimulating the creativity of children through spontaneous reaction to dance ideas. Nothing wrong in that except it made little provision for older children and teenagers through the challenge of a coherent technique to extend movement vocabulary and the possibility of wider creative expression. This limitation began to be resolved from the early 1970s through the introduction of mostly Graham-based and/or jazz techniques, changing the philosophy as well as the practice of dance in education. Fruitful as the results are proving they demonstrate also the increasing incongruity between dance and physical education and the historical error under which the two are linked together.

The entry of dance into higher education through degree courses in dance and/or performance arts at universities (Surrey and Kent), polytechnics and colleges of higher and further education emphasizes further the mismatch in the national curriculum. On the one hand, degree courses imply a proper foundation and progression of study at primary and secondary level so that tertiary study can acquire an appropriate depth, range and standard. At present, time is wasted because degree courses, whether in dance or performance arts, have to provide much of the foundation which should have been provided in schools. This foundation cannot be provided by the approach to dance in the physical education curriculum. The emphasis of the two subjects is different. To combine them misleads students and creates disparate emphases in which dance is presented as one part only of a range of physical skills. The emphasis of dance is on knowledge of body and mind through the acquisition of specialist techniques which facilitate the communication of feelings, emotions and situations, especially those which cannot be communicated in words. The HMI curriculum document emphasizes knowledge of body and mind ac-

quired in physical education through a range of skills and
frequently in competitive settings. Dance rejects competitiv
Obviously there is overlap — the need for stamina, perseverance,
self-esteem, discipline, physical competence, control, coordination
and so on — but the uses, values and emphases are different in the
two disciplines. If dance is to make its full and unique contribution to
the curriculum at each level of education this historical confusion of an
art with physical education needs to be ended.

It follows that dance, like the other arts, is not an appendage to
physical education but a particular form of knowledge and experience
on its own, a way of organizing and communicating individual
perceptions of the world. Each art, of course, is different allowing the
development of different talents, abilities and perceptions. Not to
have received a full opportunity to share in this knowledge and be
part of this discourse, including that part represented by dance, is to
that extent to be deprived of a part of education. More than this.
Dance today is not only a powerful art form of many techniques and
languages but also a means of expression and release for people with disabilities and the elderly as well as the young, an aid towards a better
society. None of this vision of dance is reflected in *Curriculum Matters
16* though it is the crux of the distinction between dance and physical
education. Both are essential in education, but dance is an art which
physical education is not. Hence the particular and special contribution dance can make to the education of citizens.

Last chapter quote

Dance as Education

The realm of dance is education of the body and of the imagination.
Responsibility for educating the imagination should run naturally
through the teaching of every subject. The arts, though, can be the
most comprehensive and direct influence on imagination with dance
adding qualities of its own. The arts, too, comprise an important part
of a wider aesthetic education. The bedrock of such an education has
to be laid in school and higher or further education, not in abstract but
in relation to past and present aesthetic and artistic development. For
this reason there is a strong case to include some arts practice within
the foundation courses of all schools and higher and further education
institutions as part of the methodology of study. The case would be
founded on arguments presented by *The Arts in Schools* and developed
further in the National Curriculum Council's Arts in Schools Project.
Published in May 1990 the report of this project identified how the
arts represent experience in symbolic form. Each art thus is a mode of
understanding. The visual mode uses light, colour and images. The
aural mode uses sounds and rhythm. The kinaesthetic mode uses

bodily movement. The verbal mode uses spoken or written words. The enactive mode uses imagined roles. A properly balanced education, seeking fully to explore and develop the potential of each young person, should provide opportunities to work in all of these modes of understanding. This lies within the aims of education itself, but shows also that arts education in schools is an essential part of cultural education.

The inadequacy of cultural education in the British educational process may be a significant reason for the racism, violence and intolerance which beset British society. Cultural education helps young people to recognize and analyse their own cultural values and assumptions; brings them into contact with the attitudes, values and institutions of other cultures; enables them to relate contemporary values to the historical forces which moulded them; and alerts them to the evolutionary nature of culture and the potential for change. It is this potential for change which perhaps frightened the authors of the 1988 Education Reform Act and led them to divide the arts in the national curriculum. Art and music are included presumably because these were traditionally recognized art subjects in the nineteenth century. Other arts, recognized today, are omitted or subsumed in other subjects. Within the general concept of cultural education the NCC's Arts in Schools Project shows six different ways in which the arts as a whole can contribute powerfully to the education of all pupils.

Through experience in different modes of understanding, arts education extends the *intellectual development* of young people helping them to widen the range of their intellectual capabilities and to make sense of the different qualities of their experience. Arts Education is concerned with *aesthetic development* deepening the sensitivities of young people to the formal qualities — and therefore the pleasures and meanings — of the arts and with extending the range of their aesthetic experience and judgment. Work in the arts contributes to the *education of feeling* by giving a positive place to personal feelings in school and by providing ways of exploring and giving them form. The arts offer direct ways of *exploring values*, of raising questions of personal, moral and aesthetic value and of discussing the ideas and perceptions to which they relate. The experience of success in achievement and of enjoyment in learning and working with others, which the arts promote, is an important form of *personal and social education* which can raise immeasurably the self-esteem and social confidence of young people. Work in the arts requires and leads to the development of a wide range of *practical and perceptual skills* with a wide application and value.

To make these contributions, provision for the arts in school timetables needs to be coherent, balanced and inclusive of each of the modes of understanding. We are concerned in dance with two modes

Plate 3 Other ways to dance. The dancer Misoshi teaching Ghanian dance to Cheshire school students in November 1989 as part of the Arts Education in a Multi-cultural Society Project. Photograph by Nick Young.

especially, the kinaesthetic mode of understanding through bodily movement, and the enactive mode. The kinaesthetic mode, like each of the other modes, embraces the six specific roles identified by the Arts in Schools Project whereby the arts contribute to the growth of young people. The different modes of understanding will appeal to, illuminate and stimulate this growth according to individual choice, interest and ability. Not to include the kinaesthetic mode, or to include it inadequately through the physical education curriculum, is to deprive many thousands of young people of a way of understanding which may be for them *the* way of understanding throughout life. Clearly, too, the limited inclusion of dance in the physical education curriculum as indicated by *Physical Education 5–16* not only cannot provide adequate opportunities to experience the kinaesthetic mode, but also omits the enactive mode and the exploration of values, rationality and creativity which accompany both modes in their unique uses of the body and the imagination.

From this outline of the situation of dance within the general concept of arts education it is clear that arguments around the place of dance in the curriculum need to be of two kinds. The general kind sees dance as part of the case for arts education as a whole not only in schools but also in higher and further education and in the community throughout all periods of life. This case is developed and carried forward in the next two chapters examining dance in higher education and in the community. The specific kind concentrates on the properties and characteristics of dance as education again through all periods of life.

The general case draws on the long dispute around the arts in education dating back at least to the renaissance in our own era and to classical times before that. The Gulbenkian Foundation's *Arts in Schools* initiative in 1982 summarized and re-presented the arguments in terms of today's social, cultural and political situation. The NCC's Arts in Schools Project amplifies and illustrates the case in 1990 after three years' collaborative and practical exploration with a wide range of local education authorities, over 200 schools and associated professional artists and arts institutions. The theoretical basis of the general case was put forward principally by David Aspin in chapters 2 and 3 of *The Arts in Schools* in 1982. It

> rests upon a view of what being 'educated' actually means and the sorts of knowledge, attitudes and capabilities which derive from this:...also on the sorts of values which we associate with this notion of education... The uniqueness of human existence consists, above all, in our capacity to appraise and communicate with each other about our various experiences of the world. We do this in many different ways, through many different modes of understanding and communication, not just one. [16]

These modes, he says, include 'languages' of number, of empirical observation and record, of induction and deduction, of morals and religion, and 'languages' in which ideas of beauty, grace, harmony, ugliness and so on are conceived, formulated and expressed. This is our aesthetic awareness. It includes languages of gesture, posture and visual expression through movement and dance. All these symbolic modes of communication have their own logic, grammar and syntax. Each is basic to human rationality by which we communicate to others our ideas and feelings about the world. Not all of these communications require words. There are whole areas of meaning and experience which have no direct need of words, and feelings, senses and emotions actually which cannot be expressed in words. Dance is a powerful example of this kind of non-verbal communication.

It follows that the rationality and capacity of those who fail to enter into any of these 'communities of discourse' will be to that extent lop-sided. They will have been short-changed educationally and, quite literally, deprived. They will be limited, sometimes severely limited, in the different ways in which their perceptions of the world are organized, communicated, understood and judged. Human rationality is not confined to one way of understanding and communication; it uses many ways. Some education in each of these ways, therefore, is necessary if each person is to have that range of intelligences, feelings and opportunities to enable him or her to realize all their potential and all the contribution they might make to the societies in which they live.

More than this. The arts, of course, are an essential element in aesthetic and creative education, meaning by aesthetic a distinct category of understanding, achievement and perception within which fall the individual arts. Through aesthetic appreciation we are able to enjoy the beauty of sunsets and are stimulated to fight to preserve the environment; we can sense the drama of great machines as well as be repelled by the ugliness they can create; we can feel the softness of material or enjoy the furnishings of a room. Arts appreciation, therefore, is not the same as aesthetic appreciation, though the two are linked closely. Each individual art has its own appeal and mode of communication. Being different and special it is attractive to some but not to others and certainly not to everyone. Because of these differences it can be misleading to talk about 'the arts' as a general category or to assume in education that everyone has an innate capacity for aesthetic appreciation or artistic appreciation. These qualities can be developed, though not always, and David Best has drawn attention to the problems.[17] The point is that the opportunity for development must be offered as part of education like other elements of knowing so that all possible communities of discourse become open to a young person from which to choose. The same applies to older people in further education. In any case the perceptions of young people are not necessarily the same as those of older people.

It is, though, legitimate to talk about the arts collectively when objecting to the exclusion of most of them from British education. As a general category of understanding and experience they have in common a number of important elements which need to be part of any education concerned to advance the welfare of individuals and society as a whole. These elements include moral purpose and values; historical understanding; capacity for artistic and aesthetic appreciation; stimulus of ideas and innovation; criticism and self-criticism; exchanges of knowing, meaning and modes of consciousness; balance in learning and leisure occupation; development of capacities for decision-making, self-discipline and attention to detail; finally, ways of understanding and making sense of the world around us. This, surely, is what schooling is about. It comprises a general training of the imagination and a broad education in culture without which there can be no social harmony, no individual humanity and much less wealth from which to nourish social living.

The arts as a whole communicate these qualities in education but, since individual arts will appeal only to some students and not to others, the presence of all the arts in education is necessary to allow choice and the opportunity to develop the choice, once made up to, and including, specialism in higher education or vocational training. A proper place for dance in education, for example, would not be concerned only with the experience of dance movement though the practice of dance emphasizes the unique nature of dance compared with other arts. In place of a pen or paintbrush or violin to create the art form dance requires the whole body and personality. This is its particular distinction, its value as educational experience and the reason why some students prefer to study dance above other arts.

The tragedy of the present treatment of dance in British education is that even these gifts to educational enrichment cannot be realized fully within the national curriculum as now conceived. There the aesthetic education of young people comprises only two of the six great expressive art forms. Therefore the arts, representing different but equivalent symbolic modes of enquiry and exploration, are marginalized or, like dance, largely ignored. What should have happened in the curriculum, as Peter Abbs points out in *Living Powers*, is that the arts should be seen as belonging together under one category of the aesthetic with options to study whichever art appeals to a young person. Thus dance would be included as a discrete subject helping to develop imagination and creativity through the practice of dance and the composition of dances. Dance practice involves mastering one's body and developing its capacities for communication and movement, using its particular characteristics. Thus dance in education is for everyone, not just for those with particular physiques or talent. Mastery of the body and its use for expressive purposes develops self-confidence with great psychological benefits. It encourages and releases original achievement which comes from conscious and deliberate choice.

The special case for dance, then, is that it brings to education the six different ways listed above in which the arts can contribute to education, plus the kinaesthetic and enactive modes with all their uses of imagined roles including mime, plus the use of the body as the instrument of communication. This last point is its uniqueness and special benefit. Other benefits, when dance is integrated fully into the school curriculum, include the development of artistic appreciation through judging the work of others and judgments about colours, shapes, patterns and the interpretation of music; education in personal relationships through working with others and appreciating the ideas of others in dance making; a better understanding of the variety of cultures in Britain and the world through studying and dancing their dances. Finally, of course, a proper place for dance in education would increase the chances of realizing a young person's full abilities in dance should he or she have the potential for a dance career.

The notion of studying the dances of other peoples carries with it obvious benefits for the study of geography as well as intercultural understanding. Likewise the study of history. No proper understanding of the contemporary world and of our society is possible without some knowledge and understanding of the roots of traditions and the culture we have inherited. What we have today — our folkdance, our social and ballroom dances, our classical ballet, modern and post-modern dance, teaching methods, dance notation and what our dance might become — all derive from the structures and experience of the past. They relate, too, to the rest of our learning at school and after school — not just history and geography but mathematics, geometry (as the eighteenth century choreographers, Weaver and Noverre, pointed out), anatomy, physiology, sociology, anthropology, physical education, sport, languages and so on. To study this past and its development into the present is to understand more clearly the nature of thinking, capacities for innovation and thus the sense of earlier societies which influence still the way we live today as well as the dance forms which remain part of our living. It is to understand better our civilization.

To realize fully the dance contribution to primary and secondary education needs to include doing dance, creating dance, learning about dance and seeing dance, especially the best examples available in our performing spaces or on video or film. At the level of higher education it needs to include all these things in more advanced forms plus a significant element of research and inquiry outlined in appendix B. This takes place already in a number of polytechnics, universities and private institutions featured in the list of organizations near the end of this book. Dance study in higher or further education can lead now to a career as performer, choreographer, critic, dance administrator, teacher, lecturer, publicist, or be regarded as preparation for a general career in business or public administration. It follows that dance teaching at all three levels, alongside the teaching of other art forms, needs to have as a central objective the communication of a sense of excellence and quality in human achievement, whether or not the student actually plans a dance career.

By excellence I mean neither the elevation of the past nor the notion of 'high art' in the 'Roman' tradition outlined at the beginning of this chapter. The arts, being dynamic modes of understanding, creation and communication, give to us today as much of value in contemporary visions of the world as they gave to civilizations 500 or 5,000 years ago. They do it differently so that excellence in each case has to do with circumstances and resources and the satisfaction of certain criteria of validity which are neither absolute nor unchanging. This is true particularly of dance with its vastly developed understanding of the human body related to human senses and the rich exchange of dance forms now possible through international communication and through the nature of Britain's multi-racial society.

Among the criteria of dance validity is a truism upon which rests much of the case for the arts and for dance in Gulbenkian's *The Arts in Schools*. 'The arts are not only for communicating ideas. They are ways of having ideas, of creating ideas, of exploring experience in particular ways and fashioning our understanding of it into new forms.' This is precisely what should happen in the dance classroom. It was impeded in the earlier child-centred approach to dance teaching because the approach placed a major emphasis on a child's own movement reaction to music. This, of course, is correct and fruitful when done with discrimination. Indeed, a senior teacher at the Royal Ballet School once said to me she would rather have a Laban-trained child, well-guided in responses to music, than some ballet teacher's pupil who had to be retrained by the School. The problem of excessive reliance on the child's own movement resources and improvisations is that these inevitably are limited. Even when guided and developed with the help of a teacher they tend to be repeated and repeated. Creativity, instead of being free and unfettered, thus becomes constricted without the further development which simple dance techniques might give. In this sense dance study, like other subjects, is a combination of past and present knowledge. Ideas developed in dance, moreover, need to be essentially *dance* ideas which cannot be rendered so exactly nor so clearly in any other forms. Through this concentration on the nature of the art form and its communication, just as other arts studies concentrate on their art forms, the student is helped to move merely from repeating experience to understanding, controlling and reshaping it in dance terms. This includes, of course, the reshaping of old ideas in novel ways to offer new sources of insight or illuminate the human condition of today or yesterday.

In this way the activity breaks apart or brings together in new ways existing patterns of ideas and belief. With dance it is the more powerful for involving the whole body and personality in the process. Perhaps this is why the Establishment generally, and many schools in particular, are so wary of the arts. It is the nature of the arts to question and disturb. Concerned head teachers and governors should welcome this quality which can give shape to the questioning of all students. They should expect that dance, when well taught by a stimulating teacher, will question existing conventions of feelings and emotions. The arts are a natural threat to all things conventional, especially deceit, hypocrisy and distortion in human relations. Moral values are a part of dance and the dance classroom. Therefore what should dance in education be about?

Dance Creativity

It is in the classroom, and especially in the dance studios of secondary and higher education, that the post-modern knot can be unravelled. Here the debate is most acute, whence it will be carried into future practice. Should dance concentrate just on itself, on dancing in the Merce Cunningham canon, or even within the more emollient canon of post-modern Rambert? There is a place for this in today's education for today's society though this should not be the whole story. It is too narrow a way to engage in dance learning — to make, to appraise, to explore, to form, to perform, to present, to seek response and to evaluate. The dance experience needs to include compassion in translating the present into dance forms and some vision of what the present might become, not starry-eyed but practical. In that way dance in the classroom becomes bigger than itself. It is not only about movement. It is about moving freely. To learn to move freely means also to learn to see, hear and understand clearly beyond the classroom.

It follows that a dance piece should have some meaning which communicates with others. Communication implies understanding on both sides. I don't mean to be pompous but a dance, or any work of art, should be about truth, however widely or imperfectly this is represented. Truth does not mean the 'truth' of naturalism, with its symptoms of the surface of things. It requires a search for deeper causes within one's life experience. Nor does it imply cosmic themes. Rather, the best understanding comes from simple situations and personal relations as Doris Humphrey pointed out.[18] Dance is suited particularly to explore the inner landscapes, which Martha Graham described, and to develop in its own way the interior monologues of modernist writers like James Joyce. It doesn't have to be narrative in form like much classical ballet, nor expressionist like early modern dance. It should be able, too, to accept experimental phases and experimenters with results not worth a second viewing, since the artist has a right to succeed or fail. Communication is between human beings — in this case not in sound as music, nor colour and shape as painting, nor words as drama, but in movement as dance. Therefore the communication must communicate — what? The arts deal in visions, in interpretation of experience, tragic or humorous. This implies something different from the way things are, implies change.

I remember a season of dance at The Place Theatre in London in the spring of 1990. Called *The Turning World*, the season took its theme from T.S. Eliot's *Four Quartets*, his greatest philosophical poem. There Eliot talks about the still point of the turning world where there is only dance. The Place Theatre picked up this image, though not in any literary way, to present a season of dance which

> is about change, about the changes that will happen faster and faster as the earth spins towards the millenium. It's about the new ways people will move, about the movements of people, about people's movements. It's founded in the belief that dance is the poetry of contemporary theatre; that dance — the most ephemeral of the arts — will best capture the moment of change, the still point.[19]

That sort of vision stirs excitement. No wonder young people fill The Place. It is the sort of vision I would like to see translated into student choreography and the dance class.

Through performance the qualities of a dance will be tested by the critical scrutiny of others so that excellence combines the 'truth' of the final work with the rigour of the creative process. This can happen at any level, not just in high art. The dance class, therefore, is a place for excellence and for thinking. It becomes an exercise in observation and experiment, in thesis and antithesis, as much as any science lesson. The special characteristic of this exercise, as with all practice of the arts, is synthesis and integration to create where most other disciplines emphasize analysis and dissection to create. The synthesis and integration are not the result of the 'merely subjective' nature of the arts compared with the 'objectivity' of, say, the sciences. They have to do with the nature of the knowledge communicated by the arts illuminating, as in a famous advertisement for a certain lager, areas which others cannot reach. These areas have to do with intuition and feeling, direct action and experience, aesthetic, religious and moral areas of knowing communicated through movement. They are as important as knowing acquired through deductive reasoning and empirical tests — not more important, but also not less important. Hence they signal the need for greater balance in education between these two sides of knowing, for considering what the two sides have in common as well as what is different, and the need for scientists and engineers, bus drivers and office workers to develop creative insight in action in the way of artists. This should be the product of schooling and is a product of dance as education.

Creative work and thinking, indeed, have become key elements in industrial and economic development. The need to stimulate such thinking throughout the work-force has lead to reorganization of many enterprises whether in factories, offices or scientific centres. No longer the vertical structures of tradition where thinking is done at the top leading to commands passed through an intermediate bureaucracy for action on the shop floor by an unthinking work-force. Rather a horizontal structure whereby experience generating new ideas can be consulted quickly at every level. A significant reason for this change — leading, for example, to much of the economic success of Japan — is a realization that creativity is not a faculty which some people have and others do not, but is a form of intelligence, potential in everyone, which can be trained and developed like any other mode of thinking. Therefore it requires discipline, experience and grounding in appropriate education. The most appropriate education is experience of the arts within which dance has the special advantage of involving the whole body and personality and of involving a second mode of understanding, the enactive. I do not mean, of course, that experience of dance or any other art is the only way to develop creativity; the arts are a particularly powerful way.

Therefore what is the nature of the creative quality to be developed? What is creativity? The Arts in Schools Report and Project, and the research behind them, are down to earth about a form of intelligence often held to be a gift from heaven. Creativity implies making or creating or thinking through something which is the personal achievement of the person concerned. It should be in some way original, different or distinctive from anything previously created in that field, including some new combination or arrangement of existing elements, and which is the result of a conscious and deliberate activity. There are, obviously, different degrees of creativity as there are different people so that the quality of the work produced, the context within which it is produced and the consistency of production also are indicators of creativity.[20] Hence the importance of an environment which encourages creativity and hence the supreme role of teacher and school in achieving the difficult balance of freedom and authority within which creative potential can grow.

To argue thus moves a long way from teaching dance steps and choreography which is the expected, but limited, role of the dance teacher. A proper place for dance in the curriculum relates to history and other school subjects; embraces values, morals, personal relationships and contact with different cultures; above all, the development of imagination, taste and creativity for application throughout all activities and phases of later life. The implication is for a broader approach to dance teaching and to dance teacher training in both the public and private sectors, a revolution in attitude and training methods to see dance in education as a way of preparing people for qualities in life shared with others, not just for a job or even for a few years of schooling. This implies in turn a closer contact with what actually happens in the art form in theatres, films, television, popular performance and youth and community dance. Hence a more creative approach to the school day with greater emphasis on stimulating imagination and on the development of young people to create and appreciate.

Such changes, possible now in individual schools, if not in local education authorities generally, would go far towards resolving the problems of aesthetic and arts education raised by Peter Abbs in *Living Powers, A is for Aesthetic* and *The Symbolic Order*. They would help young people to understand the complex issues of dance in today's society and would guide them in their own creative life. There is a need for the public and private sectors of dance education to collaborate more closely in sharing each other's expertise, particularly at a time when dance education in both sectors is under threat. Public education in Hong Kong, for example, whose primary and secondary levels are modelled on the British system, has found a way to incorporate the expertise of private dance teachers in the school timetable. Even though such teachers do not have qualified teacher status they have a dance knowledge to give young people which cannot be matched always in a public sector where dance, as in Britain, still is taught under severe restraints.

Some Conclusions

Reform is needed, therefore, of dance teacher training for all levels of education, a more adequate in-service provision for dance in schools, and more time in the curriculum to put into practice the fruits of training. The case for such reform has been argued by the Calouste Gulbenkian Foundation in association with the National Foundation for Educational Research and other agencies. It is put forward in the Foundation's *The Arts in the Primary School* (1989), *The Arts in Schools* (1982 and 1989), *Dance Education and Training in Britain* (1980), the NFER's *The Arts: A Preparation to Teach* (1985) and *Artists in Schools* (1990), the HMI survey *Quality in Schools: The Initial Training of Teachers* (1985) and the final report of the National Curriculum Council's Arts in Schools Project (1990). This powerful collective case now needs urgent implementation when community charge capping and other government cuts threaten to negate the requirements of the 1988 Education Reform Act. This lays down that a broadly based curriculum should 'promote the spiritual, moral, cultural, mental and physical development of pupils'; and should 'prepare such pupils for the opportunities, responsibilities and experiences of adult life.' Current restraints upon education have been inhibiting for some time the realization of these aims as well as ministerial claims, made in October 1988, that the arts part of the curriculum can play the most significant part in ensuring that children, when they leave schools and go out into adult life and employment, have developed emotionally in a way which complements the intellectual knowledge and skills which we all hope they will acquire. The arts then will also have provided a precious foundation which can be developed throughout their lives as adults and can be a continuing source of inspiration, pleasure and excitement.

The reality of government policy in all sectors of British life renders such words pious rather than meaningful because the arts at every level suffer disproportionately from inadequate resources of time, finance, staffing, space and materials. No need here to repeat practical measures to reform the present situation when these have been argued so powerfully in so many publications. Just a need to summarize from these arguments the reforms required to give dance its proper place in the curriculum. There are six policy priorities:

1   Every young persons should have some experience of dance during primary and secondary years of schooling, and an opportunity to choose to extend their studies in this field at sixth form level and into tertiary and continuing education.
2   The provision of such opportunities should be based on the acceptance of dance as a subject in its own right and as an art equal in status with other arts in the curriculum.
3   All young people with outstanding talent should have the opportunity of vocational training in dance. The criteria for such opportunity should rest on the basis of talent, *not* on the ability to pay fees for private tuition.
4   The inclusion of dance in the school curriculum should relate the discipline to other disciplines, to the development of the art form and to the experience of young people inside and outside schools, including experience of other cultures in Britain's multi-racial society.
5   The leading vocational institutions upon which vocational training in dance depends, but which now are facing grave financial problems from the reduction of discretionary grants, must be preserved through a comprehensive system of fee assistance covering training and maintenance for students qualified by talent to undertake vocational training.
6   Opportunities should be developed for all people in the community to continue their interest and involvement in dance after the end of formal education. This is discussed further in chapter 5.

To help accomplish these priorities at primary level:

A   The generalist teacher needs to have acquired sufficient knowledge through training and experience to understand the value of dance as part of a broad and balanced curriculum and to recognize and evaluate artistic quality in children's dance work.

B   The specialist teacher should be able to offer practical expertise in dance and be able to apply that expertise in support of non-specialist colleagues, including an introduction to the dances of other cultures as a constituent part of multi-racial education.

C   The curriculum leader and/or head teacher, alongside the skills and dance understanding of the generalist class teacher, should communicate a personal enthusiasm for dance in the arts policy of the school, in staff development and among parents and governors. Experience shows that dance flourishes in a school only when teachers *and* head teachers work together to develop it.

D   This work of the teachers needs to be supported by parents and governors with appropriate resources and greater opportunities for expressive and creative work as part of each school day.

To help accomplish these priorities at secondary level:

A   The specialist teacher needs the same enthusiastic support from the head teacher and governors as at primary level plus arrangements in the timetable to relate dance to other subjects and to develop through dance a knowledge of other cultures now part of the dance culture of Britain.

B   Dance should be accorded equal status with other major areas of the curriculum and this should be reflected in the allocation of resources.

C   Dance teachers should recognize and implement in their teaching their responsibility to develop the imagination and creativity of their students, their appreciation of all the arts, their sense of social and artistic values and their capacity for enjoyment through skills in dance performance and composition.

D   The need should be recognized for work in dance to develop into the fourth, fifth and sixth forms of secondary schools for boys and girls, with opportunities for this to happen within and outside examination courses, bearing in mind that dance is now a subject of GCSE level and 'A' level examinations leading to degree courses in higher education.

E   Measures should be taken in the school timetable to relate dance in schools to the art form in theatres through school visits to performances and through in-school visits of education units from professional dance companies with an emphasis on quality rather than quantity of contacts.

F   Restrictions in the Education Reform Act limiting provision of free attendance by schools at professional dance performance, such as schools matinees and participation in in-school dance workshops, should be abolished.

The further implication of such recommendations is for:

A   Reform of graduate teacher training particularly to provide more time to develop performance, compositional and practical teaching expertise, incorporate study of the dance forms of other dance cultures in Britain and relate training more closely with development of the art forms in public performance.

B   A foundation course in teacher training to include art, music and drama before specializing in dance and to explore the teachers' responsibilities for imaginative and aesthetic development in their pupils alongside the social and cultural values, physical skills and creativity which dance can stimulate.

C   A review of the qualifications of dance teaching staff at teacher training institutions to ensure they include the experience and knowledge to educate and train future teachers in the new dance requirements outlined above.

D   In-service training programmes which recognize the particular characteristics of dance as an art form separate from physical education and which can make available to teachers of dance appropriate courses for professional updating, renewal and additional qualifications.

E   The adaptation of these needs and principles to teacher training in the private sector, especially the Colleges of the Royal Academy of Dancing and the Imperial Society, and leading institutions like the Royal Ballet School, Laban Centre for Movement and Dance and London Contemporary Dance School.

F   A review of dance in higher education, on the one hand to develop continuity by relating courses more closely with work at secondary level; on the other hand to encourage and develop research in the study and application of dance in today's British society as recommended in the next chapter.

In sum, the object of all dance teaching in schools, maintained or non-maintained, and in higher education, should be to realize the six objectives identified for arts education in the Gulbenkian Report *The Arts in Schools*, and the NCC's Arts in Schools Project, applicable at primary, secondary and tertiary levels:

Developing the full variety of human intelligence.
Developing creativity.
Education in feeling and sensibility.
Exploring values.
Understanding cultural change and differences.
Developing physical and perceptual skills.

Notes and References

1 Calouste Gulbenkian Foundation: *The Arts in Schools*, London, 1982. Reissued 1989.
2 Ross, Malcolm (Ed.): *The Claims of Feeling: Readings in Aesthetic Education*, Basingstoke, Falmer Press, 1989.
3 Best, David: *Arts in Schools: A Critical Time*, Birmingham, Birmingham College of Art and Design and the National Society for Education in Art and Design, 1990.
4 National Curriculum Council: *The Arts 5–16*, Oliver and Boyd, London. This is produced in three volumes: *Practice and Innovation; A Curriculum Framework; A Work Pack and Slide Set for Teachers*. All in 1990.
5 Aspin, David: 'The arts, education and the community', quoting also Thucydides Histories 11.43, in Abbs, Peter (Ed.) *The Symbolic Order*, London, Falmer Press, 1989, p. 254.
6 An argument put forward many times, but first expressed in the Calouste Gulbenkian Foundation's *Dance Education and Training in Britain*, London, 1980.
7 Walvin, James: *Leisure and Society 1830–1950*, London, Longman, 1978.
8 Holt, Richard: *Sport and the British*, Oxford, Oxford University Press, 1989.
9 Calouste Gulbenkian Foundation: *Dance Education and Training in Britain*, Appendix B, 'Outline history of dance in the maintained sector'. London, 1980.
10 Walvin, *op. cit.*
11 Guest, Ivor: *The Romantic Ballet in England*, London, Phoenix House, 1954; *The Alhambra Ballet*, New York, Dance Perspectives, 1959; *The Empire Ballet*, London, The Society for Theatre Research, 1962.
12 Walvin, *op. cit.*
13 Calouste Gulbenkian Foundation, *Dance Education and Training in Britain*.

14 Foster, Ruth: *Knowing in My Bones*, London, 1976.
15 DES. *Physical Education 5–16*, DES Curriculum Matters 16, London, 1969.
16 Calouste Gulbenkian Foundation: *The Arts in Schools*, p. 18.
17 Best, *op. cit.*
18 Humphrey, Doris: *The Art of Making Dances*, New York, 1959.
19 Introduction to *The Turning World*, a programme of dance from around the world at The Place Theatre, London, 23 April–19 May 1990. Sponsored by Holsten.
20 Calouste Gulbenkian Foundation: *The Arts in Schools*.

Chapter 4

What Can Dance Do for Higher Education and Vice Versa?

Partnership

Malcolm Frazer, chief executive of the Council for National Academic Awards and very tall, seemed taller still at a degree award ceremony to students of the Laban Centre for Movement and Dance in December 1988. Most of the students' figures were neat and rather controlled beneath their BA and MA gowns and hoods. Dancers on the whole are not tall, except for some of the men. Frazer had been invited not only because Laban degrees are validated by the Council, but also because the CNAA has been the principal higher education body to stimulate and introduce to Britain degrees in dance studies and performing arts at BA, MA M.Phil. and doctoral level. When Malcolm Frazer shook the hand of each successful student the world of academic tradition — he is himself a scientist — met the world of dance and acknowledged in British higher education a partnership in the pursuit of knowledge.

The partnership began fully in 1977 when the first British BA Honours degree course in Dance Studies was validated by the Council for National Academic Awards at the Laban Centre for Movement and Dance, London. This was exactly fifty years after the first university course in dance was launched at the University of Wisconsin in the USA. Since then dance courses at degree level plus advanced research have become a normal part of American higher education. Not so in Britain nor in most of Europe where older concepts of the nature of knowledge still obtain. In Britain dance existed in higher education only in the certificate course for teacher training, then in the B.Ed. course when graduate training for teachers was introduced during the reorganization of teacher training in the 1970s.

The CNAA, therefore, was not breaking totally new ground in higher education by introducing dance as part of a new policy on the arts. Dance had existed for many years at universities as well as teacher training colleges wherever dance teachers were prepared for the physical education syllabus. Sometimes it reached a high level of creativity within these constraints but it had little to do with the wider art form and had almost no contact with the theatre dominated by classical ballet. It was, too, a subject for academic study at MA, M.Phil. or Ph.D. levels at institutions like Leeds University[1] and was accepted as a research area also at Manchester University and Goldsmiths' College, London. It entered the British university system in its own right, however, only in 1981 through a BA Honours course and a dance studies department instituted at Surrey University. Presently BA level study was extended at Surrey and the Laban Centre to MA level, then M.Phil. and Ph.D. research. This was followed in 1982 by a BA Honours course in performance dance at the University of Kent jointly with London Contemporary Dance School, proceeding also now to MA and research degree levels.

Meanwhile, at Middlesex and other polytechnics and at colleges of higher education another strand of dance studies began to be developed through degrees in Performance/Performing/Expressive and Creative Arts, also validated by CNAA. These are degrees in which a student usually can major either in drama, music or dance with the other two performance subjects as minor options. Today the pattern of dance study in higher education, therefore, embraces a wide range of approaches divided between 25 and 30 institutions of uneven quality distributed irregularly across the country. The Midlands have 8 institutions, the north 6, the south-east 8, the south-west a rather shaky 3, and 1 each in Northern Ireland, Scotland and Wales. To some of these dance is very peripheral in their programmes. The degrees they offer collectively at BA level, with or without honours, cover dance or performance arts, dance with general studies or human movement studies, or dance within a B.Ed. course linked usually with physical education. Some have been casualties of cuts or amalgamation over the years; others are newly validated. Hence the difficulty of firm statistics. Fifty per cent of all degree courses fall within the B.Ed. definition.

Most of the institutions are members of the Standing Conference on Dance in Higher Education. This was established in 1983 to act as an authoritative national voice to promote and foster dance in higher education, develop policies on dance, share information and experience and forge links with other educational bodies. The standing conference does not include, therefore, institutions offering advanced vocational training for performance during, say, a professional dance career, that is training beyond the initial courses which take a young dancer into a performing career. Britain, in fact, has no advanced institution like the Lunacharsky State Institute of Theatre Arts (Gitis) in Moscow where issues of choreography, performance, music, production, teaching, ethnic dance, coaching, staging, content and interpretation in the theatre can be linked with issues of criticism, dance history, reconstruction, research, dance administration and other matters affecting dance culture as a whole. Nor do we have yet the equivalent of the Netherlands Dance Institute, Netherlands Mime Centre and Netherlands Theatre Institute in Amsterdam. Housed next door to each other and closely linked operationally, these provide services for professional dance, mime and physical theatre throughout the Netherlands. The services include a national library and documentation centre, including audio-visual documentation, archival facilities which include notation, power to stimulate research, conference facilities and the duty to provide national and international public relations and promotion for Dutch dance and mime. This is not unlike the role which the British Film Institute fulfils for film and television in the UK. We need something similar for British dance and mime. Possibly our National Organization for Dance and Mime will grow in that direction. Meanwhile some of the necessary functions are divided between professional companies, higher education institutions or conservatoire institutions like the Royal Ballet School, London Contemporary Dance School, and the Laban Centre.

The story of dance in higher education generally to this point during the last twenty years, therefore, has been one of progress and development (albeit not enough) to create a resource much larger than is understood by the British dance and education professions and therefore grossly underused in its potential to advance national dance culture. If adequate liaison existed between the dance profession and higher education this resource could begin to provide some at least of the services provided by Gitis in Moscow and the Dutch institutes. Many of the leading British higher education institutions, after all, are linked with relevant allied disciplines like geography, anthropology, aesthetics, sociology, philosophy and cultural studies as well as traditional associations with anatomy, physiology, history, physical education, music, drama and fine art. To reach this point and to establish the criteria of dance scholarship its advocates have had to prevail in three important intellectual engagements, all of significance to the dance profession and the advancement of a national dance culture.

First, that dance makes a significant contribution to non-verbal knowledge which itself has had to win acceptance as a legitimate area of knowledge in British higher education. The acceptance of this wider concept (implicit already in music and fine art studies) through the validation of dance degrees by the CNAA and Surrey and Kent Universities represented an important liberalization of rather narrow concepts of the nature of knowledge pursued traditionally by European universities.

The second successful engagement established that research can include creative work in the arts just as it presumes already to include creative work in the sciences (see Appendix B). In other words the processes of choreography, dance teaching and dance practice involve research in themselves and are valid as areas of study for theses at M.Phil. or Ph.D. level. This has extended enormously both the notion of academic research and the range and depth of dance scholarship in higher education, embracing dance practice as well as dance theory and the application of dance in other disciplines.

The third engagement involved the nature of dance scholarship and the training of dance scholars. Britain has been slow in its development of broadly based dance scholarship compared with the USA and the USSR. This has much to do with the cultural impediments noted in chapter 3 and with the hegemony of classical ballet which delayed appraisal of wider conceptions of dance as well as the introduction of modern dance forms in the British theatre. In classical dance itself, however, in dance in education, and to a lesser extent in folk dance study, private pioneers were able to establish a basis for future institutional dance scholarship looking back to the roots of this scholarship in British social and dance history from the renaissance onwards.

I have commented on this history elsewhere[2] but three conclusions assist an appraisal of British dance scholarship. First, this scholarship is rooted in three areas of historical resource: (a) in theatre history looking back to Tudor and Stuart masques, then to the strong presence of theatrical dance in London from the seventeenth to the twentieth centuries with Russians and Americans acting as final stimuli in the creation of British classical and modern dance art forms; (b) in British folk dance and folk music dating back in recorded history to at least the eighth century and speculatively before that, researched and documented by Cecil Sharp, Percy Grainger and others leading today to a strong anthropological strain in dance scholarship alongside the scholarship of folk dance and folk music itself; (c) in educational history dating back to Thomas Elyot's *The Gouernour* in 1531, carried forward by John Colet, Roger Ascham, Erasmus, John Locke, John Weaver and the private teachers of the eighteenth, nineteenth and twentieth centuries, into the impact of Rudolf Laban on public education, the arrival of Graham-style contemporary dance and the impact of major teaching and examining bodies in the private sector.

These deep historical roots characterize British dance scholarship and define it from its American counterpart where the focus is much more on the development of a more recent national culture. They link it firmly also with Italian and French sources on which the British scholars and teachers drew. The second conclusion derives from this historical experience, that the fundamental principle of dance scholarship is a partnership between verbal and non-verbal knowledge requiring a balance between theory and practice and a broad interdisciplinary approach. This becomes a general guideline for all dance in higher education. The third conclusion follows that, in spite of the extraordinary wealth of the legacy from private researchers and critics, from as far back as John Weaver, say, but particularly since the 1930s, a privately based scholarship ultimately is unsatisfactory to underpin the development of national dance culture. 'Scholarship' here is interpreted broadly, not in the rigid terms of annotated texts favoured in academic circles but in terms of original contributions to knowledge, theoretical or practical, worked out in studios as well as in libraries, books, lectures and discussion groups.

Scholarly Beginnings, Classical

The founding fathers of British twentieth century dance scholarship are Cyril Beaumont, Arnold Haskell, Philip Richardson and Edwin Evans. This leaves out other candidates like Mark Edward Perugini whose claim is substantial but limited in its range. His *The Art of Ballet* in 1915 and *A Pageant of the Dance and Ballet* in 1946 are the extent of his contribution on dance, although the chapter on ballet in eighteenth century London in *A Pageant* later inspired Richard Ralph to undertake his great work on *The Life and Works of John Weaver* in 1985. The founding fathers, on the other hand, fulfilling the criteria of my second conclusion, were active in practice as well as theory and all four exerted a long influence on future scholarship. Three of them — Haskell, Richardson and Evans — were founders of the Camargo Society which provided the effective link from 1930 to 1933 between Diaghilev's Ballets Russes and the development of the Rambert and Sadler's Wells companies as prototypes of a British style of classical dance. Each initiated strands of British dance criticism. Evans emphasized music and exerted an important influence on the musical standards of early British classical ballet. Richardson, a collector of early dance literature, initiated serious studies of dance in the pages of *The Dancing Times*, which he edited from 1910, taking always the broad view of dance as a social as well as theatrical activity. Beaumont emphasized detailed documentation and was a founder of the Cecchetti Society. Haskell was the first director of the Sadler's Wells/ Royal Ballet School as well as an aesthetician and popular writer.

Beaumont remains continually important for his analysis of the classical repertory in his day providing essential reference for scholars thereafter, for his translation of important French texts by Arbeau, Noverre and Gautier, and for his contribution to classical teaching through a leadership of the Cecchetti Society which ended only in 1976. Richardson behind the scenes was the adept politician of British professional theatre dance and its organization, for ever emphasizing its connections with history on the one hand and with contemporary society on the other. Haskell was the first critic to write for a national newspaper[3] as well as being a brilliant if flamboyant publicist for the classical art form. He was an aesthetician who attempted to lay down criteria for dance criticism, which T. S. Eliot incidentally had begun to address during the 1920s.

Alongside these four in the early days developed an important group of private dance practitioners contributing to a wider perspective of dance knowledge. They were Margaret Morris, Ruby Ginner and Madge Atkinson offering alternative forms in modern movement, Greek-inspired dance and natural movement respectively. Although these modernist forms were marginalized in the theatre by the dominance of classical ballet, by first signs of central European 'free' dance and by the reputation of Isadora Duncan, they exerted considerable influence in education, particularly before the arrival of Rudolf Laban. They offered other ways of moving, each an original contribution to thinking about dance and human movement. The other area of early research lay in folk dance and anthropology influenced profoundly not only by Sharp and Grainger but by Curt Sachs the German author of *World History of the Dance*. This appeared in English in 1937 and remains unique in its total view of dance. Scholarship, of course, has had to mingle always and everywhere for most scholars with day-to-day criticism or other means of earning a living. There were no institutions in Britain where they might read, write, research and teach their subject as there are today in higher education. Among young writer/critics in this situation at the end of the 1930s were A. V. Coton, James Monahan and Fernau Hall all of whom became part of the rapid expansion of dance criticism after the second world war as well as adding worthwhile contributions to the growing resource of British literature on dance. For them the focus was no longer Diaghilev, Pavlova and their Russian successors but nascent British ballet itself.

One part of the second generation of British dance critics and private scholars thus emerged out of the shadow of war, responding to the growing significance of British choreography, especially by Frederick Ashton and Antony Tudor. A second part emerged mostly out of Oxford University where Clive Barnes, John Percival and Clement Crisp were students in the 1940s. A third part like Richard Buckle, Nigel Gosling (both Oxford protégés), Mary Clarke and Peter Williams emerged from the practice of editing or writing for the journals of dance criticism which arose to satisfy the post-war public interest in dance. Buckle edited his own iconoclastic magazine *Ballet* until 1952 for which Gosling began to write in 1948 subsequently following Buckle as dance critic of *The Observer* in 1955. Buckle, dance critic of *The Sunday Times* from 1959 to 1975, became an international authority on the Diaghilev period. Through his Diaghlev exhibition in 1954 and definitive studies of the period in *Nijinski* (1971) and *Diaghilev* (1979) he helped to awaken a generation of young writers and dancers to the relevance of dance scholarship. Williams, trained originally in theatre design, was founding editor of *Dance and Dancers* from 1950 to 1980 around which gathered and developed the young Oxford critics. Through *Dance and Dancers* he exerted enormous influence on British international dance relations, on the arrival and development of contemporary dance in Britain from the early 1960s and as a politician of dance through long membership of the Arts Council, dance advisor to the Arts and British Councils, author of a seminal report in 1975 on the future of dance in the UK, founder-chairman of the Dancers' Pensions and Resettlement Fund since 1975, and chairman since 1979 of Britain's annual International Dance Course for Professional Choreographers and Composers. He stands in the tradition of Philip Richardson as a writer-politician of British dance. Mary Clarke, editor of *The Dancing Times* since 1963 and dance critic of *The Guardian* since the early 1980s, has continued much of Richardson's policy without the emphasis on social dance but is author also of a substantial number of books on classical ballet history. Of these *The Sadler's Wells Ballet* (1955) can be counted a classic and an essential work of reference with *Dancers of Mercury, the Story of Ballet Rambert* (1962) an important chronicle of its period.

Besides the emergence of these critics, most of whom remain leading figures as authors as well as critics, a significant extension of private scholarship arose separate from criticism. There were three areas of study in this scholarship: early dance; nineteenth and twentieth century classical ballet; and educational dance. The study of early dance forms was led by Mabel Dolmetsch and Melusine Wood. They were joined presently by Joan Wildeblood, Mary Skeaping and Belinda Quirey, Skeaping and Quirey being pupils of Melusine Wood in this area of scholarship. The scholarship has been extraordinarily fruitful in original contributions to knowledge with two works by Dolmetsch; four by Wood; an important translation of de Lauze, the seventeenth century French teacher and choreographer, by Wildeblood who contributed also a valuable study of the historical development of manners; and an extensive research into historical dance forms recreated into stage dancing for today by Skeaping and Quirey. Skeaping, in particular, had all of the resources of the Royal Swedish Ballet and of the Drottningholm Court Theatre, Stockholm, at her disposal, thus creating an entire genre of choreography in sixteenth, seventeenth and eighteenth century styles. Some of this became available to British audiences through the Royal Ballet's Ballet for All group in the late 1960s. Quirey has built an international reputation, particularly in Europe, where her historical choreography has been presented at Versailles and on other stages. The scholarship behind these enterprises after the second world war included study of written dance records of each period and of early dance notations undertaken not only by dance historians but also on a broader scale by Ann Hutchinson Guest. Dance notation thus was demonstrated as an important source of historical dance scholarship, not just as a means of recording new choreography today.

The second area of scholarship, covering nineteenth and twentieth century classical ballet, has been led undoubtedly by Ivor Guest, a solicitor and private dance scholar. Author of more than thirty books covering the history of European ballet during the nineteenth and early twentieth centuries his is probably the most widely read scholarship of the last three decades. Combined also with chairmanship of the Royal Academy of Dancing during much of this time his work indicates another channel of research linked not with criticism but with experience of an area of dance practice. The importance of dance research linked with dance practice was emphasized by the written studies of Joan Lawson in the history and practice of classical ballet, mime and folk dance and, especially, by the writing of the Diaghilev ballerina, Tamara Karsavina. Her autobiography around St Peterburg's *Theatre Street* (1930), her *Ballet Technique* (1956) and her *Classical Ballet, the Flow of Movement* (1962) show a deep command of the English language, as well as scholarship derived from inner knowledge of dance practice. The two aspects of scholarship together provide useful lessons in translating into words an art illuminating areas of human experience which cannot be expressed easily in words. Most of the books of this post-war period from the late 1940s to the 1970s were published by A. & C. Black, Pitman, Beaumont and, later, Dance Books. Without these publishers and their nurture of a growing dance readership in schools and colleges, as well as among the general public, the development of private scholarship would hardly have prospered and we would not have today much of the essential library from which further scholarship can develop.

Scholarly Beginnings, Educational

Alongside the increase in publication went an extension of studies, of shared experience and philosophical speculation around dance training and education. *The Dancing Times* has much to do with this — Karsavina's gentle prose, for example, and much of Joan Lawson's enlightened thinking began as articles in that journal — but there was also a quite different range of educational writing outside the teaching of classical ballet. This derived from Rudolf Laban, Lisa Ullmann and their Art of Movement Studio, serving the state education system.

There were also other forms of modern dance related to what Laban had begun. A. & C. Black, for example, published in 1958 Jane Winearls' *Modern Dance* on the Joos–Leeder method, since much reproduced and enlarged. Laban's own writing was of seminal importance. It brought to Britain the experience of twenty years of creative and educational work in central Europe in a dance style which challenged most of the precepts of classical ballet. This was adapted to the theories of child-centred education dominating British education at that time and complemented perfectly the faith in expressive arts of influential directors of education like Sir Alec Clegg who proclaimed and supported the vision of creativity which could be released through educational dance.

By the time Sir Alec wrote a foreword to Violet Bruce's *Awakening the Slower Mind* in 1969 there was nearly thirty years' experience of applying Laban's modernist expressionist philosophy to British education or to areas of disability and social need. A library of books had appeared of which Diana Jordan's *Dance as Education* in 1938 was the first, hardly less influential in its day than Laban's own writing after the war. The 1940s, 1950s and 1960s were a period of intense modern dance activity in British educational circles. It revolutionized concepts of dance which had ruled schools and teacher training during the 1930s. In doing so it polarized British dance culture. On one side classical ballet, on the other Laban. In scholarship and dance literature the historical studies and aesthetic arguments of Haskell, Beaumont and others faced the philosophical theories of Laban in practical application like Marion North's *Personality Assessment through Movement* in 1971, and *Movement and Dance Education* in 1973, reissued 1990.

There were, though, initiatives between these opposites, a creativity of choreographers and dancers in the modern style appearing in theatres and small venues around the country. It influenced writers like A.V. Coton and Fernau Hall but was overshadowed by the greater resources, choreographic experience and public support attached to classical ballet. Its extent has come to light as a result of recent scholarship in *Rudolf Laban, an Introduction to His Work and Influence* by John Hodgson and Valerie Preston-Dunlop (1990) and in an exhibition of Laban's work and influence at the Laban Centre (June–August 1990), following research financed by the Centre and the Gulbenkian Foundation. This combined exploration has revealed not only that Britain had a modern dance movement in the theatre much earlier than is supposed today, albeit small and technically indecisive, but also that much of today's work in movement studies, community dance, youth dance and dance for the disabled was anticipated by earlier work adapting Laban's teaching to handicapped adults and children (Violet Bruce), the hearing impaired (Walli Meier), factory workers and their families (Marion North) and, of course, youth dance and community dance in general. Knowing this gives to these areas of dance culture evidence of deeper roots to support developments today and therefore stronger claims to public attention and finance.

There were, too, in books like Betty Redfern's *Concepts in Modern Educational Dance* and Valerie Preston–Dunlop's *A Handbook for Dance in Education* (1973), reissued in 1980, signs of the sea change in educational dance which took place during the 1970s. There was a questioning among dance teachers in schools and in teacher training colleges a need for rethinking. This was nourished in the late 1960s by the arrival of Graham-style American modern dance and the foundation of London Contemporary Dance Theatre and School. Alternative concepts of dance in schools were promoted often retaining the Laban approach for younger children but offering a discipline and vocabulary of movement more attractive to older students. The new era was confirmed by a reorganization of the Laban Centre from 1974 onwards not only to teach a range of modern dance styles from the United States and central Europe, but also to establish an institution which combined a vocational conservatoire with the higher educational dance studies which Britain lacked at that time. It was from this basis that the Laban Centre applied to the Council for National Academic Awards in 1977, to validate Britain's first degree course in dance. Since the course, and other aspects of the Centre's teaching, assumed choreographic preparation for the theatre or in the community, and since theatrical practice was the message brought also to schools by Graham contemporary dance, the 1970s began a diminution of that polarization which had afflicted British dance culture for so long. This new prospect was of profound significance for the development of dance in higher education.

Today's Situation

By the beginning of the 1980s, then, a substantial institutional resource in higher education had been established as well as the publications it needed for development. The publication continued. Macdonald and Evans, for example, published almost all the writings of Laban and Lisa Ullmann, his assistant. Faber and Faber in 1976 published an important work on choreography by Leonide Massine, one of the major choreographers of the century. Lepus Books published a study by Frank Bottomley on the significant problem for dancers of *Attitudes to the Body in Western Christendom*. Penguin pioneered in 1957 the first British *A Dictionary of Ballet* by G.B.L. Wilson since followed by others, especially Horst Koegler's *Concise Oxford Dictionary of Ballet*. Important departures took place also in thinking about physical education. A series of Lepus publications on human movement studies during the 1970s, edited by H.T.A. Whiting, indicated the range of this rethink. It included texts by Jean Williams on educational gymnastics, by Gordon Curl on aesthetics and by others who have helped to change attitudes in physical education and therefore its relationship with dance. Outstanding among these has been the work of Bob Carlisle. His *The Concept of Physical Education* in *Proceedings of the Philosophy of Education Society of Great Britain*, updated at a NATFHE conference in London in December 1988, influenced attitudes on both sides of the divide between dance and physical education.

There have been, too, a valuable range of memoirs or studies of individual dancers and choreographers. Not only Karsavina's *Theatre Street* but David Vaughan's study of *Frederick Ashton and His Ballets* (1977), John Percival's *Nureyev* (1975) and a range of studies from 1960 — Kschessinska's memoirs *Dancing in St Petersburg*, Sokolova's memoirs *Dancing for Diaghilev* edited by Richard Buckle, and Anton Dolin's *Autobiography*. Ivor Guest created personal images of romantic ballet from *Cerrito* in 1956 to *Elssler* in 1970, *Zucchi* in 1977 and *Perrot* in 1984. At the end of the decade came Patricia McAndrew's marvellous translation of August Bournonville's *My Theatre Life* (1979). This deepening mine of knowledge was supplemented from three rich veins. First, a flow of books from the United States, particularly a series of republications by Dance Horizon of important dance texts from the sixteenth century until today and, of course, books about American modern dance on which most of British modern dance is modelled. Second, photographic records as an art form in their own right by Gordon Anthony, Baron, Keith Money, Mike Davis and many others, but especially Anthony Crickmay. Third, and of immense significance for the future, the beginnings of contributions by scholars and critics from other disciplines. I have noted already how T.S. Eliot contributed to critical discussions of ballet in the 1920s. Our knowledge of early ballet history was supplemented by the scholarship of Frances Yates' *The Valois Tapestries* in 1959. Later in 1963 came Margaret McGowan's *L'Art du Balet de Cour en France 1581–1643* followed in 1982 by her long introduction to *Le Balet Comique*, 1582. Professor McGowan, author of other studies of the French Renaissance, was at Glasgow University for her first work and is now professor of French at Sussex University, formerly a pro-vice chancellor of that University, and a former chair of the board of examiners at the Laban Centre for Movement and Dance.

From the discipline of social authropology in 1979 came John Blacking's *The Performing Arts*, one of a number of books he edited or wrote, some listed in my bibliography, relating the disciplines of dance, music, ethnography and anthropology. During the 1970s and

1980s, Blacking, from his position as professor of social anthropology at the Queen's University, Belfast, became a formative champion of the development of dance as an independent discipline in British higher education. There were others. From philosophy and aesthetics related to education I have quoted already the authority of Herbert Read and Louis Arnaud Reid, but the influence of younger thinkers and writers began to be felt in the 1970s through, for example, David Best's *Expression and Movement in the Arts* (1974), *Philosophy and Human Movement* (1978) and *Feeling and Reason in the Arts* (1985), Robert Witkin's *The Intelligence of Feeling* (1974) and Malcolm Ross's *Arts and the Adolescent* (1975), *The Creative Arts* (1978) and *The Arts in Education*, (1983). In the same way other related disciplines like anatomy and physiology, music and scenic design emphasized the interdisciplinary nature of dance study, elevated its status and confirmed its significance among the arts.

This rehearsal of some of the extending literature of dance demonstrates how firm a base had been established by 1980 for the wider scholarship made possible by degree study and by the teaching staff which began to be established in its institutions. Also in 1980 the Gulbenkian Foundation published its report on *Dance Education and Training in Britain*, a work of research which aimed to assemble the facts of dance education and training at all levels. It argued the case for dance in education to government and local authorities drawing together the changes which had taken place. It offered directions for further development, especially a continuity of dance study from primary through secondary to tertiary. The concept was strengthened and influenced by the introduction of dance examinations at 'O', 'A' and GCSE levels, thus supporting the status of the subject in schools as preparation for work at degree level and for scholarship to come. The scholarship is emerging out of the new structures for dance in higher education formed since the mid-1970s. Landmark examples are offered through conferences and meetings of the Society for Dance Research formed in 1982 and through its journal *Dance Research* edited by Richard Ralph. This journal is crucial, both for scholarship standards and for dialogue with scholars abroad. It is complemented by Laban's Centre's *International Working Papers on Dance* intended to explore and exchange ideas in the discipline across national boundaries in anticipation of research. There are also flagship institutions like Laban, Surrey, and London Contemporary Dance School where research at M.Phil. and doctoral levels can be undertaken as well as study at undergraduate level. They are flagship institutions because they possess the largest concentration of dance spaces and specialist staff and because they are able to apply a proportion of resources to research directly or through postgraduate work.

The flaw in the potential of British higher education for dance research lies not only in the relatively small number of institutions including dance in their concerns. A greater problem lies in the restrictions imposed on polytechnics and colleges by official attitudes to research in these institutions and therefore to finance and staff for research. Some research, some advanced scholarship is undertaken, but not enough. The point is underlined by a new perspective for higher education institutions with dance opened by government plans to devolve arts responsibilities from the Arts Council to Regional Arts Boards. When this happens, say in 1992, the regions will need their own centres of data collection, local history, research and so on. Dance development in each region could stimulate dance activity in local higher education institutions and vice versa — that is, if dance exists in the institutions. It follows that the geographical distribution of institutions where dance is studied needs a better balance than at present, much as the location of modern scientific and research establishments in Britain needs rethinking. Less in the south-east and the Midlands, more in other parts of the country. To achieve such an objective, however, needs regional policies like those operated in France, Germany and other European countries. Such policies should aim to tap all available resources of skill and knowledge in a region, not just a proportion. Well-established dance departments at higher education level have the expertise to serve the dance information needs of a region and to nourish innovation. They are prepared to wait, too, longer than next year for a return on their investment.

It is important that each institution in this kind of way should be able to concentrate on a particular area of work while continuing general dance studies and developing cooperation with others. The University of Surrey at Guildford, for example, and the nearby Roehampton Institute are planning to establish a joint School of Dance Studies, possibly from 1991, which would be the largest institution of its kind in Europe and involve the technological/electronic resources particularly available at Surrey. This is an exciting prospect since dance has needed for a long time to begin to comprehend and use the technology now shaping our society, its leisure occupations and its arts. Surrey, too, possesses additional institutions to reinforce research. Its Labanotation Institute holds copies of almost all scores in Labanotation available in the UK and acts as a teaching and publishing centre for Labanotation. Since lack of notation is a contributing factor to the relatively low status which has hindered national dance culture, this is a crucial adjunct to dance scholarship. The other institution is the National Resource Centre for Dance which holds a growing collection of dance materials. Its principal responsibility is to develop a computerized dance database, a dance archive and published materials on dance in written, visual and aural form. Finally the university has created the first professorial chair of dance in British higher education. The discipline's establishment at university level is confirmed.[4]

The significance of the Laban Centre for Movement and Dance in south-east London is not only that it combines the functions of conservatoire for vocational training in dance and choreography with those of a higher education institute. It is the only higher education dance institution in the UK founded on a philosophy of dance inherited from one of the great dance thinkers of the twentieth century. This has guided many of its innovations in British dance studies like sociology of dance in 1978, full-time training for community dance animateurs in 1982 and studies in dance therapy at MA level in 1989. The Centre's roots in the Laban approach to dance, combined now with alternative techniques of modern dance, the involvement of related disciplines and an emphasis on choreographic creation, have produced the discipline of choreological studies which is intrinsic to the Centre's development of dance scholarship. Choreological study implies a total study of dance, neither only in practice, nor only in theory and scholarship, but synthesized in close relationship to society and social need. Such a rethinking of the nature of dance studies has emerged out of a rethinking of Laban's work at the Centre during the last few years. It has implied a strengthening of academic and vocational links with institutions in the USA, Europe and the Far East, and publications like *Dance Theatre Journal*, a quarterly journal of dance inquiry on public sale, and *International Working Papers on Dance* twice a year. The Centre maintains also a small student company whose quality has gained an international reputation emphasizing the graduate influence of the Laban Centre on choreography. Thus the two largest centres of institutional dance scholarship, one in the public sector, the other in the private sector, are very different in style and operation, but are complementary.

Other institutions are emerging with their own specialisms like London Contemporary Dance School from which *Dance Research* is published and which bases its approach on dance performance, and Leicester Polytechnic with its emphasis on arts administration. Much more than these specialisms of higher education, or indeed all the dance specialisms of all twenty-five or so institutions in Britain, will be needed to fulfil the tasks of higher education in the immediate future of our national dance culture. If each higher education institution could serve the dance interests of the region around it they could, collectively, serve and nourish national dance culture as a whole, its policies, economies and relations with the rest of national and international culture. Yet no one in the Office of Arts and Libraries, nor in Parliament, nor in the dance theatre profession has latched onto the potential of this resource. 'The arts are of enormous assistance to give

Plate 4   Other ways to dance. Members of the Laban Centre's student company, *Transitions*, in David Dorfman's *Torched*. The company tours other colleges and centres as part of its Advanced Performance Course. Photograph by Toni Nandi.

you a more balanced view of society', said Lord Goodman, former chairman of the Arts Council, on BBC Television, 15 April 1990. Well, yes! His 'you' meant everyone, but this can only be effective if the arts communicate with everyone and if the nature of their 'assistance' is properly presented. The role of higher education is crucial in this presentation. Similarly in medicine. The National Organization for Dance and Mime convened in September 1990 an international conference on *The Healthier Dancer.*[5] It was a response to an injury crisis in the dance profession which can be ignored no longer. This crisis reaches across all forms of dance, classical and contemporary, folk dance and social, non–Western solo performers to the largest touring companies. Nor does injury mean only snapped tendons, strains or broken bones. Injury embraces also body weight, eating disorders, psychological disorders, nutrition, fatigue, first aid and general illness. The conclusions of the conference produced an indication of the extensive need for further research by dance and all allied disciplines in physiology, physiotherapy, orthopaedic surgery, anatomy, foot biomechanics, chiropody, diet, psychology and other fields. Another task for higher education.

The needs of dance in the community are discussed in the next chapter. Here again, higher education has a role. There are major related studies to be undertaken on ethnic dance in British society from Scottish and Welsh to south Asian and Chinese. If it is true, as Christopher Bannerman, head of dance at Middlesex Polytechnic, remarked to a conference on higher education and the arts in Glasgow in April 1990, that 'dancers are, literally, bodies of knowledge', how do we learn that knowledge and apply it in all the languages the bodies speak from the dance cultures of the world? We shall need allies in anthropology, ethnography, music, sociology, geography, history and the other resources of higher education. Such studies would embrace dance theory and aesthetics, but dance theory and aesthetics are rarely considered in dance training. Therefore they lie almost entirely in the field of higher education or with organizations like the Early Dance Circle and the Society for Dance Research. They involve a very wide range of study. Roger Copeland and Marshall Cohen list some of the requirements in *What is Dance: Readings in Theory and Criticism.*[6] They are: definitions of dance; the nature of the dance medium; dance relations with other arts; genre and style; language, notation and identity; dance criticism; and dance relations with the societies to which they belong. Others would add to this list, but when all is done and a formidable claim for attention is presented in the councils of higher education, it would be found that choreographic achievements, dance statements, are, like poetry, not taken into account in making appointments, awarding grants and fixing salaries. Written 'publications' on the other hand open the door to academic advancement and grants. We have a lot to do to put our academic house in order.

Partly the problem is the ignorance of our peers, partly it is our own underuse of a key to dance scholarship. Dance notation has taken us out of the preliteracy of dance. Just as writing provides the ability to preserve speech and memory over time and space so dance notation allows not only the preservation of choreography, dance steps and memory in relation to music, but also the ability to study dance in depth, refer back to 'texts', argue in detail and speculate about movement in all its forms, develop a much stronger critical tradition. The possibility arises of a true history of dance, a science of dance within the history of human movement, human culture and human communication, all related to social structure and social history. There can be no genuine study of dance history and communication, nor of dissent from accepted theories, without notation and the archives which notation makes possible. Yet notation is not yet a widespread tool of dance scholarship.

It is possible, just possible, that we are entering an era in which medicine, the sciences, including political science, technology, the media and the arts — material and non-material culture working with public opinion — can put a stop to wars, poverty, starvation, disease and the persecution of human beings, animals and the environment. Everywhere there are alternatives and new directions. The nation state is disappearing into larger associations like the European Community and ultimately into a global economy and global culture. Will our national culture disappear with it? How can we defend it tied geographically as we are to Europe, linked linguistically to America and related closely still to many countries in an ambiguous Commonwealth? Must we continue to look to America rather than elsewhere or our own history and education for dance influences to sustain us in this future? How at home do we overcome the hegemony of prejudice, outdated policies and entrenched interest which inhibit dance culture? Or draw inspiration from the counter-culture of young people in dance and the interplay between generations and between intellectuals in higher education and dancers and dance teachers in the profession? How do we assess the radicalization of opinion among young dancers manifest not so much by a recent strike of the Royal Ballet as by the way the strike was conducted by the dancers themselves and the ideas they put forward? Is there, finally, an unbridgeable conflict between science and the arts, science failing to provide meaning or value for social or personal life, the arts emphasizing the development of human capacities and potential to develop a freer, richer, more meaningful life?

Only higher education in partnership with the dance profession has the resources to consider these larger questions from which to develop policies on which depend the future of dance culture at every level. It seems we need a new rationality in dance, a new cognition broader than it has been in the past evolving from a forum or partnership of all the strands of higher education and its institutions combined with dance practice inside and outside the theatre. The resources of scholarship exist provided the dance will exists. Therefore it will be helpful to summarize some issues and developmental needs of British dance scholarship today:

A broadening of the national research base to encourage, coordinate and enhance the quality of work at more centres of higher education.

A strengthening of interdisciplinary links and links between dance practice and dance scholarship.

A recognition that 'scholarship' and 'research' include the processes of dance creation and dance performance.

Improvement of the contribution of the medical profession to reduce dance injuries and close the gap between medical research and the practical work of dance companies.

Development of international links and consultation in dance scholarship, especially to broaden understanding of dance outside the theatre as well as within it.

Acceptance of dance as an ordinary, rather than exceptional, subject in higher education courses, encouraging creativity through the practice of dance activity.

Study to extend the basis of dance therapy in Britain.

Study to extend the application of dance in the community.

More coordination between institutions in the development and use of information and dance archives.

Development of a database and statistics about all aspects of national dance culture.

Closer links with media of all kinds particularly to study the presentation of dance to wider audiences through new technology.

Finally, a need to win the battle for recognition and legitimacy within the British higher education system. This implies acceptance of choreological (i.e. all kinds of dance) study as a valid discipline and area of knowledge in its own right. To achieve this means establishing once and for all the legitimacy of non-verbal knowledge as part of all knowledge to be valued equally with knowledge communicated traditionally through the written and spoken word. This means consequentially winning acceptance for the place of the arts in higher education and the funding of research and scholarship in this area by government, foundations and private sponsors equally with other areas of knowledge.

Notes and References

1   Calouste Gulbenkian Foundation: *Dance Education and Training in Britain*, London, 1980, pp. 68ff.
2   See Brinson, Peter: 'Dance scholarship in UK', paper presented at the Essen Conference on Dance Research, 1988, and published in *Documentation Beyond Performance: Dance Scholarship Today*, (1989) German Centre of the International Theatre Institute, Berlin. Also Brinson, Peter: 'The role of classical ballet in society today', lecture to the Royal Society of Arts, London, 1989, and published in the *RSA Journal*, October 1989.
3   See Sayers, Lesley-Anne: 1987. An unpublished M.Phil. thesis which should have earned a Ph.D., the study is available in the library of the Laban Centre for Movement and Dance, London.
4   Professor June Layson gave her inaugural address at Surrey University on 23 May 1990.
5   The National Organization for Dance and Mime organized *The Healthier Dance Conference* to bring together the medical profession, dance profession and opinion formers in an effort to increase understanding between disciplines. The proceedings of the conference are available.
6   Copeland, Roger, and Cohen, Marshall: *What is Dance: Readings in Theory and Criticism*, Oxford University Press, 1983.

Chapter 5

Whose Arts, Whose Community?

Like the development of professional dance and dance in education since the second world war, community dance emerged with the art of mime as a particular response to the cultural needs of post-modern society during the early 1970s. It is the third element in developing a national dance culture, carrying forward issues and practices from the theatrical art form and from dance at all levels of education. Firmly it operates an 'Athenian' approach rather than the 'Roman' approach of much established professional dance practice. To do this it has embraced populations generally not touched by theatrical dance or dance education systems, or unable to participate in these areas — working people and young people seeking to develop their own dance ability through classes, workshops and youth dance groups; elderly people; disabled people; unemployed people; people in prisons[1] and institutions; people able to *see* dance more than *make* dance like those in hospitals;[2] people able to perform and show dance from the cultures of the British Commonwealth now becoming part of the national dance culture of Britain. All this represents the application of an art form to current social conditions. It is an important development in public aesthetic education, meaning here arts activity.

At the same time such a broad constituency challenges current funding priorities by posing the claims of popular culture and alternative conceptions of art, introduced by the electronic revolution, against conceptions of art established in the nineteenth century. It poses the art interests of the many against the art interests of the few, the 'Athenian' view against the 'Roman' view, popular art (not mass art) against high art. In doing so it raises a different notion of art, including dance, in which lines disappear between production and consumption, performer and audience, creator and receiver, creation and participation, professional and amateur. Much of this is directly contrary to the principles behind the current reorganization of the Arts Council. Community dance and mime stand midway between this reorganization and the most radical implications of an alternative vision of the arts.

Community dance and mime have become established elements of the fabric of British dance culture touching at least 500,000[3] people a year. For example, Thamesdown Contemporary Dance Studio, a leading community dance project, teaches about 20,000 people a year in and around Swindon. So does Cheshire Dance Workshop based in Winsford, Cheshire. Arising out of the community arts movement of the 1960s, the community dance and mime movement has achieved in fifteen years a nationwide network, firm presence within local authority services and a recognized practice with important centres in north and south Wales, Scotland, Yorkshire, the Midlands, Lancashire and Merseyside, south central England, and London and the Home Counties. Professional dance companies like Ludus and the Kosh, Kokuma and Irie have roots in the movement and apply its democratic philosophy. It has influential partners in the youth dance movement, part educational part independent, in the powerful and growing world of Caribbean and Asian dance, in the dance involvement of disabled and elderly people and in sports and recreation. It has natural links with dance in education at all levels and with the increasingly significant dance education units of professional companies like Birmingham Royal Ballet, London Contemporary Dance Theatre and Rambert Dance Company. It has in the Community Dance and Mime Foundation (CDMF) a national organization with headquarters at Leicester Polytechnic. Significantly influencing the development of the movement are a range of supportive full-time and part-time courses in various parts of the country among which the one- and two-year Community Dance and Movement Course at the Laban Centre is both pioneer and flagship.

While the Laban community course has played a central role in training community dance workers since it was launched in 1982 there are now other sources of community animation and philosophy in British higher education. Community dance occupies an important place in Surrey University's BA Honours course. Degree courses at Leicester Polytechnic, West Sussex College of Higher Education and other institutions similarly see community dance and relationships between dance and society as areas demanding research and inquiry. London Contemporary Dance School trains its own-style animators and the Arts Council with CDMF runs specific training courses. The community dance movement is distinct in this academic relationship and training support so that the CDMF should be able to build on these connections between itself, the institutions concerned and the thinking behind their courses.

There are national networks of teaching and practice for other performing arts, all influenced by the community arts movement, but the community dance and mime network is significant additionally for its example of public aesthetic education through dance, for its encouragement of new directions in choreography and for its strong role in teaching dance as creative animation. Through the existence of the network, allied to what is happening in schools, choreography no longer is 'the rarest of the arts', as professional circles and critics claimed even twenty years ago. It is now a form of communication and personal expression open to all, and practised by many. Community choreography, however, differs from the professional stage because its four elements are different. The instrument, the body, is less trained technically or trained differently. Hence the use of the instrument, the technique, must be different with less emphasis on virtuosity, more on expression, on mime and simple movement, and on production qualities. The audience, the third element, is different, sometimes contributing ideas, often knowing the performers and always personally interested in what the choreography communicates. Therefore the fourth element, the content or nature of communication, will be different, frequently formulated in discussion with the dancers and their friends.

One might add a fifth element, the judgment or assessment of a finished piece of community choreography. This may be dancing about dancing in the post-modern style of Cunningham or Alston. More likely it will convey some fount of emotion, characterization or narrative through an humanist approach. This is clearest in youth dance but runs through most elements of community dance. Royston Maldoom reflects it in nearly all his work as one of the most experienced community choreographers. So does Wolfgang Stange, founder of the Amici Dance Theatre Company which has won an international reputation for its dance productions with mentally and physically disabled dancers. (See appendix F.) The same qualities were always found in the companies produced by Nadine Senior from Harehills Middle School in Leeds and are a regular ingredient in the work of youth companies seen at the annual National Festival of Youth Dance and in the work of the Weekend Arts College in London. They can be replicated around the country in the work of individual choreographers like Duncan Holt at Clwyd Dance Project in north Wales; Frank McConnell, a second generation community choreographer in Glasgow; the Cardiff Community Dance Project in south Wales; Linda Jasper at South Hill Park Arts Centre, Bracknell in Berkshire; Keith O'Brien of South-East London Youth Dance; Marie McCluskey of Thamesdown Contemporary Dance Studio, Swindon; Penny Greenland of Jabadao in Yorkshire; Fergus Early and Green Candle in London's East End and many more throughout Britain and Ireland,

Plate 5   Other ways to dance. Members of the Amici Integrated Dance Company in Nigel Warrack's *Mercurius* at the Tramway Theatre, Glasgow, May 1990. The company mingles able-bodied and disabled dancers. Photograph by Ian Wesley.

north and south. There is arising a distinct category of community choreographers including choreographers for youth dance and those with disabilities.

Principles and Some Practice

The principles and practice of community choreography throw light on some of the creative problems raised already in choreography for the theatre, particularly the issue of content. They have to do not only with public aesthetic education through dance but also with the moral values of present-day society. The work of Royston Maldoom and Wolfgang Stange, the one with able, the other with disabled people, demonstrates the community start point with any physique of any shape, age or size. This is the essential distinction from choreography with vocationally trained dancers in the theatrical art form. Since the instrument and movement resource are different the creative process is different with a different aesthetic in terms of 'excellence', 'art' and audience communication, aesthetic here again meaning artistic activity. The community art form builds on the capabilities and ambitions of usually untrained 'amateurs', often a term of denigration among professional choreographers. If it is true, as community artists believe passionately, that every individual has within himself or herself creative and expressive possibilities often repressed by personal circumstances, it follows that the distinction between amateur and professional artist can disappear if personal creative potential in one or another art form can be released. In any case, since community choreography is becoming recognized as a discrete area of choreographic art there are now 'professional' choreographers for the community and 'professional' choreographers for the theatre. The aim of both sides should be to work together, perhaps through the Choreographers' Committee of British Actors' Equity Association.[4]

Aged anything between 16 and 80, the ambition of amateur performers, able or disabled, is not for pointed toes and perfect line but for *dance*, that is the communication through movement and music of personal emotions, feelings, relationships and ambitions working with others of like ambition. 'You just stick a record on', learned Paul Willis[5] from a young man practising and rehearsing dance routines at home with his brother, 'and get into the groove kind of thing, like we'll work out some new moves over the weekend, and go up to the Powerhouse on a Monday and try them out like, you know ... and sometimes you'll get a whole line of people doing it ... it's really good.' When dance of this kind is achieved, either in the privacy of one's own home or in community situations through discipline, honesty and very hard work, the rewards lie in audience response, the enthusiasm of participants, the experience itself and the nature of the communication. 'We should be spoken to by our peer groups', argues Royston Maldoom. 'If I am a big fat person, I would relish being danced to by a big fat person.'[6] Stange works from his world of blind, deaf, mentally and physically handicapped people, often integrated with able-bodied people. With them he creates a performance which strengthens enormously the confidence of performers in themselves and which enhances respect and understanding in the able-bodied audience for the abilities and value of disabled people. The result sometimes can be that it is the audience which feels disabled by its inadequate expectation of what can be achieved by disability and dance.

Stange places much of his emphasis on production qualities and group work; Maldoom is able to place more emphasis on individual technical ability where this is available. Both have received enthusiastic praise for the standard of their work from critics of stage and television. Both choreographers are products of formal vocational modernist dance training now adapted to community purposes and changed greatly in the process. The same is true of a majority of other community choreographers at work throughout Britain and Ireland. All involve, where they can, the dance resources of Caribbean and Asian cultures which have enriched existing British dance cultures during the last forty years. Thus the techniques and technical training of British dance become modified. All draw also on the resources of lighting, design, video and sound, especially in multi-media forms.

There are three major political–aesthetic implications in all this for the development of British dance culture. First is its democratization of modernist and post-modernist dance aesthetic which might spill into larger audiences for professional dance theatre. Even the aesthetic which declares dance is for dance is for dancers is being used and adapted to create choreography which communicates with a broad audience, especially of young people. Although such choreography may appear to have no 'meaning' there is not a problem of communication any more than there is a communication problem within popular music. The communication is sensual, not literal, a feeling, a touching of personal moods of the moment. Often this is a result of community discussion during creation so that everyone is aware of the emotion behind the dances, knows the dancers and so brings more understanding to the performance. Maldoom declares he is 'no longer interested in the content', but this is contradicted by his experience of young people dancing.

They are very lost. Their sense of individuality has been moulded by economics. There seem very clear limits to the areas in which they can express themselves, all decided by people who make money. In the end they don't want to be 'kids' or 'teenagers' . . . They have a lot to say.

Stange's approach is based entirely on the experience of his dancers and what they want to say. All the work of his fifteen-year-old company, Amici, confronts profoundly serious personal and political issues in valid performance terms after continuing dialogue with his dancers.

The second implication is a challenge to concepts of 'excellence' and 'quality' advanced particularly by supporters of 'high art' around the Arts Council. In practical terms these concepts are meaningless. 'Excellence', remarks Naseem Khan, interviewing Maldoom, 'means many different things, but is above all the ability to transmit personal emotions through movement. . .'. To members of the Board of Covent Garden and of the Arts Council 'excellence' represents an hegemony of thought and attitude which separates one part of the art form from other parts — the 'high art' of Petipa, Balanchine and Ashton, Graham and Cunningham, from the rest of dance culture. There is thus an institutionalized, very 'Roman' view of the arts which affects all the philosophy and criteria of public arts subsidy. 'Carried to an extreme, a passion for democracy in the arts does lead to the rejection of quality', declared Roy Shaw, Secretary-General of the Arts Council, in a tortuous debate around cultural democracy and the democratization of culture in 1978.[7] In fact, a decade of Thatcherism has mocked both sides of the argument. The Arts Council's democratization of culture was to be achieved through the opening of galleries, theatres, concert halls and the Royal Opera House to wider sections of the public. Rising seat prices, charges for galleries and museums and a general reduction of state support for the arts in education and in public presentation have reduced this ambition to the smallest of movements. The more extreme advocates of cultural democracy condemned the cultural heritage of Europe as bourgeois, 'no longer communicating anything to the majority of Europe's population'.[8] This thinking, too, is shown to be fallacious by the public's own reaction to cultural festivals, exhibitions of the heritage and the needs of all those, amateur or professional, wishing seriously to dance and needing points of reference in the heritage from which to make their personal departure. Steve Gooch, a contributor to the democracy–democratization controversy in *The Guardian*, pointed out that where the argument

goes wrong is in implying that 'high' art is where all the standards are, that 'community' art is where they are not, and that all those who argue for democracy are fanatically against dissemination of the art of the past and for an art of the present whose 'standards' are invariably bad ... Many proven and experienced artists choose quite consciously to work in community arts because those are the first (and possibly last) places in this country where art is practised as art without the increasingly compromising and cynical pressure of bank-balance creativity.[9]

The third implication follows from the nature of daily life and Steve Gooch's point about morality. Daily evidence shows that monetarist morality too often follows monetarist national policy. Greed, get-rich-quick and lack of care for others now are primary stains on our society. The counter-argument is that monetarism represents self-help, self-reliance and standing on your own feet. But are not mugging, robberies, violence, homelessness, joblessness, despair and an educational emphasis on preparation for work to the exclusion of preparation for life inevitable responses to monetarist policy? In the arts, including dance, there are similar responses. A characteristic of the post-modernist reaction to modernism is that it has created few new styles. Post-modernism marks time, particularly since the arts are a low priority in official thinking. Much of the work of artists today is deflected into advertising. This feeds off the heritage of the past to write its captions and present its arguments for more sales and greater consumption. The arts, too, in this way become commodities within our culture. One could say that they were made commodities a long time ago during the Industrial Revolution. This is true, but today shows the ultimate stagnation of arts commodification. On one side of the monetarist penny segregation into 'high art' is the possession of a few; on the other side a philosophy of market forces brings the values of monetarism on to television screens. Drama portrays these values in contemporary myths of soaps and supermen. Music and song become the idiocy of Eurovision Song Contests. Each money game, each chat show, each brutality and slice of America's crime life is excused in the name of market forces to gain the largest audience. The counter to this hypocrisy is the green movement, environmental protection, social protest, a search for racial harmony, care for others and a more honest art which offers, as all arts should, a range of alternative, positive visions. This is the moral standpoint of community arts.

Thus community arts can counter the tawdriness of mass programming and complement commercial cultural forms. Through the electronic media these forms have enlarged immensely people's cultural outlook and experience even though the price to pay is extended struggle over taste and moral values. We live in a moment of intense cultural flux. Community dance, community art is influenced by 'mass culture', but also is a statement of independence and personal identity from it. Hence its huge importance for public aesthetic education, linking the aesthetic with the practical and political in everyday life. We are talking about the cultural activities of people's informal lives, countering with their own creativity the fraudulent values of consumerism.

Community dance, because its creators and performers stay so close to the living plants called grass roots, has to address itself to these issues, nourishing and strengthening the grass roots. This is in line with the general philosophy of community arts from which community dance has developed a more specific form. The philosophy sees dance as a way of knowing and understanding, thinking and investigation in the manner argued already in chapter 3. Creativity is a form of intelligence, latent in everyone and therefore capable of training and development. It is not something which blesses some people and not others but rather, as Peter Abbs points out in *A is for Aesthetic*, 'a common and everyday possession ... the condition of our existence'.[10] On the cultivation through dance of this possession rests the rationale of community dance. Community dance maintains that the innate aesthetic intelligence in everyone can be nurtured through initiation into the forms and symbols of appropriate dance for those who wish to dance. It argues that 'the future of the arts in our society depends not only on their dissemination but upon ways in which this is done and for what purpose'.[11] The community way and purpose is to develop the creativity within every person so that everybody can realize not only whatever ability they have in dance, but realize also themselves, gain in self-confidence, capacity for decision-making and innovation, relationships with others in their community. Thus they strengthen the community and themselves as active citizens in a democratic society. The ultimate beneficiary is the democratic process and, one might add, a more positive way of achieving the self-reliance and self-help which monetarism claims as its aim and virtue.

What, then, is dance? It is one among many symbolic modes of communication by which everyone may formulate and express their understanding of the world, their way of life and each other. Being non-verbal and symbolic it is a language of symbols and shapes expressed through movement for which bodies are the instrument. The symbols derive from many dance 'languages' evolved historically, like classical ballet, modern dance, folk dance, Kathak, Bharata Natyam, tap, jazz. Or they may be self-created the way young people devise their own movements in discos and dancehalls. Modern or contemporary dance, for example, uses many ways of falling to the ground. Normally the body does not fall down, but emotions do and by the symbolism of falls such emotions can be expressed. Recently, the judges of the Paul Clarke and Kerrison Cooke annual scholarship awards for dance students met to audition the 1990 candidates. The candidates were judged in the styles, techniques and symbols of professional classical and contemporary dance. There was one entrant, however, a former professional dancer, who aimed to use these techniques for community dance purposes rather than to advance her own professional dance career. She explained that her method was not to start teaching a particular technique to untrained bodies of many different ages but to start from the dance potential of each body and the wish to dance, however limited. Later she might add whatever technique might help the potential and whatever the dancer elected to learn. She showed in this way a recognition that community dance, too, has its symbols. She wanted a grant to develop her knowledge of work in communities, through dance. She got her grant alongside the others who wished to become professional dancers.

Thus community dance can adapt the existing dance styles and symbols of professional theatre to its own purpose. It can develop also its own dance symbols starting with the creative ability of its dancers to refashion the symbols of everyday movement. This can be done through the improvisation of dancers themselves or with the help of an outside choreographer. Experimentation with dance styles created in response to popular music involves its own characteristic forms of cultural work and informal learning processes.

> Amongst white youth many dance styles are initially appropriated and popularised from black youth culture. Imported from America in the case of soul, funk and hip-hop, or Jamaica in the case of reggae, they are taken up by young blacks and transmitted rapidly to young whites who incorporate them into their own repertories of cultural expression — like 'skanking', a reggae dance style.

> John: That fascinated me, and ever since then I've loved skanking. I picked up on it real fast and I'd practice the moves at home while I'm listening to my records, right. And we'd sort of mess around, me, my sister and my cousin ... and they'd show me the dances they were learning.[12]

Too often community dance animators overlook the quality and talent displayed in young people's dance forms. Nevertheless, the animator's role as community choreographer can be crucial in other circumstances in helping individuals and groups to formulate ideas and emotions which will be experienced perceptually by each dancer and communicated to spectators. Their dancing may symbolize happiness, laughter, fun, hate, love, curiosity, cunning, rejection, despair and many other emotions in the way dance has done since human beings first moved in rhythmic unison. In our own era the eighteenth century British choreographer, John Weaver, described the way a range of symbols might be used to communicate emotions to an audience. These were mimed sequences using the allegories of classical mythology as framework for his dances. We too need frameworks appropriate to our time and our communities. Today mime is combined with dance or presented separately as an art in its own right. Whatever the method it is clear that the act of communication places responsibility on the artist for what is communicated. Therefore the symbolization of a personal or collective vision in an appropriate style of movement is more important than the early mastery of a particular technique as the improvisation of young people shows. Dance uses millions of symbols and thousands of styles around the world. British dance culture uses the symbols and styles appropriate to its history and people. No one form should have a monopoly, neither classical nor contemporary nor folk nor jazz nor Asian nor community nor reggae nor anything else. Dance culture needs a plurality of forms including dance forms recreated from historical periods and from other cultures. Community dance can be anything the initiative of local people want it to be.

It follows that the grammar of community dance, however adapted to meet the needs of a community, will be enriched by reference to existing dance techniques and other art forms. Hence community dance needs a proper preparation of its instruments of communication, its bodies, to extend communication through a vivid articulation of feelings, which is aesthetic activity in movement. One way of doing this might be the home practice of thousands of young people. Another way can be regular and rigorous dance classes in which the teacher participates alongside the dancers. Participation in the creative activity of students enriches that activity rather than the methods of community teachers who stand back in the hope that 'creativity' will happen of itself. It won't. The same approach is needed to develop appreciation of dances, the creative act of seeing, understanding and responding to dance. Often this is neglected in community dance. It should rank equal in importance with practical creation, using films, video and discussion to extend understanding. Community dance implies not just the act of community dancing but a community of dance and mime in which performers, creators and spectators can share emotions and perceptions to extend through dance and/or mime the creativity inherent in everyone. Thus the ability of all can be strengthened to know better, understand and control the circumstances of daily living.

Mime exerts its power through the arts of gesture and mimicry. It is a part of the non-verbal physical theatre to which dance belongs with an history which has influenced profoundly both dance and

117

drama. It is a link between dance and drama, a basic skill for both and yet an art form in its own right. It is one of the modes of understanding, the mode of enactment, identified by the NCC's Arts in Schools Project. Mimicry can absorb, as it were, all the skills and advantages of that which is imitated; it can destroy by ridicule; it can seem harmless and protective yet be deadly in its affectations. It works through humour and tragedy, farce and exaggeration, derision and travesty, mockery and burlesque, irony and irreverence, clowning and buffoonery, caricature and satire, comedy and vulgarity, acrobatics and physical extravagance. It belongs in the circus and streets and community spaces and popular festivals as well as in the theatre. It reaches people in ways which dance cannot use, plainly, directly, down to earth, with its own artists and teachers. It has wide international links. At the same time its great traditions are fragmented today in many different schools so that its appeal is less than it could be. Yet it is another way of knowing and understanding the world, therefore an important addition to the armoury of empowerment the arts can give to ordinary people. Hence the community dance movement thinks of itself in terms of community dance and mime linked together in one Community Dance and Mime Foundation. Mime is an essential, influential and historical element of national dance culture. It is also economical in the most practical terms. It can be presented in limited spaces with very few artists. Thus it can represent a significant extension of dance, drama and mime appropriate to limited budgets.

Practical Applications

Community dance and mime, then, conduct aesthetic education in a range of general community situations as well as specific areas of youth dance, dance for the elderly or disabled or action to introduce to British dance culture the dance forms of Britain's racial minorities. In this sense 'aesthetic' is conflated with artistic activity, the activity moving sometimes beyond dance into social action out of understanding gained from dance. Such community dance and mime is generated in many forms. There are over a hundred professional community dance animateurs actually in paid appointments throughout the United Kingdom. Most are members of the Community Dance and Mime Foundation. They work through, or in contact with, a wide range of community organizations with a fluctuating membership as well as contact with professional companies. There is the support of individual volunteers and sometimes quite separate activities of local authorities usually working through leisure departments. To this must be added work with adult education or extra-mural departments, the growing activity of education units in professional dance companies and the burgeoning number of youth dance groups. In all, the classes, workshops and performances of this activity involve each year between half a million and a million people in the creative practice or appreciation of dance outside professional theatres and not counting the millions attending commercial dancehalls and discos.

The activity is dependent almost entirely on support from local authorities, local education authorities and regional arts associations although such supporters often have difficulty with the mercury of community arts. Community art, including dance, revolves around local culture which funding bodies are ill-equipped to handle because of conflicting definitions of art and culture. The more local it is the more questionable the 'art'. It would be better if all criteria were rethought in terms of culture rather than art. At present, if a project does not receive funding it may not achieve the status of 'art' or its nature, such as street dance, may not match the funder's conception of dance even though the dance is a long-standing expression of local culture. The British suspicion of culture runs deep. Funders prefer 'arts' so that Glasgow's city of *culture* in 1990 is something of a breakthrough. Yet funding might be fairer and less divisive if 'cultural activity' was the criterion rather than 'arts activity'.

This approach and reticence in funding may need revising in 1992 since 'culture' rather than 'art' is the criterion most often adopted by funding bodies in Europe. The extension in the last ten years of Arts Council and regional funding for youth dance, black and Asian dance and arts for the elderly and disabled are real, if partial, victories in favour of a cultural approach. All these are part of the community field and are referenced in appendices C, D, E and F. The cultural movement represented by all these elements of community dance and mime amounts in sum to a movement for ecology of the body comparable with the green and environmental movements. These have placed the study and preservation of plants, animals, the earth and the environment in the forefront of contemporary thinking. They have sounded an alarm which is transforming the attitudes of nations. In a world of issue politics they have made the ecology of planet earth a primary issue. Few people yet talk about an ecology of the body in the same way. Yet ecology of the body is needed to reform, even rescue, the human body and brain to play a more positive role in the conservation of the world. It could be a task for dancers to lead the way.

In the industrial nations of North America, Europe and Japan the human body and brain have formulated the policies which have created the global crisis. In the context of life from birth to death they are the capacity and the resource from which every person can help to refashion their part of the world to turn crisis into salvation. Yet the education of mind and body to such ends in industrial society is faulty from the start for reasons outlined in chapters 3 and 4. It concentrates on knowledge verbally acquired or expressed and concentrates on training for vocation in preference to training for the whole of life. It omits very largely the non-verbal knowledge acquired and expressed through aesthetic experience, the practice of the arts and the physical development of the body in harmony with the senses, notwithstanding physical education. Dance cannot provide a whole answer to this enormous problem but it can provide a paradigm through the community example. In concert with community arts movements in other countries community dance could point the way towards a better balance between the physical, intellectual, aesthetic and sensual elements of education and daily life. It could proclaim the need for an ecology of the body and for this to be a task of the 1990s with dance and mime providing principles and direction. Principles and direction derive not only from the experience of community dance and mime but from the community arts movement as a whole in Britain. Community dance and mime arose from this experience and from the circumstances of their historical context. It follows that this project for the 1990s needs to be on the agenda of the Community Dance and Mime Foundation and of all community art organizations.

The Context of Community Dance and Mime

The second world war destroyed long established communities and much of remaining British working class culture as Richard Hoggart showed in *The Uses of Literacy*.[13] It created instead a huge mobility — employment mobility as people moved from destroyed cities to new towns; educational mobility to new schools; cultural mobility bringing visitors and refugees from overseas into established British living. The mobilities created new communities of people who knew their neighbours no longer, who were set adrift in uncongenial situations like high rise dwellings, whose children were separated from relatives and friends on whom they had relied. To try to overcome these problems a new profession of community work arose towards the end of the 1940s, seeking to create new communities to replace the past. Presently, in the 1950s, there was added community education.

Community education was not a new concept as such. Its name and notion have a long history looking back to working men's institutions in the nineteenth century and the whole radical tradition in British politics. The Workers' Education Association and the extramural departments of universities are part of it. So is Dartington where Laban, Jooss and Leeder took refuge in the 1930s. Henry Morris applied the idea to create an educational philosophy which initiated a series of Village Schools in Cambridgeshire during the 1930s. They became the prototype of Community Schools and Colleges found today in many parts of Britain. Leicestershire developed them, for example, after the war. Many higher education institutions maintain departments of community education. The philosophy assumes education to be a communal all-age activity balancing intellectual learning with the development and growth of social, political and cultural awareness and sensitivity. It assumes that schools for the young should offer access to older people to expand interests, skills and experience of leisure pursuits and to participate in local and national decision-making. The school thus becomes a focal point for the whole neighbourhood and accountable to it. In a community school the staff should see the community as a valuable educational resource and the community should see the school as a great educational opportunity.[14] Although community workers did not see things that way in the 1950s this philosophy underlay the introduction of education and the arts to supplement their work.

Community workers early discovered a growing need to support individual people in a post-modern world where organization had grown bigger and more impersonal in every sense. Amalgamations, mergers, conglomerations and the spread of transnational companies made workers less and less able to relate to management. The health service, housing service, education service, employment offices and other branches of the welfare state all represented huge bureaucracies requiring formidable paperwork for ordinary people to complete. The same was true of local government and familiar tasks like shopping. The growth of supermarkets proclaimed increased choice for the customer, but the disappearance of small shops and the size of the supermarkets in fact turned the customer into an impersonal consumer. In such a situation it became necessary to rescue the individual.

Community education therefore developed during the 1950s the practical purpose of assisting individual people to cope with the pressures of new social and economic organization. People needed help to interpret the jargon of official forms from central and local government as well as private employers and others. Claimants' unions were formed to help claim benefits, rebates and pensions in areas of need inadequately explained by administrators. Those for whom English was a second language needed language help. A whole range of issues in civil rights including voting rights, civil liberties and social responsibility arose from new legislation or, more often, from its interpretation by the bureaucracy and the police. Especially was this true in the increasingly dilapidation of inner cities. Community education thus added theoretical, legal and cultural elements to its initial practical purpose. In doing so it overlapped with traditional areas taught by university extra-mural departments and the Workers Educational

Association. I remember from personal experience that this was particularly true in the cultural field. Here demand for sessions in arts appreciation and arts practice, including dance, grew significantly during the late 1950s and early 1960s. This foreshadowed a further extension of community work to embrace the arts.

The community arts movement may seem now to be particularly a product of the cultural upheaval of the late 1960s in all industrial countries. In Britain at least it had deeper historical roots in the working class culture of Scotland, Wales, the north of England and London; and in poetry, songs, banners, plays, music and dance which were part of a strong culture based on working class life. The political and social thinking of the radical 1960s gave this tradition a particular direction. The objectives and manifestations then introduced disturbed deeply established arts practice, arts teaching and arts funding. One dance manifestation arising directly out of adult education was the formation of the Royal Ballet's Ballet for All group in 1964. Aiming to take the performance and appreciation of an elite art form to areas which larger companies could not reach, its purpose and appeal to new audiences worried classical ballet's conservatives. Similar manifestations developed in film through the Film Society Movement and in painting and music linked with amateur practice. By the early 1960s all this had created a climate in which the aesthetic education of the public through greater access to established arts became recognized as a necessary political objective. Consequently, the Arts Council began to receive regularly increased government funding from 1964 onwards. Inevitably this created its antithesis. Within the search to improve quality of life for all the nature of arts and of access to them more and more was questioned. The questioning took shape in the community arts movement, a third stage in British community development.[15]

Arising in the late 1960s, and developing through the 1970s, the primary aim of the community arts movement at its foundation was to provide opportunities which might stimulate and release the creativity of ordinary people through artistic experience. That way, it was argued, the arts would replace their elitist image and limited access with an artistic democracy which would open the arts to all. There would, too, be important social repercussions in the sense that releasing individual and community creativity can strengthen the self-confidence of people and provide an important means of communication and self-expression. Thus the stimulus of artistic creativity would empower individuals and communities to play a more positive role in the democratic process.

Although there have been many ideas of the form community arts should take, an interpretation gaining more support than most was produced in a policy paper by the community arts advisory panel of the Greater London Arts Association in the mid-1970s. This argued that

> community arts enjoins both artists and local people within their various communities to use appropriate art forms as a means of communication and expression in a way that critically uses and develops traditional arts forms, adapting them to present day needs and developing new forms. Frequently the approach involves people on a collective basis, encourages the use of a collective statement but does not neglect individual development or the need for individual expression ... Community arts proposes the use of art to effect social change and affect social policies, and encompasses the expression of political action, effecting environmental change and developing the understanding and use of established systems of communication and change. It also uses art forms to enjoy and develop people's particular cultural heritages...community arts activists operate in areas of deprivation, using the term 'deprivation' to include financial, cultural, environmental or educational deprivation.[16]

Such was the context, the ambition and the immediate way ahead argued in countless battles within the movement and in many applications to potential funding bodies. The early movement tended to be concerned with process and cultural action rather than specific arts practice. Part of it emphasized creativity, enjoyment and participation; part emphasized politics. It had been started by community workers mostly in run down areas of inner cities and by graduates from art and drama schools seeking new audiences and new means of reaching audiences which lay outside established galleries and theatre spaces. Their canvasses became the sides of houses, walls and places where people meet. Their stages were streets and the floors of community centres, old people's homes, youth clubs, prisons. Collectively they gave the arts a new slant and perspective questioning the role of the arts in society and affecting the perception of the arts by people. The new role was advanced particularly in the late 1960s by the formation of Arts Laboratories housing many forms of arts and social activities, including social and sexual protest. Their significance at this stage was overlooked by almost all funding bodies and arts-support organizations. Essentially, and in a most direct form, they pitted an 'Athenian' view of the arts against the prevailing 'Roman' view of the established approach to arts management.

To realize further the vision of arts for the people new organizations were created for particular community art forms — artists reinforcing media communication through murals, posters and exhibitions; community photographers and video artists doing the same thing in their own way; drama projects, dance groups, printing organizations and the like. Presently these were extended to encompass larger fields like community broadcasting, multi-media projects and national organizations like the Association of Community Artists formed in about 1972. All these organizations needed money to fulfil their purpose. The ACA campaigned and argued such funding on behalf of a movement which spread throughout the United Kingdom and believed its projects deserved a proper share of the increased funds then going to established arts structures.

While funding bodies like the Calouste Gulbenkian Foundation sympathized with the new movement and funded it from the early 1970s as liberally as they could, including the placement of professional artists in schools, the decisive response lay with the Arts Council. It was to the Council that community arts ventures looked for regular revenue funding. Two problems emerged. First, the applicants as a group or category lacked a philosophy and agreed objectives around which arguments could be framed, definitions made and criteria developed. Every applicant made a different case from a different position in terms of arts need, or social or political position. This weakened enormously the establishment of a strong common case in early funding discussions and inhibited also the response of potential funders. Early on these funders emerged as the Arts Council, local authorities, foundations, private business and individuals.

The funders, too, were confused. They agreed about the need to open arts access to more people, but not about the reasons or the method. In their demand for a tidy philosophy they overlooked a wide consensus which held the movement together, though not in any formal sense. This emphasized the need to preserve popular art forms as part of wider access, and especially a need to interpret arts access as arts practice more than arts appreciation. Arts practice, moreover, was understood generally as an aid to social change. Only the Gulbenkian Foundation among funders at first seemed willing to acknowledge the implications of such an understanding.

The reservations of funders were supported by the legal position, especially the rules of the Charity Commission. These made clear that funds from charitable bodies like the Arts Council or British-based foundations could not be given for political or campaigning purposes and that generally speaking recipients also should hold charitable status. Few community arts enterprises in the early days distinguished between arts need and social or political action. Most of them acknowledged a campaigning purpose, especially in local politics. Almost none held charitable status. The influence of this dilemma on the movement was profound and helped ultimately to determine its development into today's structure. In particular, it meant that community arts tended to be kept on the sidelines as awkward fringe activities. They were left to beg money rather than become a recognized category receiving regular funds for clearly understood purposes like, say, a social service or the local theatre. Too often also this placed community arts in a hostile climate in relation to funding bodies compared with other applicants.

A great part of these difficulties arose because community arts were integral to the radical cultural movement of the late 1960s. This movement was concerned to break down established social codes through new standards of dress and behaviour, youth power, popular music and political aspirations for change, all resting on an economic boom which people thought perhaps had arrived to stay. The rivulet of community arts became larger and stronger through tributaries from the black consciousness movement with its influences from the USA; the feminist movement with its energy and critique of existing social relations; the gay and lesbian movement with its focus on social and sexual minorities; and the student movement around Vietnam, the Bomb and related issues. Funding community arts thus became deeply problematic. Within this complex situation and precisely because the movement never was an organized movement, community artists overlooked potential allies outside the protest movements. The most promising of these lay in local education authorities. Several authorities, with Leicestershire setting an example in music and the performing arts, developed well-funded policies to carry arts appreciation and practice to young people and their families mostly through an extension of educational institutions. Such activities were guided by advisory teachers in each authority, often with views close to the objectives of community arts projects. These teachers often were crucial supporters of artists-in-residence schemes influencing the artists as much as staff, pupils and the local community. Very few projects, however, explored the possibilities of collaboration. The movement tended to isolated itself in its poverty, looking inward rather than outward. There is no need here to give a detailed history of the way things went, but it is important to outline how Arts Council and Regional Arts Association funding developed to accommodate the swelling tide of applications representing the many interests of community arts.

The Council began by establishing a New Activities Committee in 1969 followed by an Experimental Projects Committee in 1971. When this method of funding proved inadequate to the need, a working party on community arts was established under Professor Harold Baldry to make recommendations. The recommendations and arguments in this report,[16] published in 1974, have guided ever since Arts Council policy towards community arts even after these were devolved to Regional Arts Associations in 1979. The reorganization of the Council and RAAs following the Wilding Report[17] in late 1989 therefore seem likely to be the first major change in a relationship which now has run its course. It is a relationship which has to do with individual arts much more than it has to do with an overall national arts policy, still less to do with a national cultural policy. The Arts Council never really came to terms with a need to see community arts as part of a national policy reaching and serving every section of society. Its approach was piecemeal.

The Baldry Report took from Europe the notion of *animation culturelle* as the process through which the community arts movement was seeking to achieve its objectives. Unable to define the movement and its functions more precisely, the notion of cultural animation, then propagated particularly by the Council of Europe, began to guide the attitude of the Arts Council because it was the only philosophy the Council could ascribe to community arts. This saw the animators operating in particular neighbourhoods, often from arts centres or resource centres, but sometimes touring from place to place. In this sense community artists were drawn into the existing structure of arts funding and arts practice whereas community artists really were seeking to change the practice through new processes of group creation stimulating individual and group creativity. In so far as the community arts movement had any common philosophy it argued a cultural democracy in which creative arts opportunities, enjoyment and celebration would be available to all and stimulating to all. Essentially this was a doctrine of empowerment. The Arts Council's philosophy argued alternatively a democratization of culture through which the population might learn more about the arts through greater access. The difference was fundamental and was articulated in 1978 through publication of *Artists and People* by Su Braden,[18] commissioned by the Gulbenkian Foundation. Reviews of the book, in which Braden defended cultural democracy, brought the argument into the national press and into the annual reports of the Arts Council. It encouraged also the ultimate devolution of community arts from Arts Council to RAAs during 1979 and 1980; an assessment system of grant-giving which emphasized the Arts Council's commitment to democratization of culture; and a rejection of cultural democracy which thereby affected profoundly the nature of public aesthetic education.

There was and is, therefore, a philosophical confusion about the role and purpose of community arts. Many funding agencies saw them as social provision, educational provision or a form of community work rather than the process of art-making in which most community artists believed, a process in which quality and standards mattered. Hence the continuing hesitant attitude towards community arts. This questioned the argument of community artists that, since they worked to stimulate the grass roots of creativity and artistic understanding, their work had an overriding claim to money from taxpayers and private benefaction. The funding response to this argument was clouded by a mistaken belief that community arts implied the second-rate in creative work and was a form of activity more to do with politics than the arts.

By the beginning of the 1980s a position had been reached whereby devolution split the national character of the movement, such as it was, and the campaigning element of community arts projects was emasculated by the insistence of most funding organizations on charitable status before funds would be forthcoming. This neutralized the early community arts emphasis on community activism, replacing arguments for cultural democracy with the Arts Council's preference for the democratization of culture. In pursuit of this commitment the Arts Council required all subsidized national bodies like galleries, drama and dance companies to provide public education services about their work. Local authorities and regional arts associations adopted similar policies which broadened access to existing cultural provision in their areas. Thus one positive result of the community arts movement was a willingness to extend provision and access. In the event this was limited by government financial restrictions so that provision still hardly reaches people in towns and villages whom community artists sought originally to empower through arts practice. Nevertheless, a major part of early community arts practice and aims was taken over in this way by government-funded bodies. The movement, in fact, became divided in its approach to community arts. Earlier attitudes and aims, including political commitment, were sustained by the continuity of projects founded in the 1960s and early 1970s. Later projects, and a degree of professionalization through training introduced for new community artists in the 1980s, tended to emphasize the integration of community arts with local funding structures and policies. Yet the ambition remains that community arts, by helping to release local creativity, will stimulate self-confidence in wider fields of living, encourage an ability for decision-making and social concern and thus contribute fundamentally to the democratic process through a greater ability of people to run their own affairs.

It is clear that the nature of community arts has changed. The notion and work have become largely institutionalized through the appointment of community arts officers at various levels and through professional training courses in polytechnics and colleges. The concept has become much broader alongside the concept of community work and community development generally. Today it embraces voluntary action schemes, community awards schemes, community arts projects of many kinds, arts for the elderly and the disabled, carnivals, festivals and other celebrations, community arts projects sponsored by business concerns, youth arts and the misnamed 'ethnic' and 'minority' arts. In particular, community arts with few exceptions have moved under the umbrellas of local authorities and regional arts associations. Community arts have broadened to become arts and the community and tend to be dismissed in official thinking as 'not real art — just social and educational'.

The development of community dance and mime illustrates the mistake in this judgment, supported by the further judgment of the Devlin Report.[19] No one, except high art dinosaurs, seriously questions today that community arts are a process encouraging arts creativity leading therefore to an art product. If the process leads also to livelier, more socially active communities or individuals so much the better. Nothing can be wrong with the notion that the development of arts creativity can stimulate also greater self-determination through which groups of people might gain or regain some degree of control over some aspects of their lives while realizing talents they did not know they had. This calls in question: (a) political and social action associated with community arts; and (b) the established notion that art is the product of solitary creative work.

It is natural that these questions should arise in a society where pluralism issue politics and mass consumerism have become the norm. Therefore alternative approaches to art creation need to be explored and supported by funding bodies concerned with the arts. Art and artistic creation have to do with values. Community arts (or art projects in the community) have to do with community values, recognizing these values and communicating them through the arts. Are arts in the community considered to be fringe art because individual communities are seen to lie on the fringe of social and economic organization? The 'fringe' view of community arts so far has not changed whatever vision, talent, craftmanship or technique is incorporated in their creation, whether they are the product of individual creativity or part of a community's pleasure and celebration. Art in any event is always communication. Therefore the arts becomes a stimulus and framework for activity whether presented in galleries, opera houses or localities. Therefore the cry, 'Is it art?', asked frequently at the birth of community arts, is a nonsense. Such arguments apply to community dance as much as to other arts in the movement.

Much of the problem lies in a failure by funding bodies to recognize the extensive changes in arts communication which have taken place since the second world war. They see the arts still in categories of live performance — opera, ballet, drama, orchestral music, exhibitions of painting and sculpture. These offer a great deal to many people as I learned through years of taking Ballet for All to miners in Coalville, stockbrokers in Guildford, schools in Scotland and the elderly in Devon. To performance arts of this kind have been added now arts on video, film, television, sound tapes. Live perform-ance is overshadowed by electronically recorded performance which huge numbers of people can share and copy for themselves. Shared consumption leads often to shared participation. This was established in a survey of youth leisure carried out in the London Borough of Lewisham between 1982 and 1985 by the Laban Centre for Movement and Dance. Listening to popular music stimulated music-making by young people, either through the formation of independent bands or through study at the informal Lewisham Academy of Music, a model community arts project. This led in turn to young people recording their own music and marketing their own labels. Consequently, fund-ing priorities today need to include not only the subsidy of seats for minority opera-goers but also subsidy towards resource centres of cultural facilities for majority interests like video-making, film-making, print-making, dance-making and music-making. This also is creative work. It uses symbols and symbolic materials in informal community settings, drawing on personal experiences. It releases and supports forms of art which are present already in people making their own statement to other people.

The historical justification for this community approach is the old craft guilds where creation was largely a communal act. Today popu-lar culture remains largely a collaborative act in music, dance, drama, film, television and journals. Even creative writing cannot be carried out except in relation to outside experience, often in consultation with others, and always requiring readers. The creation of art, therefore, like most other creativity, is not solitary. Its solitary image is a nineteenth century myth against which young artists rebelled in the 1950s and 1960s. Art is always a result of collaboration with others both in itself and in organization and planning. It follows that the working methods of community arts not only are important in themselves, but also lie in the mainstream of cultural production and should be supported as such. Creativity is a social rather than a solitary act.

It follows further that community arts should be seen as a system of assisting the infusion of local cultural traditions and art sources into the national or regional art system through methods which imply shared activities, shared creativity and goals, and implicit acknowledg-ment that membership of a community carries consequent responsi-bilities. This again is to relate community arts to broader concepts of community. Community implies a set of relationships and mutual communication, including arts communication. These together form local social organizations reflecting the attitudes, needs and interests of each locality. In these social organizations community arts play a vital role because they contribute individual and communal visions of living, ways of seeing the world and each other which are essential elements of democratic living. These elements are not fulfilled by receiving the vision of one artist, or even a group of artists, in passive reception at a concert or performance. Therefore performances of Shakespeare, opera, dance, spoken poetry, music, painting and so on acquire extra importance to the extent that they stimulate local, community and individual responses which in turn can illuminate further what has been seen or heard.

This community aspect of the activity of theatres and concert halls often is overlooked in national or regional arts policies. The places for performance are seen more often as rendezvous to which individuals go for individual or family satisfaction without losing an individual or family isolation. The community aspect is addressed only as a fringe activity through community or education departments. But take away the community aspect, by which I mean local activity run by local people, and a vital part of the equation of all arts activity is lost. It follows that community arts projects should be seen to serve the interests of communities and that workers on these projects, whether or not professionally trained, work *with* people not *on* people. They may feed their own skills, experience and ideas into each project, but they should draw much more from and with the community. Community arts projects of any kind, especially dance, imply participation and genuine collective creativity. Therefore community arts activity can embrace groups of any size, large or small, and need to be concerned not only with the process but also with the content of what is communicated.

Cultural localism in the operation of choice and the reflection of differences should, therefore, play an important part in national and regional arts policies. It is essential in any cultural democracy (which I presume is how government approaches arts policy) that people should be able to question the social organization in which they live, question the information they receive and offer alternative interpretations of the world around them based on local experience. This can be done significantly and effectively through the arts and has been done traditionally through working class culture. This culture is collective, participative and often oral. 'Official' culture, descending originally from court taste, is frequently individual and presentational. Usually it is defined as 'good' art or 'high' art with working class culture defined as non-art. Discussion of community art cannot avoid this issue because such definitions underlie all national, regional and local arts policies. It is, surely, a form of discrimination like racism or sexism. It affects also attitudes to the arts of Britain's cultural minorities. Most often these are characterized as minority or ethnic arts thereby implying a lower category and indicating discrimination. Yet from the point of view of communities and the significance of cultural localism they are of supreme importance. Often, too, like the dance forms of south-east Asia, they are drawn from long traditions of high art in their country of origin.

It follows that any relationship between communities and the arts has to question the notion that art is handed out from above with very little choice for the consumer and very little provision to help understanding at local level. The present organization of provision suggests a hegemony of one view only of the arts. Greater devolution proposed in the Government's arts reorganization provides an opportunity to question this hegemony provided new Regional Arts Boards see community arts as the priority they are. The opportunity should lead to greater emphasis on regional creativity in which community creativity and the role of the amateur will be essential elements. This community approach to the arts should seek to hold a balance between receiving cultural production and participating in cultural production. Both are valid. Both communicate knowledge, understanding and values, but the participation is more significant than the reception, short and long term.

All this affects the issue of funding. Money can never be neutral, nor can requirements for accountability. Community arts imply plurality and a large measure of independence not always in accordance with the views of funding bodies. To operate they require a right of access to the means of communication and to the skills necessary to effect communication. Hence the need for socially owned resource centres to provide the means and the skills. The other essential need is recognition of the principle of co-authorship or co-creation. This implies teamwork on a project producing not only shared art production but also shared understanding of creation, content and ultimate use. The use includes the effect of the art work on people and its means of distribution. The result is not only a team creation whose techniques can produce 'professional' results but also a way of attracting and inspiring other local talents not in the team, as well as developing the talents of the team. These two needs should be recognized by funders as a powerful stimulant to arts creation and a major extension of public aesthetic education.

At the same time the history of community arts suggests that the views of single funders can prevail over the preferences of a community to an extent that the nature of a project becomes changed. Grant aid, whether from public or private sources, is no bad thing provided there are no strings or implications distorting a project or work with a community. To avoid this possibility, sustain independence and recognize the present climate of funding it is desirable that funding sources should be plural rather than single. The origins and funding sources of community mime and dance today illustrate changes in the national movement and the position of individual art forms twenty years after community arts were launched in Britain.

Developing Community Dance and Mime

The Association of Community Artists (ACA), formed about 1972, sought to establish itself as the national body for community arts, campaigning and arguing the case for a larger share of arts funding. Frustrated by the rules of charitable status it sought to circumvent these rules by itself becoming a charity called The Shelton Trust. Thereby it became a valuable forum for the movement but lost its campaigning capacity. The dance equivalent of ACA was the National Association of Dance and Mime Animateurs (NADMA) developing from the late 1970s and learning from the experience of the first ten years of community arts. Dance, of course, had been always one of the arts, usually incidental to music and theatre projects or an important part of festivals. But it had no interest group the way video, drama and mural artists were organized. This was largely because classical ballet ruled the art form without serious challenge until the arrival of contemporary dance from America in the late 1960s and the development of a British New Dance Movement in the 1970s. Contemporary dance demonstrated early on its readiness for social commitment, first at the London School of Contemporary Dance from 1966, then at the reorganized Laban Centre for Movement and Dance from 1974, but it took time to become established. The New Dance Movement added an essential element of British roots and a link with the dance profession.

By 1976 a combination began to evolve of experience from artist-in-residence schemes, experience from the community arts movement, the questioning implied in New Dance and the social interest of contemporary dance graduates from the two schools to create a concept of dance animation. The first animateur projects were appointed in Cardiff and Cheshire in 1976, with a third project in Swindon a year later. These were partly a result of individual initiative and partly the fruit of local interest with local or Gulbenkian funding. At the same time individual initiative established independent projects funded either communally or by the adaptation of funds for related purposes like further education and health needs. Outstanding examples of these were Shape, founded by Gina Levete, and what is now Amici, founded by Wolfgang Stange, both beginning through dance in hospitals. Shape is now a national organization applying all the arts to social need; Amici is an internationally recognized dance company further described in appendix F.

Thus from its beginning the community dance movement work-ed within the constraints of charitable and local authority funding. There was little of the political activism known to the rest of com-munity arts, unless one includes the rather cloudy new thinking and dance relationships towards which New Dance was feeling its way. The dancers, in fact, had no option since by the late 1970s the argument over cultural democracy or democratization of culture had been won by the Arts Council. With the devolution of responsibility for community arts to RAAs after 1978 a new situation with new priorities emerged. Community artists began to discuss working con-ditions and pay, clearer definitions of their role within the commun-ity, working methods and preparation or training for the job, profes-sionalism, and the quality and nature of the art they stimulated.

Under pressure from the growing dance animateurs' movement and the success of early projects the RAAs accepted responsibility in 1982 to develop more dance posts across the country. A steering committee was established by the Arts Council the following year to evaluate the growth of what was by then a recognized and credible new form of dance activity to which became allied the art of mime. From the recommendations of this evaluation in July 1985 came a national organization to represent the dance and mime animateur profession, financial support for that organization and a range of development, conference and training initiatives.

Unlike earlier community art forms and the community arts movement as a whole, community dance and mime thus became integrated with existing national arts structures and funding systems from the beginning of its work. Indeed, if one recalls Gulbenkian funding of its first dancers-in-residence in 1976, it grew out of this system and the system has shaped its present structure. The dance animateur movement, therefore, is in contrast with the earlier in-dependent protest of community arts against the hegemony of the arts establishment. It made its own protests in its own way, but the movement's national organization — first the National Association of Dance and Mime Animateurs in 1986, then the Community Dance and Mime Foundation from 1989 — represents the movement's interests within the system, especially to the Arts Council and the Regional Arts Associations.

The benefits of this integration are clear. The dance animateur movement has developed with astonishing speed as a discrete section of a community arts movement which no longer has its own national forum. Dance and mime animation runs its own developmental train-ing courses and summer schools with Arts Council and RAA support. It has issued professional *Guidelines* to employers supported by an offical *Handbook for Dance and Mime Animateurs*. The CDMF provides a national forum, consultancy service and exchange centre of information and experience. It has a regular bulletin, *Animated*, which supplements for its membership publications with a wider reference for community dance like *Dance Theatre Journal*[20] and *DICE*.[21] It sees itself as a campaign body for dance and mime, for the employment and training of a growing number of dance animators and for their pay and conditions and place in the national dance structure. As backing it seeks to create a data base for information and research, widening contacts with dance animation in Europe and a funding portfolio which looks to private sponsorship to supplement core funding from the Arts Council, Sports Council, Welsh and Scottish Arts Councils and Regional Arts Associations. Its social objectives include the promotion of multi-cultural dance and equal opportunities. In sum, the record is impressive.

On the other hand the semi-official position of CDMF inevitably removes from its priorities the kind of political and social critique which provides the sharp edge of other work in community arts. There is a tendency to be inward-looking at the still very variable employment conditions of community dance and mime animateurs. The nature of their work and the overriding obligation to provide regular classes wherever community dance and mime are based means that grass roots animation often attracts those who have simply missed out as dancers when younger and want to catch up rather than those who need the stimulus of community dance to ameliorate social conditions or isolation in inner city or rural poverty. This legitimate balance is hard to maintain and needs a regular monitoring not yet provided. There is a need to stress the independence of community dance and mime from official influence, particularly through an independent think-tank role which can review official policies and examine possible developments like the ecological link, and closer international ties and the problem of competition from sports centres and local government leisure services at standards lower than are acceptable to professional animateurs. There is a need, too, to embrace a larger dance aesthetic remembering that the body is a medium of expression used in many ways all of which dance can touch. People decorate their bodies with style and fashion. Bodies cannot be separated from activities like keeping fit, musical interest, personal taste and meeting people. These wider areas of dance and body communication remain largely to be explored by community dance animateurs whose role should be to receive ideas equally with offering, but never imposing them. In a word the community dance and mime movement, stretching wider than its Foundation's membership, needs to think hard about its role and larger influence in the development of British dance culture. In particular it needs to give major attention to the politics of dance and to the effect on small groups and community dance of the reorganization of national and regional arts funding now in hand by the Government.

Against this background and potential future the links of the community dance and mime movement with the wider dance and mime profession need to be recalled. Community dance and mime are not only children of the community arts movement in the 1960s but also part of a movement of professional dance and mime artists to break loose from the constraints of working only within established companies and theatrical settings. Their movement is the same as the movement of artists and actors which led to community arts. Thus the dance and mime movement is in every sense a *professional* movement taking professional dance and mime standards to new audiences in small venues through solo or group performances or involving large numbers of people in professionally conceived community animation and celebration. It does this in two ways: through local dance animation with a professional animateur resident in the community; and through the touring performances and workshops of small professional dance groups. The line is very thin, therefore, between, say, the much admired Cholmondeleys company touring nationally its contemporary dance creations; the Indian classical dance group of Shobana Jeyasingh; the small classical ballet group Ballet Creations, also touring nationally; David Massingham Dancers resident as animateurs in Northumberland; Janet Archer, the one, but very lively dance animateur in Welwyn Garden City; solo professional dancers like Laurie Booth and Julyen Hamilton performing in Britain and abroad; and occasional large scale festival or dance projects with many local participants devised by choreographers like Geraldine Stephenson or Rosemary Lee. All should be seen as part of a national dance provision, supplementing larger companies, and funded in partnership between the Arts Council, Regional Arts Associations, local authorities and private initiative.

The dance art works manifest in each case, whether by touring groups or resident animateurs, are all the result of professional dance activity and training reflecting influences from Laban, classical ballet through Ballet for All, New Dance, ethnic dance, London Contemporary Dance School and the community arts movement. Collectively these influences have opened new forms of dance activity during the last twenty years which need now formal recognition by funding bodies as integral to coherent dance cultural expression. Hence salaries, training and other support need to be commensurate with the rest of the dance profession. Failure to recognize this is a reason why talented solo artists like Julyen Hamilton need to live abroad and why there could be a drain of some of the best British dance groups to Europe as European integration becomes reality. The network of small professional dance groups touring Britain and the network of locally based community dance animateurs are one complementary national service, neither extra nor fringe, but a professional and permanent expression of British dance culture created by, and appropriate to, British society at the end of the twentieth century.

Notes and References

1 Motionhouse in the West Midlands is one among several dance companies to visit prisons.

2 The national organization Shape, is responsible for organising the application of the arts to a wide range of social need.

3 Estimates vary up to one million people a year. It depends on definitions. The lowest figure is 500,000.

4 The Equity head office is at 8 Harley Street, London W1N 2AB (Tel 071 636 6367). A useful *Handbook for Choreography*, by Ann Whitley, has been published by the National Organization for Dance and Mime, 9 Rossdale Road, London SW15 1AD (Tel 081 788 6905).

5 Willis, Paul: *Common Culture*, Milton Keynes, Open University Press, 1990.

6 In an interview with Naseem Khan, *The Sunday Correspondent*, 24 December 1989.

7 *The Guardian*, 30 December 1978.

8 Braden, Su: *Artists and People*, London, Routledge, 1978.

9 *The Guardian*, 4 October 1978.

10 Abbs, Peter: *A is for Aesthetic*, Basingstoke, Falmer Press, 1989.

11 Aspin, David (1989): 'The Arts, Education and the Community', in Abbs, Peter (Ed) *The Symbolic Order*, Basingstoke, Falmer Press, 1989, p. 255.

12 Willis, Paul: ibid, p. 66.

13 Hoggart, Richard: *The Uses of Literacy*, London, Chatto and Windus, 1957.

14 For a post-war application of these notions see Jones, Donald: *Stewart Mason. The Art of Education*, London, Lawrence and Wishart, 1988.

15 For a fuller exposition of this early period and its theories see Kelly, Owen: *Community, Art & the State*, London, Comedia, 1984.

16 Arts Council of Great Britain: *Report of the Community Arts Working Party*, (The Baldry Report), London, Arts Council, 1974.

17 Wilding, Richard: *Supporting the Arts*, a review of the structure of arts funding, (The Wilding Report), London, 1989.

18 Braden, Su: *op. cit.* p. 18.

19 Devlin, Graham: *Stepping Forward*, (The Devlin Report), London, The Arts Council, 1989.

20 Published quarterly from the Laban Centre for Movement and Dance, Laurie Grove, London SE14 6NH. Contains regular community dance information.

21 *DICE* (literally Dance in the Community Exists) is a quarterly journal for community dance in London from 79a Broomsleigh Street, West Hampstead, London NW6 1QQ.

Chapter 6

Whose National Dance Culture?

I have referred often to a political aesthetic or an aesthetic of politics. The phrase draws attention to the political implications of an approach to aesthetics, to the arts and to dance which takes a wider view than usual of the aesthetic field. This view rejects any ivory tower, elitist, intellectual and privileged approach to the arts. Such an approach suggests that the arts comprise a special kind of excellence to be appreciated by a specially qualified minority. This minority exists and has powerful advocates in government, the Arts Council, the media and other sources of influence. Arnold Haskell, one of the first British ballet critics, was such an advocate and was proud to be so.[1] Not surprisingly the greater part of the population rejects arts of this kind which play no part in their lives. Yet there is a popular, lively culture, including dance culture, forming and being formed by majority taste. I remarked on it in chapter 1, developed it in chapter 5 and ask now the question: Whose dance culture are we discussing?

An extreme view of dance excellence — more extreme even than Haskell's — was expressed by Nicholas Dromgoole, critic of *The Sunday Telegraph*, on 6 May 1990. He argued that classical ballet is 'mainstream while contemporary remains a tributary'. He overlooked the close interchange today between classical and contemporary dance training, overlooked history and the social origins of classical and contemporary/modern dance which establish these and other dance forms firmly in our culture. He suggested, without evidence, that 'a surprisingly high number of contemporary professionals are ballet rejects' and referred to 'the serious limitations of the contemporary technique' as if there are no limitations in classical technique. His critical duties presumably did not require him to notice in the work of choreographers in both disciplines the ever-developing enrichment of modern dance by classical technique and of classical technique by modern dance.

Misleading allegations in such a quarter are irresponsible as well as cheap. They air Dromgoole's apparent prejudice against contemporary dance but amount also to a kind of dance apartheid. One aspect of dance is promoted above all others as 'excellent' where a balanced dance culture for the majority requires pluralism. The taste and preferences of a powerful minority are elevated to a hegemony which could starve of resources both contemporary dance and all that is being achieved in public dance education. Dromgoolization is bad for dance in general but is sinister especially in its political implications for dance funding. Early proposals of the arts minister to reorganize the Arts Council, for example, assure secure central funding to the Royal Ballet leaving the rest to be negotiated. Convention has it that politics has no place in the arts, least of all in dance. The arts are held to be above politics, or at least at arm's length. This is a cover-up because reality shows the opposite. The Arts Council's current reorganization is intensely political in practice. At a theoretical level almost all the papers in *The Symbolic Order*[2] carry political implications though they have to do primarily with aesthetics in The Falmer Press Library on Aesthetic Education. Louis Arnaud Reid, Roger Scruton, Peter Brook, Michael Tippett, David Best, Ernst Gombrich, Peter Fuller, Ted Hughes, Peter Abbs, David Aspin and others all are critical of the established order in one way or another, or put forward alternatives to strengthen aesthetic education in ways which require an exercise of political will.

The politics of dance have deep historical roots looking back to Plato and Aristotle. In our own era renaissance princes up to Louis XIV developed ballet for political reasons; performances of ballet played a role in the French Revolution,[3] the French Empire and the Italian Risorgimento; Hitler went to special lengths to curb the influence of central European modern dance under Laban, Jooss and others; varieties of dance experiment reflected aspects of the Russian Revolution until suppressed by Stalin and Zhdanov. The British Foreign Office, like other foreign ministries, uses dance companies to further British political, economic and cultural relations abroad, even sending Sadler's Wells Royal Ballet to strengthen relations with the Marcos regime in the Philippines a short time before the regime collapsed. Robert Hutchinson wrote a persuasive exposé of relations between government, Arts Council, Royal Opera House and other national theatres in *The Politics of the Arts Council* in 1982.[4] He lifted the lid not only on political relations between government and the top state insitutions of the arts but also on the double standards applied when experimental or community ventures outside recognized art categories apply for subsidy, whether national or local. All community arts workers have experienced such difficulties, often cloaked under the excuse 'It isn't art!' It would be reasonable to argue on this evidence, therefore, that a political aesthetic exists at all levels. The subject was explored in major controversies before and after the second world war between Ernst Bloch, Georg Lukács, Bertolt Brecht, Walter Benjamin, Theodor Adorno and their successors.[5] The debate continues in today's different context. 'Culture is not something separate from the general struggle', said the South African writer, Albie Sachs, early in 1990. 'Culture is us, it is who we are, how we see ourselves and the vision we have of the world.'[6]

Paul Willis uses the term 'grounded aesthetics' in his recently published report *Common Culture* and its accompanying booklet *Moving Culture*.[7] By grounded aesthetics he 'aims to convey some sense of scepticism about the "flight" of conventional aesthetics ... We want to bring aesthetics back to earth ... in the "earthiness" of the normal conditions of everyday life'. The normal conditions in this case are the cultural interests of young people in Britain. 'If activities of this kind were not conventionally described as "artistic"', said Simon Richey, assistant director for education at the Gulbenkian Foundation which commissioned the Willis study, 'this perhaps said more about our narrow use of the term than about the nature of the activities themselves.'[8] Political aesthetic is not quite the same as grounded aesthetic but it is close enough to benefit from Willis's thorough research. His work considers not only youth culture and young people's attitudes to music and dance, but also has implications for community dance and the projection of high art as elements of cultural policy. As Salman Rushdie pointed out, 'no aesthetic is a constant'.

I don't want to confuse the arts with the general culture of which they are a part but the issue is the same in both areas. Choreography is not an art which waves banners easily and makes direct political statements. The few examples I have seen were rather tiresome, although there have been moments when dance and choreography have needed to enter politics. David dancing before the Ark was a political act. Most *ballets de cour* had a political subtext. So did a number of choreographic interventions during the French Revolution, noted by dance historian John Chapman.[9]

Isadora Duncan used her genius to demand that dance address itself to contemporary issues so that war, revolution, liberty and human rights were expressed on stage in ways rarely attempted since. Experimental choreographers of the Russian Revolution addressed similar themes in the 1920s and there were strong political implications in much of the work of Rudolf Laban, Kurt Jooss and other German expressionists. In a sense the grand dance displays which precede many Olympic and Commonwealth Games carry political messages about the host country's culture and the need for peace and harmony between nations. The real issue, though, as I pointed out in chapter 2, has much more to do with humanism and creative purpose, the way choreographers see themselves, the vision they have of the world and its translation into dance form. This vision is conditioned positively or negatively by the cultural climate and political atmosphere of their time, in particular the hegemony of public thinking around them.

By hegemony[10] I mean the domination of ways of thought and attitude over public life accepted by a majority of the population. The consent of the majority, however, is induced and influenced by education, the media, tradition, custom and so on. Education and the media are the dominant factors but tend to reflect the choice and ideas of relatively small, unrepresentative groups of people particularly in media like television, radio and the press. These choices by controllers of the media 'often reject, as a matter of course, all the choices that have been made by the majority of people with whom they happen to disagree'.[11]

Education, too, encompasses in its broadest sense much more than the process of formal education. It carries always an essentially arbitrary cultural scheme derived from the hegemony of particular ways of thinking which represent actually, though not in appearance, an exercise of power. This power, and its ways of thinking, may explain some of the alienation which many young people demonstrate during formal education. In any case, as Willis points out,

> common cultural forms, in one way or another, accompany young people into the classroom every day of their lives. For many young people they may be a more profound influence on their sense of self, identity and possibility than is the formal curriculum.[12]

This view was confirmed by a study of young people's leisure in the London Borough of Lewisham, referenced in Chapter 5.[13] Consequently educational institutions increasingly are in tension between the hegemony of formal education and established cultural institutions and the counter-culture of large sections of the population most vividly expressed by young people. Artists, more often than others, respond to this tension by questioning hegemony and its use of power to favour some rather than others. In British cultural practice, for example, dancers of the Royal Ballet receive salaries substantially higher than other professional dancers partly because of their organized strength but also because they provide the acceptable dance image of British high art. At the other end of the scale the notion of community art often is rejected by establishment representatives as 'not art'. Consequently its practitioners are poorly paid. Both are examples of influence of hegemony.

This issue of hegemony in national and dance culture becomes more urgent the more the growth of a global economy stimulates the growth of a global culture. The beginnings of this global culture are here already in the universality of pop culture, the transnational organization of media (especially films and television under the hegemony of the USA), international fashions such as jeans, and the reduction of consumer difference between one advanced industrial country and another. Will the intensification of global contact under the economic imperative of transnational companies produce increasing tolerance of other cultures, or reactions in the form of fundamentalist and nationalist movements? What about the emergence of 'third cultures' such as international law, the financial markets and international dance and music? Global culture follows global economy which follows global culture. They interlock. What chance for Britain's cultural traditions and for a British dance culture in face of such overwhelming global power? This issue, raised in chapter 4, is a matter for government policy, all arts practitioners and the study of higher education institutions.

The evolution of the global market, for example, has overturned world strategic settlements of fifty years ago, flawed experiments with the social market and command economies in individual countries, demolished what had looked like impregnable political barriers and includes now the construction of new integrations, among them cultural globalization. Thus capitalist expansion follows a new path. No longer the way of trade, missionary activity and military conquest, but the formation of transnational companies to organize production and exploit markets on a transnational scale. This requires in return the development of a universal consumer society conflating in a common life-style formerly local ways of life, values and cultures. Questions of cultural value, therefore, figure more and more prominently in wealth creation: on the one hand the material element of capital investment, corporate growth and profitability; on the other hand the non-material element of education, the environment and the arts.

Consumer culture, spreading across the world, has collapsed former distinctions between culture and commerce. As a result all cultures, even those which are remote or belong to relatively small communities, acquire two use values. First they need to become more accessible and vigorous in local appeal if they are to survive. Second their quality becomes often the image of the community's products projected to consumers, or potential consumers, across the world through supermarkets, advertising, television and radio, travel brochures and trade fairs. London Contemporary Dance Theatre, for example, was the dance element of the British Government's largest-ever trade fair in the USSR in June 1990. It illustrated the importance of a vigorous national dance culture, among other arts, if a nation is to sustain its identity at home and abroad in face of global pressures. The arts, especially dance, are a particularly important statement of national identity on the global scene. Dance exemplifies national distinction in the clearest form because bodies cannot divest the physical and temperamental characteristics of their nature and nurture within the nation. Whatever they perform, in however unusual a dance language, the movement will retain always the national characteristics of the dancers who perform it.

Cultural localism, therefore, becomes the immensely important corollary of cultural globalism. In a world of shared cultures local cultures acquire a new interest and value the more they can demonstrate locally unique qualities. It follows that nourishment of the arts at all levels — popular forms as well as minority forms — is crucial to the survival of national identities in a world of interlocked economies. The arts and sport, both broadly interpreted, become almost the only way national identity can be preserved and asserted.[14]

An illustration around the current economic development of Europe drives home the point in local terms and in terms of national cultural policy. At one time Britain was the workshop of the world but suffers now in the poverty of its inner cities and declining industries from failure to think new, think big and value its cultural image. Growth, in the 1950s, shifted to the Ruhr, the Saar and the industrial areas of the Netherlands. Since the 1960s there has been a further shift. The golden areas of Europe have become Baden-Wurtemberg, Bavaria, Lombardy and Catalonia, not any more the Ruhr–Saar, leaving Britain more and more on the fringe. These golden areas emphasize their cultural attractions as much as their economic and industrial endowment. The three elements go together. In Britain, by contrast, Glasgow's achievements as European City of Culture look like being a one-off. The title will shift elsewhere in Europe and the stimulus for Britain will subside. What is needed is continuity, the eye-catching projection of local cultural images year by year from different parts of Britain not just to the rest of Britain but to European and international audiences. This would invigorate our arts, including dance, and restore our battered local and national pride.

To achieve such a change in traditional neglect of the arts requires an imaginative national cultural policy in the interests of our own people and of our entry into Europe on equal, cultural terms with other nations. John Myerscough has demonstrated already the direct economic value of the arts to Britain in his carefully researched study *The Economic Importance of the Arts in Britain*.[15] The arts, as he shows, do not cost the nation money, but earn it money as well as prestige and affirmation. In Europe the growing significance of the arts, economically, socially and culturally, was insufficiently appreciated when the Treaty of Rome brought into being the present drive towards European integration. There is no cultural remit in the treaty so that such matters cannot form part of Community stimulus and investigation in the manner of the Community's economic and social policies. Nevertheless it is clear from the document reproduced in part in appendix G that the Commission of the European Community has perceived the need for a cultural policy to put it in touch with cultural activities throughout the continent, especially the arts. 'Cultural policy', it says, 'will be crucial in the coming decade.'[16]

The dance proposals in this European document are slender and conventional. They need imaginative expansion to embrace the many forms of dance activity outlined in this book, including commercial and popular dance. The positive tone of the document, however; the certainty that dance, which has no language barriers, will be required to play an increasing role in cultural exchange and national representation in future; combined with the proven value of the arts to the national economy, emphasize the directly destructive affect of British government arts policies over a decade of cuts and restrictions. The destruction results also from the hegemony of traditional thinking. Unlike French thinking, British politicians and administrators, with few exceptions, have never over a century and a half considered the arts important to national interests, dance least of all.

Against these difficulties the Arts Council has achieved remarkable results and advances during the last fifty years in spite of many faults in the system. Current proposals to reorganize Arts Council responsibilities for national arts funding offer opportunities to remove some of the faults, although general signs for the future are not encouraging. The proposals give to the Council a general responsibility to continue to distribute, monitor and supervise government expenditure on the arts. This will be done mostly through delegation to enlarged regional arts associations rechristened Regional Arts Boards. Certain national companies and arts organizations will continue to be funded and appraised directly by the Arts Councils, such as the Royal Ballet. Others will be delegated to Regional Arts Boards. The Council also will encourage artistic innovation; be responsible for preparing and implementing a national arts strategy; will establish and operate an enhanced system of accountability in which RABs will have to agree their plans and spending programmes with the Council; will have overall responsibility for touring; will establish a comprehensive basis for the collection, analysis and dissemination of information about the arts; and will develop its work in the fields of education, training and equal opportunities. In a wide context it will encourage international arts in Britain, develop closer links with the European community, encourage a greater use of radio, television and video to disseminate the arts, develop the application of effective marketing to the arts, offer personnel and other professional advisory services to

RABs, and assist the development of public policy in the arts, relating to Parliament, government departments, local authorities and other public agencies.

There is much here to be applauded like encouraging innovation, the possibility of a coordinated national touring system, the establishment of a proper information system and data base for the arts, more attention to education, training and equal opportunities, a more extended and planned use of electronic media and closer links with international arts developments. Much depends, though, on how the revised remit is interpreted. The encouragement of innovation, for example, has been an Arts Council function for many years, especially in the dance department. What will not be acceptable is an interpretation of 'encouragement' as 'control' to exclude really radical innovations politically unacceptable to the government of the day. Equally unacceptable would be the devolution of national companies and organizations like London Contemporary Dance Theatre, Rambert Dance Company, the National Organization for Dance and Mime, and Dance Umbrella to a body like Greater London Arts. Greater London Arts has the London region as its priority and is not equipped to become a mini-Arts Council responsible for national dance bodies.

There are other worries like the need to upgrade and train regional arts board staff for their larger responsibilities, especially in dance where many RAAs have dispensed with dance expertise as an economy measure. The proposed reorganization of Arts Council staff looks as if it may dispense with art form officers in favour of advisors, thus losing the expert advice and guidance which has been as valuable to dance development in the past as funding itself. The principal worries, though, lie in the disposition of funds and the interpretation of criteria. The new responsibilities of Regional Arts Boards imply a need for additional funding. This appears unlikely to come from government which argues local authorities and local business should contribute. But local authorities are being cut back in their expenditure and business interests have shown unwillingness to fund what should be public responsibility. They have their own interests of publicity and prestige. Are, therefore, community arts, small companies and small ventures generally going to be sacrificed in order to sustain regional flagships and established arts concerns out of inadequate regional budgets? Are the phrases 'artistic criteria' and 'artistic excellence' really a way of preserving high art for the few and favoured rather than excellence of provision for the many? There is not much practical attention to access *for all* in the reorganization proposals nor to crucial areas like assistance to new art forms from Asia and the Caribbean which now are part of British culture.

There is, therefore, the suspicion of a subtext, an aim to preserve the high arts and their 'excellence' at the expense of the large-scale public aesthetic education and reform of arts funding which are needed. Arts for the few rather than arts for the many. Consider the new situation. Today there is more leisure time for wider sections of the population at all levels partly from longer holidays but also from new relationships between work/non-work and from falling ages of retirement. Therefore there need to be new approaches in presenting the arts, coordinated with educational and other authorities able to facilitate and enrich the new leisure time. The whole public arts constituency is balanced differently from the time the Arts Council was established nearly fifty years ago. It is larger, there are new perceptions and manifestations among sections of the population hardly touched by the high arts. These new audiences and new creators were alerted to the arts first by radio then in more persuasive forms through television from the 1950s. They remain still a minority of the British people but it is a growing minority. Their tastes and points of view, however, continue to be conditioned by the old-style controllers of art forms who have guided the policies of the Arts Council since the 1940s through a tight control of funding. There is a growing gap between potential audience, administrators and artists. Changes in the Arts Council charter and useful changes of practice, like the addition of an education policy during the secretary-generalship of Sir Roy Shaw, have tinkered with a problem which needs root and branch reform plus additional funding to recognize the enlarged arts constituency. The current proposals, however apparently radical, really amount to further tinkering because the basic philosophy of funding is not rethought. Hence it will not satisfy the growing constituency of artists and audience, producers and consumers who consider the character of the arts and their funding to be now an important political issue.

The Arts Council dance department achieved what it did to reach new audiences in the 1970s and 1980s in spite of the traditionally low status and finance accorded to dance. The proposals for reorganization appear to threaten even these achievements. The arm's length principle is ditched implicitly, if not explicitly, at local as well as national level. The close consultation between practising artists and Arts Council officials, which pressured and enabled limited expansion of the system since the 1960s, is to be restricted or eliminated. Although funding responsibilities are to be delegated to new Regional Arts Boards, power will be consolidated at the centre in a small executive committee of officials under the Chairman of the Arts Council. This will have a power of veto over regional funding plans and decisions. Meetings of the Arts Council itself will be reduced to four a year. In the policies of the new RABs business interests, seeking prestige publicity, will begin to play an influential role alongside representatives of local authorities but with very restricted opportunities for popular representation or representation from practising artists. This diminishes very much the positive aspect of a larger role for the regions which is a principal merit of the reorganization.

Very few English regional dance boards dispose the expertise and administrative resources to accept responsibility for dance companies which, for reasons of economics, spend most of each year touring the whole country. Hence contradictions are bound to arise between the interest of regional boards, accountable for funds to their constituents, and the national commitment of dance companies earning most of their box-office outside the region. This will be so even if the Arts Council, fulfilling its responsibility for touring, pays the bulk of touring costs outside the home region. These costs are likely to be so large in relation to regional resources and company budgets that the big companies might as well return to national funding. The devolution of large dance companies and national dance organizations is a flawed argument.

For small dance companies the proposals are even more threatening. In the climate of falling government subsidy many regional arts associations have begun to economize on dance. They have ceased the habit of regular consultation with local dance interests and have ceased to employ a dance officer, or made only a junior appointment with little influence on regional funding policies and little expertise to encourage regional dance activity. This means that regional opportunities for small dance companies are deteriorating. Yet the 100 or so small dance companies which criss-cross Britain each year provide the bulk of dance performance outside main theatres as well as a substantial element of public dance education and community service. The year-round funding which makes this possible usually is shared between a region and the Arts Council through project grants. The Arts Council element often covers the administrative costs and the touring schedule outside the home region. The home region often insists that its money goes only to services within the region and rarely covers administrative costs. Take away Arts Council funding, as is proposed, and existence becomes impossible. No dance company can find enough year-round work within a region. History shows a list of failed attempts. At best, therefore, small company support by the regions alone will be patchy and uncertain without central support. The national pattern of small company touring, funding, new dance development and educational service, created over many years, seems wholly at risk because the local interests of future Regional Arts Boards are bound to take precedence over national commitments.

Thus the Arts Council's reorganization appears to curtail the general funding of dance, except to the established art of the main companies, and to introduce piecemeal regional development at a time when the issues in choreography and in education, raised in previous chapters, require a national vision and synoptic planning. All this diminishes greatly the obvious advantages in regional devolution. Even the advantages tend to be negated by contradictions within the proposals and by impediments arising from other government policies in other fields. The most obvious negation comes from the overall intention to save money rather than support further the growing place the arts have earned in national life.[17] Anthony Everitt, secretary-general of the Arts Council, argues that

> people taking the decisions will be better informed of the audience's needs and about the artists and that will be better news for both tax payers and artists ... Regional arts associations have shown that they are very good at working with local authorities and persuading them to spend more money on the arts and will be able to develop partnership funding with local authorities and the private sector because they will be there on the ground.[18]

This notion of happy partnership is flawed before it starts by community charge-capping, the demands of the poll tax and the unwillingness of the private sector to take a leading place in arts funding. The private sector's judgments are based on commercial, not arts, considerations. Consequently arts funding may become as fitful and uneven across the country as the award of discretionary grants in education. Or everything may change again if there is a change of Arts Minister or Government, or a different emphasis develops in Arts Council policy.

Such a system is unlikely to develop worthwhile 'excellence' at every level nor will it nurture talent on any planned basis. As a system it is divisive, pitting the local needs of community arts against the needs of major arts organizations in the regions, and translating Dromgoolization into national policy. There may be twenty or fifty flagship organizations, centrally funded. The rest presumably become second class citizens. Moreover the greater accountability, which proponents say is a benefit of the new system, means financial accountability not artistic accountability. Thus the reorganization of the Arts Council looks suspiciously like a plan for tighter control over troublesome artists rather than an extension of public aesthetic education and arts opportunity for all. At risk at once are controversial programmes at The Place and Institute of Contemporary Arts, Chapter in Cardiff, Dance Umbrella, DV8 and a range of other ventures around the country.

Dance is at risk for other reasons. It needs centres where there are dance teachers and dance classes; proper spaces for dance with sprung floors; physiotherapists and other medical specialists who understand dance injuries; regular experimental performances and visiting dance companies to stimulate standards and new ideas; other dancers in other disciplines with whom to exchange ideas; above all, sympathetic dance environments and audiences. At present these needs are met fully only in London. Such centres might be created outside London in time if the regional dance agencies proposed in the Devlin Report come into being. At present there is no sign of funding for such agencies which, in any case, would take time to mature. In the meantime dance groups transplanted by devolution into new territories seem likely to wither for insufficient funds and inadequate resources, if their move is not accompanied by careful planning and the assurance of relocation funds. Any relocation of dance companies, large or small, needs to be accomplished slowly with RAB and local authority commitment to provide an appropriate infrastructure. This cannot be achieved within the two years allocated for reorganization. But it can be done as the regional dance centre in Glasgow shows and in the way another centre is developing in Birmingham with the relocation of Sadler's Wells Royal Ballet in the autumn of 1990. The Glasgow development took twenty-five years and the Birmingham development has taken already not only years in planning but millions of pounds in relocation funding. Given time and money, however, the potential benefits of relocating major dance companies are enormous with a national extension of the dance profession and career opportunity, greater projection of dance in the lives of communities, greater opportunities for dance participation and a positive influence on local dance teaching. It is no less important to safeguard the devolution and standards of smaller companies by ensuring at national level the continued existence of national development organizations which help them such as the Arts Council's central project funding, the Community Dance and Mime Foundation, the Black Dance Development Trust and the Association for South Asian Dance, Aditi.

Behind this questioning and potential lies always the special problem of dance funding. Historically most of today's dance companies came late into the Arts Council's funding circle after the hegemony of classical ballet was established and after most of the new money granted to the Council in the late 1960s had gone in other directions. Both the Arts Council's own policy report in 1984, *The Glory of the Garden*, and the Devlin Report, *Stepping Forward*, in 1989 confirm that dance remains underfunded at all levels, mostly operating on shoestring budgets and unable for that reason to devote enough time to creating new work. A briefing paper by the National Campaign for the Arts[19] in July 1989 recommended an increase in funding of £4 million (i.e. 30 per cent) for dance in England with a proportional increase for Scotland but rather more substantial increases for Wales and Northern Ireland which start from lower bases. Further funds should be made available to regional arts associations to enable them to spend about 10 per cent of their budgets on dance. Although this runs directly counter to the economies claimed in the current reorganization, it would be still not enough to place dance funding on a level with other arts.

The Campaign welcomes the notion of Regional Dance Agencies because these would help small companies to develop their potential and widen access through developing audiences and encouraging a grass roots dance culture. It urges that funding is needed to develop middle-scale companies such as Diversions in South Wales and small companies such as Motionhouse in the Midlands 'to ensure increasing creative input and output and to help create a network of such companies across the nation'. Funding, moreover, especially of the major touring companies, should be index-linked to inflation. 'Experimental work, by companies from the Cholmondeleys to Rambert, should be regarded as a key growth and development area for dance and should be funded accordingly.' Special provision should be made for the funding of Black and Asian dance at all levels (not just one or two flagship companies) in order to help these dance forms take their full place in national dance culture.

The Campaign points out three necessities to underpin such a national dance policy: (a) the development of a comprehensive training and educational infrastructure for dance, locally and nationally, particularly in-service training for choreographers, dancers and administrators; (b) the provision of suitable performance and rehearsal spaces for dance companies throughout the regions; (c) the improvement of the present low pay and poor conditions of dancers to levels where company salaries match at least the Equity minimum rate and dancers can contribute to pension and resettlement schemes for their future. The Campaign emphasizes also that dance needs to remain 'a key part of a child's education' with guarantees of 'the place of dance within the National curriculum — both in terms of performance and appreciation'.

The implications of a comprehensive training and educational infrastructure for dance, additional to recommendations at the end of chapters 3 and 4, are improved pay and conditions for teachers of dance; mandatory rather than discretionary grants to dance students; in-service training for artists and administrative staff; and grants to facilitate overseas visits and exchanges as in other areas of education and training. In the development of suitable venues operating through Regional Arts Boards, the Arts Council needs to recreate its successful Housing the Arts Fund and set aside a fixed proportion for dance. A National Dance House (surely a flagship concern?) is needed in London, as recommended in the 1984 Drummond Report, not only to present major national and international companies, but also where the issues of choreographic development and artistic responsibility raised in chapters 1 and 2 can be debated and tested in a suitable dance environment. All this rests on proper salaries for dancers, choreographers and administrators. Many 'salaries' are actually below the recognized poverty line with companies unable to meet basic employment rights and dancers unable to contribute to essential pension and resettlement schemes to assure their futures. Scott Clark, an experienced dancer now with the Siobhan Davies Company and distinguished over many years as a lead dancer on the international circuit, told me in May 1990 that working with Siobhan Davies was the first time he had ever been paid for rehearsal!

There is no recognition of these issues in the Wilding Report or in the reorganization proposals of the Arts Council and no sign of an informed understanding of the infrastructure necessary for a healthy dance profession and a growing national dance culture. The approach is static, redistributing what exists in 1990, often increasing the problems rooted in conventional thinking which overlooks, for example, that the majority of British dance companies are not building based but peripatetic. There is no allowance for growth or development whereas the arts are dynamic, always changing, reaching out. Consequently there is grave risk of the loss or dispersal of the dance expertise which has guided growth nationally and regionally over the years. The thinking behind the proposals is short-term and inadequately researched with a confusion (even conflation!) of the social and aesthetic roles of dance, niggardly staff provision for the changes intended, and no attention, other than verbal reference, to the cultural implications of closer European integration after 1992, especially in the community field. It is dishonest, too, to argue, as the leadership of the Arts Council does, for more 'excellence' in leading dance companies and to accuse experimental or community dance groups of not achieving excellence if the funds necessary for this purpose are reduced or eliminated.

How to change all this? How to fill the gaps? How to consolidate and develop our national dance culture in its many forms in spite of dismissal by public prejudice and our own lack of organization? How to stop the art drain of dance artists abroad and the graduates of our leading dance schools to places around the world? How to create a future for ourselves?

Plainly the dance profession in all its forms with all its allies must take action. Its forces are formidable once assembled. 'Dance companies are brimming with talent', noted the National Campaign for the Arts. 'The potential for the flowering of a highly developed and sophisticated dance culture is enormous. This potential needs to be fulfilled.'[20] Within the last twenty-five years the profession has extended in so many directions it has transformed the character of national dance culture. Today, in order to seize the opportunities, as well as resist the possible destruction of much of what has been achieved, the great and small organizations of this culture need to work together in ways rarely discussed and never practised before. In my own dreams of this unity, so that national dance culture is accepted and contributes to British national life in all the ways it could, I imagine sometimes for myself a fantasy. It is of the forces of dance arrayed against the constraints of prejudice, hegemony, inadequate aesthetic education, poverty of resources and internal division. The aim is to replace these constraints with alternative values where prejudice and the rest will wither. The battlefield extends beyond the United Kingdom to all the world where we have allies and into the airwaves of radio and television. We are assembled under the National Organization for Dance and Mime in a unity which has been always our hope.

Out front in our battle formation are the reconnaissance squadrons of young people in discos and youth dance companies probing, inventing, exploring — thousands of them with their music. In alliance are squadrons of music theatre companies punching holes in enemy resistance and courageous cabaret dancers used for decoy and diversionary tactics. Behind them are a vanguard of small companies ranging the country, gathering support and reinforcements in many hundred places, like the Cholmondeleys, the Featherstonehaughs and Adventures in Motion Pictures. In the centre are regiments of professional companies — the Royal Ballet, Birmingham Royal Ballet, Rambert, London Contemporary Dance Theatre, Northern Ballet Theatre, Scottish Ballet, London City Ballet, Adzido, English National Ballet with their commanders and choreographers. In support are the light cavalry of middle range companies like Diversions, Phoenix, Kokuma, Shobana Jeyasingh Dance Theatre, and Siobhan Davies and Dancers, making sorties, winning local battles. Behind them are the short and medium range artillery of managements, unions, television producers and gala organizers alongside communications units of press and publicity in touch with media and critics. Further back is the long range artillery of dance researchers and thinkers in universities, polytechnics and specialist colleges. On the left flank are reserves of handicapped and disabled companies like Amici, disproving prejudice and ready to reinforce their able colleagues. On the right, guided by organizations of the Friends of Companies, are the ranks of audience arriving with timely help, as Blücher did for Wellington at Waterloo. In special reserve for special purposes are units of folk dance troupes operating usually on their own but sometimes with the professional regiments and the heavy cavalry of ballroom dancers massed and ready at a moment's notice to overwhelm the enemy in strong formations. Over the enemy lines are dropped parachute sorties of dance animateurs to organize resistance, raise morale and pass back information. Beneath the enemy lines work engineers like Dance Umbrella and other new dance festivals, laying mine fields to explode surprises which upset hegemony. Scattered among friend and foe are critical snipers with their special targets. Some way behind these forces, carefully camouflaged, work a combined general staff of the major organizations responsible for battle plans — the National Organization for Dance and Mime, the Royal Academy of Dancing, the Imperial Society, the British Ballet Organization, the Community Dance and Mime Foundation, ADiTi, the Black Dance Development Trust, the Council for Dance Education and Training, the National Dance Teachers Association, the International Dance Teachers Association, the English Folk Dance and Song Society and the Standing Conference on Dance in Higher Education. These are advised by intelligence services of experimental choreographers for ever devising new forms of dance, by the planning of senior dance administrators and the strategic thinking of local authorities and Regional Arts Boards, working with medical support services and long supply lines to dance schools, private studios and colleges, training recruits and sending forward reinforcements.

Fantasy perhaps, but it illustrates the wide and powerful nature of our dance culture. Many parts of this culture did not exist twenty-five years ago. Other aspects were not appreciated adequately by traditional sections of the dance world. I mean not only the intellectual and critical aspects but also even dance in music theatre and television shows and the wide-ranging forms of social dance, national folk dance and historical dance. All these in every part of our dance culture need to be drawn together to form a dance lobby so powerful that its proposals and actions overcome traditional prejudice in national and local government, education and the older generation. Our arguments and dance forms must vanquish the historic hegemony of established thinking and attitudes.

There is not much time. Of all the dance companies and organizations introduced in a week of performing and planning at the beginning of this book only the Royal Ballet now can look forward with confidence to the future. The rest are threatened by reduced grants, uncertain locations or elimination. Drama and music similarly are threatened. The theatres, halls and spaces in which performing arts appear around the country record falling audiences because taxes, high interest rates and inflation have reduced money for theatre visits. Sponsorship is declining because sponsors too are squeezed by interest rates. The annual Arts Council grant, lifeline for all, is scheduled to increase in 1991/2 by only 2.5 per cent against inflation of around 10 per cent guaranteeing the disappearance of some theatres and companies. This afflicts dance in particular because national funding for dance is a disgrace, especially compared with other European countries. Out of a total Arts Council budget of approaching £200 million, only just under £15 million goes to dance and mime. Details are not easy to extract from the annual Arts Council report. Of this dance total about half, around £7.9 million goes to the Royal Ballet which needs more. The rest is split among thirteen other companies and organizations of dance development. Only about £0.1 million, for example, goes each to new dance projects, Black and Asian dance forms and dance development.

Thus the cultural legacy of the Thatcher years threatens to be a wasteland of missed potential, unfilled promise and declining audience. This is due to hegemonic thinking as much as lack of money. I referred earlier to the Wilding Report's treatment of dance companies as if most of them are building-based whereas almost all are peripatetic. The error symbolizes the hegemonic thinking we have to overcome. Such thinking has impeded dance development since the nineteenth century for all the reasons outlined in chapter three. It continues to do so today particularly in present Government circles, the civil service, the church, many other organs of state, the media and much traditional family thinking. Kenneth Baker, Conservative Party Chairman, illustrates the way this thinking influences policy. He compiled in the spring of 1990 a 'roll of shame'. This was a list of Labour Councils which he argued had spent foolishly or excessively. The only 'Shame' he could impute against the London Borough of Lewisham was to have spent £11,000 on appointing a dance officer particularly to help young people in one of the most disadvantaged areas of the country. To a traditional-thinking chairman, who seems to exploit commonly held prejudices, this was a 'shame' he knew might gain support from other traditional thinkers.

Hegemonic attitudes of this kind create a major problem the dance world must address[21] if national dance culture is to develop further. It is reflected, for example, in nineteenth century concepts of theatre-going rooted in traditional theatres and civic buildings. Yet we are moving into the twenty-first century. Many theatres, galleries and museums are responding to new cultural demands which locate the arts in more informal settings, local festivals, fringe events, small venues and community centres. We are moving away from monuments. As Peter Wright, director of Birmingham Royal Ballet once remarked, 'there's a heritage belonging to Ashton and Diaghilev. But there are also the contemporary works which dancers must have the right to enjoy ... whatever happens on stage, dance must *live* — I can't stand museum ballet.'[22] The civil servants of the Office of Arts and Libraries do not recognize yet this transformation of attitude among the public as well as artists. They are unwilling to concede the autonomy of the aesthetic realm or that the arts are about change. If not about change they are about nothing. One important change is a realization that dance is not now, if it ever was, an art of the opera house but of the city, the town and the village in direct communication with citizens. It is a means of understanding, intelligence and knowing through the senses which needs local presentation to achieve its full aesthetic impact. Our aim must be to open this understanding to everyone.

If then, dance is about change, what kind of change? There are achievements and signs to indicate the future in spite of a gloomy present. There is courage to draw from twenty-five years of expansion and creation to today's national dance structure notwithstanding inadequate funds at the Arts Council. This has been a triumph of management and creativity by choreographers and companies as well as by the Arts Council's dance department. The creativity of companies and choreographers continues in the programmes being announced for 1990/1. African, Caribbean and south Asian dance forms continue to grow and build audiences. Equally important, young dancers from Black British and Asian backgrounds are enriching British dance culture not only as dancers in contemporary dance companies but also in classical companies. The growth of dance based in the regions continues albeit needing more care and planning to create local infrastructures, as Birmingham Royal Ballet again shows.

The resource organizations for community Black and South Asian dance become more established. Dance Umbrella continues its missionary work. Experiment, new dance forms and visitors from abroad draw young people to fill seats at the South Bank, Riverside Studios, The Place and Bonnie Bird theatres in London. We must build similar centres outside London. In education dance teachers unite around the dance deficiencies of the national curriculum; dance companies strengthen their links with the education profession through programmes in schools; private dance schools struggle against the injustice of discretionary grants; dance in higher education is established and dance research is a reality. All this provides power bases for action because action will not happen unless the dance world itself acts. It can take comfort from the world situation. The cultural climate is never separate from the material climate and the changes in eastern Europe, disarmament, the dissolution of the Cold War, suggest a more positive climate for the future influencing the situation in Britain. A future for all dance in Britain, however, for those who enjoy dance by seeing or participating and for young people to benefit from increased dance opportunities in education depends on the unity of the dance world, all of it not just some of it. It means consolidating our national dance culture by burying ancient rivalries in the common interest. I hope that great teaching and examining bodies like the Royal Academy of Dancing, the Imperial Society, the British Ballet Organization and the International Dance Teachers' Association can work together in confederation towards more rational organization of syllabi, examinations and standards; that institutions in contemporary dance and higher and further education like the London School of Contemporary Dance, Laban Centre, Surrey University, the polytechnics and colleges can confer more closely to advance the dance cause in their joint areas of interest; that commercial dance interests might sit down with private dance interests; and that our journals of dance like *Dance and Dancers, Dance Theatre Journal, The Dancing Times, Dance Research* and the journals published by dance organizations can join with critics to advance the cause in written ways. Into this I hope the radio and television media can be drawn.

They key to the exercise of such power is the largest of all dance resource organizations, the National Organization for Dance and Mime. It is a dancers' organization bringing together dancers, choreographers, educationalists, medical specialists, writers, dance companies, teaching bodies and many others. As if realizing its responsibility NODM is revising its constitution to extend its work, influence and membership. Needed, I think, is an organization with faculties or departments covering discrete interests but able to combine these interests in national programmes of campaign and pressure to realize needs identified in this book — like dancers' pay, conditions and resettlement, issues affecting creative work like artistic responsibility, and issues around the future of national dance culture itself like the hegemony of the past and the extension of public aesthetic education in dance. That way lies our future.

Notes and References

1 Haskell, Arnold: *In His True Centre*, London, A & C Black, 1951, but also all of Haskell's range of critical writing on classical ballet. We were friends, fellow wine-writers, but looked at dance from opposite points of view. He was a mixture of attitudes. Staunch supporter of the young British ballet when support was needed, champion of Soviet ballet, he was also a supporter of the Cuban Revolution and its dance policies.
2 Abbs, Peter (Ed.): *The Symbolic Order*, London, Falmer Press, 1989.
3 Chapman, J.V.: Dancers, critics and ballet masters: Paris 1790–1848, Unpublished Ph.D. thesis, London, Laban Centre, 1985.
4 Hutchinson, Robert: *The Politics of the Arts Council*, London, Sinclair Browne, 1982.
5 New Left Books: *Aesthetics and Politics*, London, New Left Books, 1977.

6   *The Guardian*, 10 May 1990.
7   Willis, Paul: *Common Culture*, London, Open University Press, 1990;
    Moving Culture, London, Calouste Gulbenkian Foundation, 1990.
8   Richey, Simon: Introduction to Willis, Paul, *Moving Culture*.
9   Chapman, *op. cit.*
10 I have applied the concept of hegemony by the Italian Marxist, Gramsci,
    to the dance situation in Britain because of its relevance. Like Marx's
    identification of surplus value in economics one doesn't have to be a
    Marxist to acknowledge value in many Marxist contributions to social
    and political theory. See (e.g.) Gramsci, Antonio: *Selections from Prison
    Notebooks*, trans. Hoare and Smith, London, Lawrence and Wishart 1971,
    and Sassoon, Anne Showstock: *Gramsci's Politics*, London, Croom
    Helm, 1980.
11 Willis, Paul: *Moving Culture*, p. 52.
12 *Ibid.*, p. 60.
13 Undertaken mainly with finance from the Greater London Council and
    unpublished on the GLC's dissolution.
14 Brinson, Peter: *Dance and the Arts in Hong Kong*, Hong Kong Govern-
    ment, 1990. A study *inter alia* of the influence of the global economy and
    the growth of global culture on a particular area of the world, illustrat-
    ing the connection between culture and identity.
15 Myerscough, John: *The Economic Importance of the Arts in Britain*, Lon-
    don, Policy Studies Institute, 1989.
16 Committee of Cultural Consultants: *Culture and the European Citizen in
    the Year 2000*. Final report, Brussels, European Community, 1989.
17 These passages and criticisms have been compiled after extensive discus-
    sion with Arts Council and regional officers (often as much in the dark
    as dance organizations), former officials, academic researchers and dance
    organizations likely to be affected. I have had the benefit also of hearing
    a long question and answer session with Peter Palumbo at the Royal
    Society of Arts, 11 April 1990. The gist of this session is reproduced in
    the RSA's *Journal*, September, 1990. I am indebted also to an interesting
    article by David Lister in *The Independent*, 22 May 1990.
18 Quoted by Lister, *op. cit.*
19 National Campaign for the Arts: *Dance Policy Statement*, London, 1989.
20 *Ibid.*
21 For further discussion of the problem of hegemony see Brinson, Peter:
    Dance as a lifelong pursuit: The Ideological Dimension in Proceedings of a
    conference organised by Dance and the Child International and the
    National Dance Teachers Association, August 1990. Available from
    either organisation in the list of organisations at the back of this book.
22 Pascal, Julia: An interview with Peter Wright, *The Guardian*, 4 May
    1990.

Part 3

Aspects of National Dance Culture

Introduction

National dance culture embraces obviously the art forms of dance and mime seen in the theatre and outside the theatre as well as folk dance and social dance and dance education wherever this takes place. It is not remembered always, though, that national dance and mime culture embrace other aspects of these arts sometimes inadequately considered and supported. These other aspects receive inadequate consideration because they are seen still to be marginal to professional performance or to the network of national folk dance activity or to formal educational provision notwithstanding unrest around the dance element of the national curriculum. Yet these aspects become more and more important the more our society changes its values under the impact of new economic and social structures and technological change. There is no way that a book of this nature could present the detail of each of these aspects to which references have been made in the general argument. The portrait of national dance culture would be incomplete, however, without some extra indication of why I drew attention to these aspects in the first place and why they are significant, socially and artistically, to the rest of the dance culture of which they are a part. I present here, therefore, a taste — no more — of seven such aspects in appendices about the dance and physical education controversy, dance and dance scholarship in higher education, images of community dance, new cultural contributions to British dance, youth dance, dance with the elderly and handicapped, dance and cultural policy for Europe.

Dance in the School Curriculum

Proposals for the national curriculum marginalize the arts by failing to identify them as a coherent aesthetic discipline worthy of a place as such in the education of all young people. The arts are divided in the proposals. Music and art are within the curriculum in their own right; drama is placed under English Studies; dance is placed under Physical Education; the rest are nowhere. The four major professional organizations of the dance education world have responded with a joint document of protest and explanation partly against the treatment of dance in the curriculum proposals, specifically against the characterization and presentation of dance in a publication, *Physical Education 5–16*, from the Department of Education and Science. The four professional organizations are: The Council for Dance Education and Training, the National Association of Teachers in Further and Higher Education (Dance Section), the National Dance Teachers' Association and the Standing Conference on Dance in Higher Education. Their joint documents are presented below: first the general case for dance in the school curriculum; second the specific criticism of *Physical Education 5–16*, a widely circulated HMI document presumably indicating they way dance will be regarded in the national curriculum. Both documents are reproduced with permission from the organizations concerned. Finally, the actual press release, membership, terms of reference and notes are reproduced of the Physical Education Working Group established by the Secretaries of State for England and Wales to illustrate the objections of four professional organizations.

1 Dance in the School Curriculum

Developments in Dance Education

Over the last twenty-five years dance has become established as a valuable part of the curriculum in a large number of primary and secondary schools throughout the country. The increasing number of current dance courses in schools — GCSE, TVEI, 'A' and A/S level, and the development of undergraduate and postgraduate courses in dance studies, demonstrate that dance has an important contribution to make to education. The numbers of candidates entered for 'O' level, and now GCSE, have approximately doubled each year. This indicates the increasing level of commitment to the subject. In addition, the creation of new dance advisory posts and INSET courses illustrates the way in which local education authorities are supporting this subject.

Dance is now much more evident in our culture than it was twenty-five years ago. Community dance classes with a range of dance styles, small touring dance companies, dance on television, and the emergence of regional and local youth dance companies, indicate a thriving level of interest.

At this crucial point in the development of dance education and dance in the community, it is vital to ensure its future in the school curriculum. This paper is a response to the fears of dance educators that this momentum will be lost unless a place for dance is articulated within the national curriculum.

Why Dance in the Curriculum?

Dance makes a distinctive contribution to the education of all pupils, in that it uses the most fundamental mode of human expression — movement. The body as the instrument of expression is unique in its accessibility. With the other arts it provides considerable potential for the expression of personal and universal qualities. Through its use of non-verbal communication, dance gives pupils the opportunity to participate in a way which differs from any other area of learning. In a broad and balanced curriculum this important area of human experience should not be neglected.

In What Particular Way Does Dance Contribute to the Curriculum?

Through **artistic and aesthetic education**, dance:

provides initiation into a distinct form of knowledge and understanding.

gives access to a unique expression of meaning.

develops perceptual skills.

develops the ability to make informed and critical judgments.

develops creative thought and action.

provides opportunities for creating and appreciating artistic forms.

develops performance skills.

introduces pupils to dance as a theatre art.

Through **cultural education**, dance:

gives access to a rich diversity of cultural forms.

offers insights into different cultural traditions.

develops understanding of the different cultural values attached to dance.

introduces processes of cultural generation and change.

Through **personal and social education**, dance:

gives opportunities to explore the relationship between feelings, values and expression.

promotes sensitivity in working with others.

develops self-confidence and pride in individual and group work.

encourages independence and initiative.

provides opportunity for achievement, success and self-esteem, for pupils with and without learning difficulties.

Through **physical education, health and fitness**, dance:

promotes a responsible attitude to the body and its well-being.

develops coordination, strength, stamina and mobility.

encourages physical confidence and control.

provides a leisure pursuit for fitness in life after school.

Through **cross-curricular learning**, dance:

develops communication skills through movement and visual images.

encourages collaborative teaching and learning strategies.

uses problem solving through alternative and non-linear methods of thought and action.

develops active and independent learning.

provides a stimulus for cross-curricular projects.

reinforces learning in primary and secondary theme-based work.

provides a context for considering attitudes and values of society.

reinforces language development.

Through **prevocational education**, dance:

gives access to further and higher education in dance, the performing arts and physical education.

gives access to dance in the community.

gives access to professional training in dance, the performing arts, and the entertainment and leisure industries.

The Future for Dance in the Curriculum?

Dance has evolved within the PE curriculum and many of the pioneers of dance education have been specialists in that field. Undeniably, dance contributes to the physical education of pupils, but to define it solely in these terms is to limit severely its potential in education.

Recent curriculum development has seen dance taking its place not only within PE, but also with the other arts, in performing and creative arts departments, or as a separate subject on the timetable. Initial training for teachers of dance is now becoming equally eclectic.

The 'dance as art' model in education — *performance, composition and appreciation* — has taught pupils to learn the skills of dancing, to create and perform in dances, and, through watching their peers and professional artists, to learn to respond, enjoy and make discerning judgments.

The emergence of dance animateurs and dance company education units with education officers, has given teachers and pupils access to the world of dance in ways which were never possible before in the curriculum. Never have we had such a wealth of collaboration between the professional and educational dance worlds.

So what is next for dance? Dance educators seek assurance that guidance will be given to school curriculum planners. Headteachers, however committed to the dance at present in their schools, will neglect it if clear statements are not made as to how and where dance may be included.

2 Physical Education 5–16, Curriculum Matters 16, HMI Series 1989: Joint Response by the CDET, NATFHE (Dance Section), NDTA, SCODHE

1 General Comments

1.1 The overriding concern of our national dance associations is the outmoded language in which dance is characterized and presented in this DES document. Its content fails significantly to recognize, and capitalize upon, the very considerable progress that has been made in dance education during the past decade — a decade in which the validation and implementation of 'O' and 'A' levels in Dance, together with several GCSE Dance Syllabuses, have succeeded in establishing dance as a respected and autonomous subject as well as a valuable component in Creative Arts, Performing Arts and PE Courses in our schools.

1.2 Implicit in this concern is the document's failure to establish the fundamental nature of dance as an art form — as a distinct domain of study which has its own unique concepts, criteria for judgment and distinct cultural context. It follows from these that the curricular aims and objectives, together with the assessment of dance, will necessarily be specific to dance as an **art**.

Regrettably what the DES document does is to fuse the aims and objectives, course content and principles of assessment of a wide variety of disparate activities under the umbrella of 'Physical Education' presumably in the belief that these activities are somehow homogenous. We believe this approach to be profoundly mistaken and serves only to distort, in our case, the aims and purposes of dance in education.

1.3 The outmoded framework in which dance is described in the DES document evidences itself in the specified curricular objectives which appear as the 'expression of feelings' and the 'evocation of emotions'. This conception of dance undoubtedly influences the content, methods of teaching and assessment of dance, and will do so in the new national curriculum unless modified. Dance will be relegated to the now antiquated period of 'expressionism' in the arts — a period which dominated the 1920s. Dance today, we believe, has a much **wider** range of aesthetic purposes than that of 'expressionism' and current practice in education must necessarily reflect this eclecticism if it is to keep in touch with contemporary culture.

We are therefore concerned that, following a period of exciting progress and development in dance education, its future within the national curriculum will be shackled to outworn ideas and obsolete practices unless radically reformulated.

1.4 We find no mention of interrelated arts work in the Primary and Secondary Schools in this document, nor mention of dance as a vital part of cross-curricular work in Primary Schools — both as a stimulus and a reinforcement of learning in other areas of the curriculum. We regret this omission.

2 Specific Comments

2.1 At no stage in the document is there adequate reference as to how the school dance experience might relate to dance in the wider community and contemporary culture.

2.2 There is only one mention of the 'aesthetic' in the section on dance and yet this we believe to be the **central** purpose of dance which unmistakenly identifies its *raison d'être* and unique educational value.

2.3 The alliance of the content of dance and gymnastics we believe exposes a confusion of intention.

2.4 'Choreography' and 'performance' in the document are not adequately distinguished and 'appreciation' lacks definition. Similarly, the skills of choreography, performance and appreciation are not clearly identified. Progression between the age ranges is tenuous (i.e. choreography appears out of the blue in the objectives for 16-year-old pupils).

2.5 There is no mention of the important elements of Design (set, costume, lighting); music is not mentioned in sufficient detail.

2.6 Technical skills are mentioned but there is no indication as to their precise nature (i.e. what technique or style in dance).

2.7 When the 'craft of composition' is mentioned, there is no attempt to set this in the context of a style or genre; inevitably, principles of composition vary according to each of these.

2.8 Regrettably there is no mention of examinations in dance and reference to assessments is narrowly tied to 'bodily' aspects.

2.9 The use of video in dance education we do not believe should be a 'rare event'. It is an invaluable aid to pupil self-assessment of performance and choreography and at the same time sharpens observation and critical skills in both judgment and appreciation.

2.10 We believe that dance for boys needs special mention.

2.11 The particular needs of dance in terms of resources, equipment and space might well have been mentioned.

2.12 'Social dance of different cultures' is mentioned in para. 24, p. 10, but no mention is made of a wide variety of highly sophisticated dance art forms which have relevance to our multi-cultural society and are a valued part of dance education.

3 Final Comment

The anomalies and inadequacies of the DES document *Physical Education 5–16* in relation to dance will be apparent from our comments. In the light of this we would urge that a parallel document entitled 'Dance Education 5–16' be speedily formulated and published in which the content, aims and objectives and assessment of dance be more clearly and comprehensively articulated. Such a document would, we believe, serve to contribute to the reaching of national agreement about the role and status of dance in the national curriculum.

On 11 July 1990, after this book was with the publisher, the Secretaries of State for Education and Wales, announced terms of reference and membership of a National Curriculum Working Group for Physical Education. This is the Group which will make recommendations for statutory and non-statutory elements of physical education in schools. On the whole it is a depressing document for dance in schools. It does not appear that the secretaries of state have paid attention to the representations of the dance teaching profession, but every appearance that the emphasis is to be on competitive sport, on elevating Britain's international sports standing and on continuing the Harrow headmaster's conception of sport in the 1890s quoted on page 59. Moreover the hurried nature of the Working Group's programme — interim advice by the end of 1990 and a final report by June 1991 — suggests that the secretaries of state are not concerned greatly to extend consultation to the education profession. These, therefore, are not in any sense terms of reference to provide an adequate dance education for young people although one hopes the Working Group will be more positive and imaginative than the HMI document quoted above. In particular it may be that the discretion to be given to schools will allow some new development and some schools to emphasize dance in their programmes. If so, this will be an exceptional use of the curriculum. The struggle to achieve dance as a subject in the curriculum on a par with music and art will need now to be developed on a very broad front, outside as well as inside the education profession. The announcement of the secretary of state on 11 July 1990 was as follows: Education Secretary John MacGregor today announced the membership of a National Curriculum Working Group for Physical Education. The Working Group will advise on the programmes of study and attainment targets for physical education to be included in the National Curriculum.

The Working Group will be chaired by Ian Beer, the Head Master of Harrow School and a former England rugby international. It will include sportsmen such as the footballer John Fashanu and the athlete Steve Ovett as well as educationalists, academics and representatives from business. John Fashanu is a striker for Wimbledon FC and Steve Ovett, the Olympic gold medalist and former world record holder, is presently a writer and broadcaster on athletics.

Announcing the Working Group today, Mr MacGregor said: 'I want to stress the importance which the Government attaches to PE in school, including sport. PE is the major means we have available for ensuring that young people are physically fit and understand the importance of regular exercise in maintaining a healthy life.

'I want as many children as possible to have the opportunity to participate positively in a range of PE activities.

'I am glad that the Working Group will include a range of expertise, including professional sportsmen, practising teachers and educationalists, as well as representatives from the business world.'

Details of the membership of the Working Group are attached. The terms of reference for the Group (also attached) point out that PE includes active physical education, competitive sport and dance and that PE contributes to other subjects and cross-curricular themes such as drama and music, health education and personal and social education.

The Working Group has been advised that the attainment targets and programmes of study for Physical Education should not be as prescriptive as the core and other foundation subjects already announced. Schools and pupils should have considerable latitude to develop their own schemes of work.

The Group will start work in the next few weeks. It has been asked to give interim advice by 31 December 1990 and to submit a final report by the end of June 1991. Physical education will be introduced as a statutory National Curriculum subject in the Autumn of 1992.

Notes

1 The Working Group has been established jointly by the Secretaries of State for Education and Science and for Wales.
2 Guidance on the approach which the Group should adopt is included in the terms of reference attached. In addition to advice on statutory attainment targets and programmes of study, paragraph 4 of the terms of reference asks the Group to make recommendations for *non-statutory* statements of attainment calibrated into ten levels.
3 Details of the membership of the Group are attached.
4 The Education Reform Act 1988 established a National Curriculum comprising ten foundation subjects (eleven in Wales) including English, mathematics and science (the core subjects), as well as technology, history, geography, a modern foreign language, music, art and PE, and, in Wales, Welsh.
5 National Curriculum working groups advise on the knowledge, skills and understanding ('attainment targets') which pupils should be expected to have acquired at different key stages, taking account of differences in ability. Groups also advise on the essential content ('programmes of study') which should be covered to enable pupils to reach agreed attainment targets. Paragraph 2 of the terms of reference indicates that, because of the nature of physical education, the Secretary of State intends that the attainment targets and programmes of study will not be prescribed in as much detail as for other core and foundation subjects.

Working Group on Physical Education: Terms of Reference

Background

1 The Education Reform Act 1988 provides for the establishment of a National Curriculum of core and other foundation subjects for pupils of compulsory school age in England and Wales. The Act empowers the Secretary of State to specify, as he considers appropriate for each foundation subject, including physical education (PE), attainment targets and programmes of study. Taken together, these attainment targets and programmes of study will provide the basis for assessing a pupil's performance, in relation both to expected attainment and to the next steps needed for the pupil's development.

The Task

2   The Secretary of State intends that, because of the nature of the subject, the objectives (attainment targets) and means of achieving them (programmes of study) should not be prescribed in as much detail for PE as for the core and other foundation subjects. He considers that schools and teachers should have substantial scope here to develop their own schemes of work. *It is the task of the PE Working Group to advise on a statutory framework which is sufficiently broad and flexible to allow schools wide discretion in relation to the matters to be studied.*

3   The Group should express an attainment target in terms of what is to be expected of pupils at the end of key stages. This expectation should take the form of a single statement of attainment in broad terms for each key stage which may comprise components covering different aspects of the subject. Each statement should represent what pupils of different abilities and maturities can be expected to achieve at the end of the key stage in question. These statements are intended then to form part of the *statutory* order for the subject. The statutory assessment arrangements for PE will not include nationally prescribed tests (except in the case of GCSE examinations at the end of Key Stage 4).

4   In addition, the Group should make recommendations for *non-statutory* statements of attainment calibrated into ten levels. It is intended that these should form part of guidance to teachers to help them to plan for continuity and progression and to identify both high attainers and those in need of extra help, including pupils with special educational needs. It will be necessary for these ten levels to be defined in such a way that they can be used consistently with the statutory statements for the end of key stages.

Submission of Reports

5   The Working Group is asked to submit an interim report to the Secretaries of State by 31 December 1990 outlining and, as far as possible, exemplifying:

   i)   the contribution which PE (including dance) should make to the overall school curriculum and how that will inform the Group's thinking about attainment targets and programmes of study;

   ii)   its provisional thinking about the knowledge, skills and understanding which pupils should be expected to have attained and be able to demonstrate at key ages; and the profile components into which attainment targets should be grouped; and

iii) its thinking about the programmes of study which would be consistent with the attainment targets provisionally identified.

6   By the end of June 1991 the Working Group is to submit a final report to the Secretaries of State setting out and justifying its final recommendations on attainment targets and programmes of study for PE.

Approach

7   In carrying out its task the Group should consult informally and selectively with relevant interests and have regard to the statutory Orders on mathematics, science, English and technology and to the reports of the other subject groups — history, geography, and modern foreign languages. The Group should in particular keep in close touch with the parallel music and art groups. Additionally the Group should take account of:

i) the contribution which PE, including active physical recreation, competitive sport and dance, can make to learning about other subjects and cross-curricular themes including, in particular, expressive arts subjects (including drama and music), health education and PSE and which they in turn can make to learning in PE; and

ii) best practice and the results of any relevant research and development.

Membership of PE Working Group

Ian Beer (Chairman)	— Head Master of Harrow and former England rugby union international.
Professor Denys Brunsden	— Professor of Geography at Kings College London. Contributor to a report by Lord Hunt on outdoor education.
John Fashanu	— Footballer with Wimbledon FC.
Ann Harris	— Head of Binfield Primary School, Berkshire.
Susan Jackson	— Deputy Head of Connah's Quay High School, Clwyd.
Tim Marshall	— Lecturer at Birmingham University Medical

School. Member of Sports Council and of DOE Review Group on sport for people with disabilities.

Elizabeth Murdoch — Head of Chelsea School of Human Movement, Brighton Polytechnic. Member of School Sport Forum.

Philip Norman — Senior marketing manager with Nat West Bank. Former Olympic oarsman.

Steve Ovett — Olympic athlete and broadcaster on athletics.

Maggie Semple — Director of Arts Council Project on Arts Education.

Keith Sohl — Senior manager with IBM.

Margaret Talbot — Head of Carnegie PE Department at Leeds Polytechnic.

Michael Thornton — Deputy Head of Greenfield Comprehensive School, Newton Aycliffe, County Durham. Formerly PE teacher at the same school.

Academic Research

The introduction of performance arts degrees by the CNAA since 1975, especially in dance, has begun to enlarge traditional conceptions and criteria for academic research beyond that which was accepted traditionally for the humanities and sciences. They include now processes of creative work in the arts recognizing, for example, that choreography or the writing of a play can represent research. Since then these extensions of research have been adopted by a number of universities. The relevant passages from the CNAA's 1989 regulations for the award of Master of Philosophy and Doctor of Philosophy show also some extension beyond the Council's earlier regulations in 1983. They are, with italics which are mine, as follows:

G1.3   Programmes of research may be proposed in any field of study subject to the requirement that the proposed programme is capable of leading to scholarly research and to its presentation for assessment by appropriate examiners. *The written thesis may be supplemented by material in other than written form* . . .

G3.3   Candidates may undertake a programme of research in which the candidate's *own creative work* forms, as a point of origin or reference, a significant part of the intellectual inquiry. *Such creative work* may be in any field,* but must have been undertaken as part of the registered research programme. In such cases, the presentation and submission may be partly in *other than written form*. The *creative work* must be clearly presented in relation to the argument of a written thesis and set in its relevant theoretical, historical, critical or design context. The thesis itself must conform to the usual scholarly requirements and be of an appropriate length (see G3.9.9) below. The final submission must be accompanied by some permanent record[†] of the creative work, where practicable, bound with the thesis...

The notes accompanying the regulations state:

* For instance, fine art, design, engineering and technology, architecture, creative writing, musical composition, film, dance or performance.

† For instance, video, photographic record, musical score, diagrammatic representation. (Author's comment: This would certainly include also dance notation.)

G3.4   Candidates may undertake a programme of research of which the principal focus is the preparation of a scholarly edition of a text or texts, musical or choreographic work or other original artefacts. In such cases the completed submission must include a copy of the edited text(s) or collection of artefact(s), appropriate textual and explanatory annotations and a substantial introduction and critical commentary which sets the text in the relevant historical, theoretical or critical context.

G.3.9.9   Where the thesis is accompanied by *material in other than written form* or the research involves *creative writing* or the preparation of a scholarly edition, the written thesis normally should be written within the range:

for Ph.D.	30,000–40,000 words
for M.Phil.	15,000–20,000 words

(Author's comment: 'Creative writing' may be assumed normally to include choreography.)

An oral examination is mandatory in all cases additional to the written thesis.

I am grateful to the Council for permission to reproduce these extracts.

Images of Community Dance

The Community Dance and Mime Movement plays a more influential part in British society than is suggested by the Wilding Report or the funding it receives through the Arts Council, local authorities, Regional Arts Associations and private sponsors. At its centre is the Community Dance and Mime Foundation, the only national organization of community arts. This embraces community dance companies and projects as corporate members together with individual dance and mime animateurs. These are defined in the Foundation's handbook as

> professional dance and mime activists working in a community context and who are in receipt of public subsidy ... This definition excludes those whose sole function is as a teacher within Statutory Education or anyone whose main function is a performer or choreographer in a dance or mime company.

Dance and mime animation thus represents a new profession. It reaches outside this professional conception, however, to cooperate with or stimulate dance in statutory education and the education units of professional companies, youth dance, Black and Asian dance and dance for the elderly and disabled often stimulated today by local authorities. It uses professional dance groups, like David Massingham Dancers in Northumberland, to work in residence to build local interest and knowledge, or touring groups like Ballet Creations of London to bring dance performances to remote venues. Currently, too, it is exploring all-important links with community dance in European countries postulating the possibility of a European community dance and mime movement.

In Britain community dance and mime reflects this wide variety of influence in hundreds of local projects. To name just three: Cheshire Dance Workshop, Jabadao in Yorkshire and Green Candle in London's East End. Cheshire Dance Workshop is one of the oldest community dance organizations, established in 1976 from a successful dancer-in-residence placement at Sutton Comprehensive School near Ellesmere Port. Today it defines itself as

> a group of dance animateurs who devise and lead dance pro-
> jects and activities. These aim to create a flow of experience
> and enthusiasm between the educational, professional and
> community dance worlds. Activities include regular classes,
> youth groups, work with the elderly, residencies with profes-
> sional companies, training provision and residential courses.

The Workshop works closely with local professional teachers as well as with professional dance companies and individual professional artists, nearly one hundred of which have contributed to its fourteen years of life. Consequently it is linked strongly with educational and arts organizations throughout the north-west receiving support from Cheshire Education Services, Cheshire Arts Services, North-West Arts, Merseyside Arts, Macclesfield Borough Council, Crewe and Nantwich Borough Council, Warrington Borough Council and Halton Borough Council as well as the Arts Council of Great Britain and the Calouste Gulbenkian Foundation. This range of support helps to ensure the continuity of the project balanced, as it is, between education, arts and local authority interests. Thus Cheshire Dance Workshop is something of a paradigm in community dance funding.

Jabadao across the Pennines in Bradford is best known nationally for its leadership in community dance for people with disabilities be they visual impairment, physical or mental disability or other special needs but its range is much wider than this substantial reputation implies. It interprets 'community dance' very broadly dividing its activity into training work and creative project work. Its 1990/1 training programme, for example, includes courses in dance and visual impairment, dance in mental health, dancing in special care, dancing with young people with physical disabilities, dancing for parents and toddlers, Indian dance in special needs settings, and dance in the community reviewing the whole range of community dance in three days of seminars and practical work. Looking beyond dance the programme includes also a workshop in Women's Creative Space for 'women involved in any sphere of creative activity'; workshops in Making Celebrations covering decorations and special moments celebrating food and organising ceilidhs; a workshop for Men moving Together; a conference on Conductive Education and another on special care; a two-year, part-time diploma course accredited by the Royal Society of Arts in dance for personal and community development; and a range of other training ventures for all of which students pay appropriate fees. There is also the beginning of a new policy concentrating creative project and training work in particular areas over a three-year period. Currently the area is Calderdale seeking 'to use dance to contribute to community development work alongside the existing agencies in the area, responding to request and suggestions, including celebrations'.

The focus and methods of Jabadao thus differ from those of the Cheshire Dance Workshop and yet are loosely parallel. Both projects, for example, attract to their regions national and international specialists to teach and create. Founded in 1985 to serve the whole of West Yorkshire Jabadao has been a rapid and outstanding success funded by Yorkshire Arts and West Yorkshire Grants, the consortium of local authorities formed to fund voluntary and social projects of all kinds throughout West Yorkshire. Hence Jabadao's creative projects usually are local while its training programme serves the whole region including a resource centre to buy or hire training materials and an important annual summer school of workshops and conferences. By contrast Green Candle, the youngest of these three examples, founded only in 1988, is London-based at Oxford House in Bethnal Green, but national in its projects and tours. Much influenced by the New Dance Movement of the 1970s and perhaps also by Ballet for All with which one of its leading members worked in the late 1960s, Green Candle is essentially a performance company. It is funded in its East London work by Greater London Arts and London-orientated foundations, and in its national work by the Arts Council, the Gulbenkian Foundation, business sponsors and the regions it visits during a year.

The Company's aims are

> to be an effective part of a process of reinstating dance to a central position in this society, thereby restoring the birthright of all to communicate, express themselves and enjoy themselves through dance; to use the performance and teaching of dance as a tool to enhance people's innate creativity, to improve people's mental and physical health and to act as a model of life as it could be to bring dance, as performance and as practice, to all parts of the community who have least access to it; to present dance as a central part of a creative spectrum involving (at least) dance, music, visual arts and theatre; to represent in all aspects of the company's work, as well as by the example of the company's own structure and practice, a clear non-racist, non-sexist model, and one which opposes all forms of oppression.

To achieve these aims the company's artistic policy annually creates and presents 'vivid, exciting and moving dance theatre performances targetted to specific community groups, using original choreography,

Plate 6 Other ways to dance. From left to right: Sally Davies, James Thomas, Fergus Early and Lati, in Green Candle's community dance work, *Songs for the Beast.* Photograph by Teresa Watkins.

design and music to a high level of excellence'. It runs workshops in community venues in conjunction with its performances, or separately, using materials from is productions to teach all sections of the community — old and young of all ages, mentally and physically disabled, different racial groups, teachers and group leaders or participants seeking to extend their own creativity and performance ability. It runs residencies in schools, colleges, community centres or other appropriate centres, provides a backup resource of advice for groups to create their own dance projects and 'requires all venues to provide information on access provision for disabled audiences and performers and improvement plans for these facilities'.

As a touring performing company Green Candle is different again in its community dance approach from Cheshire Dance Workshop and Jabadao but, like them, plainly fills a need which could not be met in other ways. Its 1988/9 activity took it to work and perform in Lincolnshire, Humberside and Cambridge as well as London giving a total of 66 performances of 2 different productions plus 111 workshops — 177 events in all to a total audience of nearly 9,000 people by a group of 4 dance artists (2 men, 2 women) organized by 1 administrator. Not bad for a first full year! The year 1989/90 is organized on similar lines to different areas of Britain.

Appendix D

Arts Education for a Multi-Cultural Society

Like the community arts movement the numbers and achievements in Britain of artists of all kinds from Asian, Caribbean, African and other backgrounds outside Britain are much greater than usually is acknowledged. These are *British* artists, often second, third, fourth or more, generation citizens, enriching Britain's culture and economy as the Huguenots did in the seventeenth century and Jewish and other immigrants did in the nineteenth century. Today's British people descend from a very, very mixed past. At present, however, the hegemony of British society works against artists from Black and Asian backgrounds so that their arts become marginalized in the same way that community arts tend to be marginalized. There is, too, undoubted and continuing discrimination throughout British society. One of the most significant achievements of the Arts Council's dance department during the last twenty years, therefore, together with Regional Arts Associations, the Gulbenkian Foundation and some other funding bodies, is that against this hegemonic tendency they have helped to establish Black and Asian dance firmly within the day-to-day practice of dance performance, teaching and workshops alongside other dance art forms.

Much of the credit for this new development in British dance culture belongs to the artists themselves and to their companies for the quality of their work and, all too often, for their dedication in face of inadequate funding in spite of Arts Council support. Companies such as Phoenix, Irie, Adzido and Kokuma, dancers and choreographers like Darshan Singh Buller, Tamara McLorg, Pushkala Gopal, Unnikrishnan, Shobana Jeyasingh, Pratap Pawar, Carl Campbell and Nahi Siddiqui, to name only a few, testify to the validity of their places within British dance. Schools, moreover, are training more and more British dancers from backgrounds outside Britain to deserve a place in existing British dance companies alongside their white compatriots because of the quality of what they can contribute. Dancers

179

from Caribbean and Asian backgrounds were part of London Contemporary Dance Theatre and its school from their beginning in 1967. Such dancers today from London Contemporary Dance School and from the Laban Centre continue to provide much of the force in British contemporary dance generally. In classical ballet, dancers from Asian backgrounds have appeared for years with British companies and are supplemented now in the Birmingham Royal Ballet with the first classical dancer from a Caribbean background trained at the Royal Ballet School.

In spite of all this there remains much to be done to overcome prejudice and habit. The place for action lies obviously in education. Many teachers over a long period have sought to instil better racial understanding among their pupils often through the use of the arts. I remember in the late 1970s visiting schools and education centres in the Midlands, Yorkshire and Greater London to see these efforts in practice. During the 1980s dance institutions like the Laban Centre introduced regular classes in Caribbean and Asian dance forms into some of their courses. Some education authorities did the same. I have before me an ILEA leaflet from 1989 announcing African dance classes at the Tower Hamlets Institute. There have been many similar initiatives throughout the country.

Dance, though, particularly in this context, needs to be seen as one among all arts in a multi-cultural society. To advance this concept the Calouste Gulbenkian Foundation, Arts Council of Great Britain and Commission for Racial Equality sponsored jointly a series of conferences to explore the possibilities of developing arts education along these lines. The conferences were large-scale affairs held in Manchester, Birmingham, London, Glasgow and Cardiff during 1980 and 1981, the dances of India, China, Africa and the Caribbean playing a prominent role. As a result of the need these events demonstrated and the discussions they provoked the three sponsors went further. They decided to launch a major curriculum development project over three years called Arts Education for a Multicultural Society (AEMS). This took a long time planning but was launched in 1988 to conclude in 1990 after working with many local education authorities and schools in different parts of the country. In some ways, therefore, the project resembles the Curriculum Development Council's Arts in Schools Project and may have a similarly profound effect on the arts curriculum. Already it has brought to public notice the large number of Black and Asian artists working not only in the performing arts but also in spoken, written and visual arts, craft, design, film, video and photography.

The project aims to find ways to give effect to existing policies of multi-cultural education (many of which are not fully implemented) and to encourage multi-cultural awareness in the arts curriculum. The initiative, therefore, is of immense importance to public aesthetic education as well as to race relations. To achieve its purposes AEMS works in partnership with local education authorities, regional arts associations and practising Black and Asian artists, accepting and incorporating an anti-racist approach. Its principal strategies are to identify areas of need; to remedy these needs through research, curriculum development projects, training programmes for teachers and artists and the provision of resources; and to create a national forum for debate, shared experience and information about effective practice. To date the project has worked in educational establishments across all phases, covering all the arts including dance. Therefore it has created a fruitful dialogue between teachers, students, artists, local education authorities and regional arts associations.

From this dialogue has begun to emerge a philosophy to underly not only multi-cultural education but the business of living in a multi-cultural society. After all, the United Kingdom has never been an homogeneous society. Differences of custom, culture and speech always have been important and continue to be visible, for example, in different dance forms in different parts of the country. It is true that improvements in communications and increasing centralization have reduced regional and national distinctions, yet diversity remains a characteristic of British life enhanced in past centuries as a result of migration. In the same way the post-war period has seen substantial numbers of people migrate to Britain from territories of the former Empire. Almost all these people can be distinguished easily by race and colour often making them targets for discrimination and attack. At the same time the post-war period has seen substantial changes in the international position of the UK and the growth of a global culture. This creates a contradiction between the fact of discrimination, whether at the point of entry to the UK or in housing, jobs, education or the law, and the need for multi-culturalism to match the trends of international economics and the increasing recognition of the value of cultural diversity. It is becoming accepted that the predominant ethnocentricity of British society and education is a product of historical development and that mono-culturalism is neither an inevitable feature of all societies nor good educational preparation for an interdependent world.

The UK today is a multi-cultural and multi-racial society within this world. Consequently its education system must serve the particular needs of such a society and equip young people to live within it. This means adjusting present educational provision to help all students understand the cultural diversity they will meet in life and the way diversity enriches British society today as it has done in the past. Unfortunately, the new core curriculum makes no specific provision in this area anymore than it does, say, for the closely related field of human rights education or for dance as a separate art form. It is left to individual schools to fill the gap so that their students can comprehend the new composition of British society and the values of its ethnic groups, old and new. This is important in all areas of Britain, not just in those with a high concentration of new immigrants. Therefore we need to develop a curriculum which draws positive advantage from different cultural traditions. A powerful way to achieve this is through the arts which involve life-styles and attitudes and can epitomize the essence of different cultures. Within this conception the value of dance alongside other arts is clear because of its movement, colour, music and non-verbal mode of communication, extending aesthetic education and understanding through its particular portrait and language of the society from which it comes.

Paul Willis observed in a passage already quoted (p. 116) about British youth culture today that 'among white youth many dance styles are initially appropriated and popularised from black youth culture'. The efforts of everyone concerned with building Britain's multi-cultural society for the twenty-first century will have succeeded when this example is followed so completely that all dance styles from south Asia, China, the Caribbean and elsewhere, now seen as unusual or exotic, become facets of one British national dance culture alongside Welsh, Scottish and English traditional dances or, for that matter, the waltz which came from Austria.

Forward with Youth Dance!

Fifteen years ago the youth dance movement began to draw together to make a national impact. The occasion was the first national festival of youth dance organized by the Leicestershire Education Authority in 1975. Out of that developed in due course an annual national youth dance festival in different parts of the country and a National Youth Dance Company. The latter is one of the organizations which the reconstructed Arts Council really must retain as a national commitment not devolved to a particular region. Of course the notion of youth dance is much older than fifteen years. If it had not existed strongly in 1975 there could have been no national festival. Youth dance rests also on the truism, known since humanity began, that 'young people enjoy dancing. They enjoy learning and perfecting new skills, creating and performing their own dance and being a member of a group.' That quotation is taken from an introduction by Susan Hoyle, dance director of the Arts Council, to *Young People Dancing*, the first full statement by the Arts Council of an extensive consideration and research into youth dance and its needs.[1] This confirms through research by Penny Rea the evidence on page 116 from Paul Willis's study of today's youth culture in Britain.

The place of youth dance in national dance culture, though, rests on more than young people's known love of dancing or the proliferation of youth dance groups around the country or even the growth of an established youth dance movement. Youth dance provides an important guide to the direction of national dance culture because of young people's ability to accept and incorporate change into their lives. Today, as I have pointed out often in this book, we live in a culture in which the ever-changing arts (and much else besides) are constrained within the nineteenth century art conceptions of politicians, administrators and the arts establishment. The result is a hegemony of personal attitudes which dance, in particular, must overcome if it is to grow into a national force. I have not seen anywhere an analysis of this phenomenon although Paul Willis's *Common Culture*[2] begins the process. The contradiction within the situation, and its implications for the future, are illustrated by the needs and development of youth dance as part of youth culture generally, although much of the youth dance movement *per se* lacks contact with what actually happens in discos and popular dance centres.

The dominant factor in the arts today is the commodification of culture. Resources and materials for all the performing arts as well as fine art, design, literature, photography are mediated by the electronic environment and resources provided by the market. The old institutions of opera houses, concert halls, repertory theatres and galleries reach far fewer people than are reached through television, radio, film, videos, sound tapes, compact discs and the electronic press, or will be reached by new electronic forms consolidating the global market and global culture. This affects dance as much as every other art. It is a perspective hard to grasp by the over-40s, but not by young people who grow up within a consumer society. They understand and respond to the new cultural situation because it surrounds them and is what they know. They are sceptical of established, especially formal, institutions wishing rather to make their own sense through their own interpretation of the environment mostly through an *informal* cultural practice of their own versions of art forms which attract them. Hence the enormous importance of providing in the school curriculum opportunities to experience all art forms as part of aesthetic education.

Informal art practices such as youth dance help young people to make more sense of their own lives in ways not possible through traditional institutions ruled by established conceptions of the arts. An informal do-it-yourself cultural practice can release their own creativity in different and new directions in which different values, the probable values of the future, are implicit. This allows a more optimistic approach to the future than is assumed generally because the values of the future often are mediated by the cultural values of the present. It is also a means to the empowerment of young people as intelligent contributors to the democratic process. Thus all those assisting youth arts carry a great responsibility.

One responsibility for the Arts Council, regional arts associations, local government and education authorities is a shift of priorities to give more support to informal manifestations of the arts such as youth dance. If Britain's national dance culture is to grow it must be through recognition of the informal dance practices of young people as much as formal presentations on stage. A revolution is taking place in arts creation and presentation led by young people, needing support and understanding by the adult world. Instead of looking back to golden ages of the past, therefore, it is more constructive to help forward golden ages of the future. This is the way to inspire young people, including young dancers and choreographers, because it is relevant also to the new art forms of the economic environment and the new ways of sharing older art forms which technology now makes possible. It is also an essential reconsideration within consumer culture of ways to extend the social role of the arts among a population unable to afford ever-rising seat prices in theatres and concert halls.

The nature of youth dance certainly involves the adaptation of post-modern forms to youth perceptions, often through the influence of advertising and choreography in popular television. Paradoxically, youth dance sources include also the continuing influence of high art because of widening, if occasional access through youth proms, schools matinées, touring dance groups and the visits of education units. If youth culture relates closely to the electronic environment it remains related also to traditional arts because these two are part of the cultural environment communicated by parents, teachers and the media. Young people's interpretation of the world through their art forms balances tradition against the will to change. Important conclusions follow from this assessment.

One, obviously, is that funding bodies, especially statutory bodies like government, the Arts Council, the Sports Council, local authorities and regional arts associations, need to give more attention to funding the future through youth arts. Another is that the youth movement generally, statutory and voluntary, needs to recognize more imaginatively the importance of informal youth culture and youth art forms, modifying accordingly their conception of 'youth work'. This view is born out by the Lewisham Youth Leisure Study already mentioned (p. 129). Most of the programmes offered by youth organizations in the borough were conventional, unimaginative and limited by lack of funds and resources to pool, ping-pong and the like. There was inadequate provision for minority interests and few attempts to open creative opportunities or recognize the real environments in which young people live. Exceptions were the Lewisham Academy of Music, a remarkable introduction to musical creativity for young and old, able and disabled; South-East London Youth Dance based at the Laban Centre; the drama, dance and video activities of the Albany, the borough's major cultural centre; and photography, screen printing, pottery, painting and other art work in a few youth organizations around the borough. This balance is haphazard but reflects a pattern in the rest of the country from considerable work for youth arts achieved already by organizations like the National Youth Bureau, the Arts Council, voluntary youth organizations and other bodies.[3] Many of these, like the initiatives in Lewisham, have suffered closure or reduction as a result of government policies.

The third conclusion is that youth dance projects, alongside other youth arts ventures, need to see themselves more clearly as part of national youth provision in general, seeking a share of this provision from the social service, education and sports and leisure budgets which underpin provision. To do this implies confronting established attitudes in two directions. First to overcome narrow conceptions of youth work and youth interest which persist among those administering statutory and voluntary youth organizations. Second to eliminate practices within some youth dance groups where choreography is undertaken only by the adult leader. Occasional pieces by an adult leader, or even by an important professional choreographer, provide useful experience but too much of such practices can stifle young people's own choreographic creativity. The other side of this adult penny is neglect of the dance creativity and dance forms evolved by young people in their own leisure time or in commercial dance spaces, illustrated by Paul Willis. Much of this creativity is untapped by youth dance groups whose technique classes reproduce only the modern or classical styles of professional dance. Such classes are an essential basis for movement expression, but to concentrate only on professional styles limits the innovative element of youth dance and its attractiveness to a larger circle of young people.

Two illustrations make the point. The first is from an area of economic and cultural poverty in Leeds. At Harehills Middle School, and in Chapeltown — which became the base of the Mara Ya Pili project — arose two examples of dance for young people of all abilities, many of them with little prospect of employment or creative interest. Both projects were educationally based involving not only classes and performance which combined contemporary, Caribbean, jazz and other dance forms, but also support from those able to make and design costumes, props and publicity, in other words, the community. The aim never was to produce professional dancers but always to release individual creativity, stimulate dance interest and enlist the help of grant-giving bodies for this purpose. In the process some of the many young people involved discovered a talent they never knew they had, making possible professional careers in dance. Harehills, in particular, became a national example of creative youth dance, originator of today's professional Phoenix Dance Company and the main stimulus towards forming a Northern School of Contemporary Dance in 1988, providing further opportunities to carry forward young people's dance interest. A wider dance interest not only in Leeds but in Yorkshire generally, including classical alongside modern dance, led to the formation of a Yorkshire Dance Centre.

The other illustration is the Weekend Arts College in Camden, north London. Also educationally based, this was established in 1978 specifically to find and help young people living in the Greater London area aged between 14 and 21 years, who hope for a professional theatre career. WAC stands in contrast, therefore, with Harehills' broader purpose but it arose out of a similar need to make good the inadequacy of arts provision in the general school syllabus, particularly for poorer pupils. It recognized three problems for young people in general education. First many young people are never offered the opportunity to experience dance, drama and music during their formal education. Second, as a result, some young people discover an interest or potential in these subjects only after leaving school when they lack the means or place to catch up. Third, even in schools where opportunities to experience the performing arts exist on a relatively generous scale, the school has to be concerned with the needs and level of the majority rather than with the minority who wish to advance further and faster perhaps towards vocational training. WAC seeks to fill the gap by providing weekend classes for teenagers who are thinking about a career in the performing arts. It runs also a Weekend Arts Club providing dance and drama classes on Saturdays for 5–13 year olds. All this is done by professionally qualified teachers at minimum cost to students through funding raised from statutory and private sources. The classes run from September to June in term time and cover mime, drama and improvisation, voice training, singing, body control, contemporary (modern) dance, classical dance, dance composition, jazz dance and tap, general music, musical composition and jazz rock and reggae music. There is also career counselling and an important course in audition techniques. For performance experience there is the London Fusion Orchestra, WAC's jazz ensemble, and Fusion which combines dance and drama in one company. All the works performed are devised by members of the company not only diminishing the divisions between drama and dance, but fusing also the ideas, attitudes and feelings of young people from different cultural backgrounds in London's huge population.

Reviewing the situation and present development of youth dance in the context of national dance culture, ten priorities emerge. Since these are elaborated in the Arts Council's *Young People Dancing* alongside Penny Rae's research I offer a summary. Youth dance needs:

1 To start from young people's own dance and dance ideas, not from those of adults.
2 To be more willing to accept the unconventional and the unexpected.
3 A definition of youth dance which clarifies its qualities and uniqueness as an activity in its own right essential to national dance culture deserving more central and local government support.
4 A data base of youth dance throughout the country flowing from professional research, regularly updated.

5 To see youth dance as an important element in the struggle to achieve dance as a separate subject in the national curriculum.

6 A new and better deal for dance teachers in teacher training, in-training and in schools to bring dance into line with rising technical and artistic standards, multi-racial education and more concern for disability.

7 To agree and proclaim a philosophy which makes clear to the dance world and to those in positions of authority the value and role of youth dance to young people in education and in leisure time.

8 A central backup organization, recognized as the national responsibility of the reorganized Arts Council, to provide information, advice, support and a public voice.

9 This to be organized probably through a regional network in ways which accord with young people's wishes and methods of organization.

10 Strengthen links with Europe and youth dance in other countries through exchanges, festivals, courses, newsletters, videos and other communication methods.

Notes and References

1 Arts Council of Great Britain: *Young People Dancing*, London, 1990.
2 Willis, Paul: *Common Culture*, London, Open University Press, 1990.
3 Two documents from the 1980s illustrate the possibilities for youth arts alongside the impediments which flow from traditional attitudes and organizations. The possibilities can be seen in *Youth and the Arts*, a report in 1982 of a regional training conference for artists, arts administrators and youth workers organized jointly by the Arts Council, the National Association of Boys' Clubs and the National Association of Youth Clubs in cooperation with the Southern Arts Association. Published by the Arts Council, the report covers dance, drama, mime, music and photography. The impediments are illustrated in *An Introduction to Voluntary Youth Work in England* by the National Council for Voluntary Youth Services. Published in late 1984 and reporting on the Council's plan of work for the 1980s, the document lists the 45 full members and 15 observer members of the NCVYS. Of these 60 members, covering the largest voluntary youth organizations in the country only eight — Inter-Action Centre, the Methodist Association of Youth Clubs, the National Association of Boys' Clubs, the Religious Society of Friends (Quakers), the United Kingdom Federation of Jazz Bands, and the Woodcraft Folk among full members, the Commission for Racial Equality and the Cooperative Union among observer members — actually reckoned it important to mention the arts among the services they offered. We know there are others who include the arts, like Youth Clubs UK, but it is clear the arts rate low in official youth work.

Appendix F

Dance, Disability, Ageing

Since a large part of dance is, or should be, about joy and celebration it is no marvel that some dancers seek to communicate this joy to the sick, the disabled and the elderly in many forms. The many forms reflect the many ideas of many people who undertake such caring work. Their multiplicity was outlined in the Carnegie Trust's report *Arts and Disabled People* in 1985. One part of the work lies in the world of arts therapy. In its formal sense this involves the arts with hospitals, local authorities, health districts, training establishments and academic institutions. In dance, for example, one of the leading academic courses is the MA in dance and movement therapy at the Laban Centre for Movement and Dance in London. Leicester Polytechnic holds occasional disability awareness courses for arts administrators including dance administrators. Hertfordshire College of Art and Design holds a computerized data base of the arts and disability throughout the European Community. This was started in 1984 as part of the European Training Initiative Research Project at the College with funds from the European Social Fund and Hertfordshire County Council. Today its comprehensive directory holds details of over a thousand organizations concerned with the arts and disability underlying, incidentally, the indispensability of cooperation with Europe if this field of care is ever to gain sufficient muscle to induce governments to provide adequate resources. The project publishes also a journal *Atria* to provide an information Arts and Disability Exchange, Europe-wide, three times a year on a low subscription basis.

I write, though, not about arts therapies, their professions and their organizations. Rather it is about artists, especially dancers, choreographers and dance organizations, who see dance as an area of expression and creative work for disabled and elderly people to enrich 'the world of art itself by their greater involvement'.[1] The number of disabled and elderly people in our society runs into millions. We overlook that they comprise not only a significant audience but also a creative resource of dance-making which expands our restricted notions of dance. The disabled and elderly tender to our national dance culture ideas and forms of dance which could enrich our whole society.

As in other spheres this potential contribution is made within the larger context of arts in general. Particularly it is concerned with issues around the integration of disabled people and the elderly into the arts, into employment and into society at large. In each of these fields it challenges able-bodied assumptions about disability and old age. To this end Graeae, formed in 1980 and now Britain's best-known professional company of actors who are disabled, maintains a professional theatre company, an amateur company and an education programme. All are aimed at raising the level of public awareness about disability as well as integration. A number of other drama companies, through training and employment, similarly challenge theatrical standards and argue a wider campaign for change.[2]

In visual arts the way was led in 1973 when a painter, Peter Senior, offered to brighten a Manchester hospital by hanging a few pictures on its walls, or actually transforming the walls themselves with images. The response was so immediate and enthusiastic it sparked a movement led by Peter Senior, funded by the Gulbenkian Foundation, health authorities and others, to bring a wide range of arts to hospitals and health centres throughout the city. Hospital Arts was evolved from this as an organization whose example is followed now by hospitals and health authorities throughout the country.[3] Other health initiatives struggle or flourish, too, in photography, sculpture, video, music, film, literature and crafts.

Stimulated enormously by Carnegie's Report, but existing already, of course, before 1985, the movement to extend the arts among disabled and elderly people embraces now statutory and voluntary bodies with a national remit. The arts councils of Great Britain, Scotland, Wales and Northern Ireland adopted early in 1986 a Code of Practice on Arts and Disability, and the Arts Council of Great Britain appointed a full-time Arts and Disability Officer with an assistant. A number of regional arts associations and arts centres have begun to take action within their own areas to follow this example. Foundations like Gulbenkian[4] and the King Edward's Hospital Fund have increased support. Voluntary bodies like the Disabled Living Foundation and Shape have found their long campaigns and projects gaining more attention among a wider audience. Television companies increased their coverage and programmes about a subject which concerns large sections of the public like Central Television's regular programme, 'Link', on the Independent Television Network.

There remains a long, long way to go but in all these beginnings dance exerts noticeable influence. Part of its influence derives from Shape started by a dancer, Gina Levete, in 1975 with help from Westminster Hospital and the Gulbenkian Foundation. Today many other supporters have come forward and Shape has grown to be a national service seeking to develop and provide the arts of every kind wherever need and talent exists, arts for socially deprived people as well as the sick, disabled and elderly. Funding comes mainly from local sources through combinations of regional arts associations, local authorities and regional and district health authorities as principal providers. Is it not natural that the dance world, so concerned with healthy bodies, might be concerned also with disabled and ageing bodies? Ballet for All tried regularly to open its performances to disabled people in the 1960s although few venues in those days had means of access for people with physical disabilities, let alone for wheel chairs. A small group of Royal Ballet dancers in the late 1970s began taking short performances to hospitals. During 1989 several Royal Ballet dancers worked with visually impaired children from Clapham Park School, London, as part of the company's education programme culminating in participation in a festival of achievements in the arts by disabled people at the John F. Kennedy Centre in Washington, DC. More recently Ballet Creations of London with Ursula Hageli and Richard Slaughter have included performances for disabled and elderly people in education and performance tours of classical ballet around Britain — see illustration facing page 43.

The contemporary and modern dance world and the dance education world generally accept a concern for the disabled. The City of Aberdeen and Arts in Fife became the first local authorities in Britain to appoint arts and disability officers in dance. Both were trained in contemporary dance and both were assisted financially by the Scottish Arts Council. The Laban Centre's community course includes preparation for work with disabled and elderly people in both its study and practical elements. Arts Centres around the country and almost all community dance projects include commitment to the disabled and elderly as priority in their work. Specialist dance companies like Common Ground, including hearing-impaired members, tour workshops and performances around Britain, appearing also at the first Scottish Festival of Youth Dance in Stirling in 1988. The Indian dancer, Bisakha Sarker, includes work with disabled children in her workshops and performances as part of the Arts Council's Arts Education for a Multicultural Society project. She is one among many artists working with this project to develop this commitment. Two of the best-known dance enterprises in the community field are Amici, mingling able with disabled dancers, and Jabadao, serving the elderly and the disadvantaged as well as the disabled in West Yorkshire. Both have been discussed briefly in chapter 5 and in Appendix C but a word more about particular issues raised by their work.

Discussions by the Community Dance and Mime Foundation at training sessions or members' conferences return often to the issues of integration and public performance. Should people with disabilities be integrated with able performers on stage or work separately in their own groups? Is it morally right, is it helpful to disabled people, to expose disability through public performance on stage, however sympathetic? Amici, through a track record of ten years, offers answers alongside other companies in drama and dance facing the same issues. Its week-long season at Riverside Studios, London, in June 1990, following appearances in Glasgow, added two new dance works to its repertory, *Mercurius* by Nigel Warrack and *Passage to Sanity* by Wolfgang Stange. After ten years there is a string of creations of this kind in what can be seen as a distinct genre of dance increasing annually since the first performance in 1980. This is turn was preceded by classes in creative dance where Stange noticed the remarkable development of disabled students in self-confidence and dance ability as a result of class and performance experience. Amici has received now a Digital award to develop further its stage productions in 1991.

The development of students, many with mental as well as physical disability, is part answer to the moral issue of exposure through public performance. There is, though, a related issue. Accepting the benefit to disabled performers, is it right that the result be treated as an ordinary theatrical presentation for which the public pays like any other piece of dance theatre? Putting to one side the full houses each season which cannot represent only relatives and committed supporters — and therefore is part answer from the public — the performer–audience issue raises central questions about the nature of dance performance and the extension of dance culture through the creativity of disabled people. Does it matter that bodies are not perfect, even disorted? 'Amici dancers move only when they have something to convey, not for the sake of filling the stage with movement: their stillness is compelling', wrote Jann Parry, dance critic of *The Observer*, after the 1989 season.[5] 'The power of intensely felt gesture is something that needs to be learned by able-bodied dance companies searching for a new form of physical theatre.' This surely is the point. Here is a different dance genre. What does it communicate? Don't look for virtuosity. Do look for insights into an alternative world of human existence, strange on sight, ignored by many. If the sight makes for discomfort so do many other works of art. This art comes from the vast world of disability presented in a dance language whose accents inevitably are different from able dancing. They are not thereby invalid any more than is the music, created in part by disabled musicians. Therefore, it could be argued, this is the beginning of a dance genre with much potential for development in which the disability of able audiences to comprehend disability becomes eroded. It is in this sense an extension of the aesthetic dimension and of public aesthetic education.

Jabadao applies dance in broader social contexts of which performance and disability are important elements but not the only ones. It is a community dance and training resource described already on page 175 in Appendix C. In its use of dance it tries to make visible the power of dance to strengthen the human bonds which lie at the heart of community life; to show the healing power of dance; and to demonstrate dance and movement as sources of insight, knowledge and learning. What sounds like a too idealistic approach to survive in a materialist world is realized through an intensely practical programme. The long-term objective is to develop a greater understanding of the value of creative, non-verbal approaches within selected areas of work. At present the priority is elderly people; people with learning difficulties, mental handicap; and people with mental illnesses. As the work grows other groups are brought in like mothers and toddlers with difficult relationships, family therapy, rape crisis, sexually abused children, young offenders, prisoners. To all of these the long-term objective is applied so that Jabadao, the only resource of its kind in the country, attracts enormous interest in arts, social service, health and community work.

The aim for the elderly is to replace the norm of variety shows and singsongs with performances and participatory work which stimulate and strengthen individuality and status. Reminiscence is an important factor, sometimes producing published work as it did from a three-month residency among the older members of the east Leeds villages.[6] In promoting community work through dance Jabadao often provides 'taster' examples through visits to a particular locality to stimulate later local initiative. This might be backed up by courses or workshops for potential leaders. The technique is well established. Free Form in Hackney, London, and Community Arts Workshop in Lancashire used much the same methods in their work during the early 1980s. Jabadao have extended this in other directions and on a larger scale. Its emphasis on working with people with learning difficulties is not only to work with the learners but much more to develop skills in anyone who can promote greater independence for people with learning difficulties through creative dance and movement.

Jabadao's way of working, then, advertises and explores community dance generally and specifically in relation to social need. Its service to the elderly supplements agencies and specialists active already in this field. There is a growing, but still inadequate, network of such provision from well-known individual specialists in dance and movement for the elderly like Seona Ross and Jasmine Pasch to specialist organizations like Extend and Medau, to national bodies like Shape and the Disabled Living Foundation, to local initiatives like the Dark Horse Venture in Liverpool and touring dance groups like Ballet Creations illustrated on page 43.

These, and many other ventures, statutory and voluntary, try to serve the ever-expanding needs of early retirement and creative leisure which should go with retirement and old age. There is no point in medical services helping people to live longer if they have nothing to do with their extra time. As in other fields the arts in old age can stimulate courage, freedom and confidence to do, to create, and thus sustain self-confident elderly citizens contributing still to the community through their own modes of expression. Dance adds to all this the priceless ability of movement without which age becomes restrictive and disabling. To raise such a vision, though, points the lack of coordination and links between arts ventures seeking to help the aged. Bodies like Jabadao, local authority leisure departments like Lewisham, community arts projects around the country, community dance training of various kinds — all bring individual practices and ideas to bear with very little central study or coordination. There is some practice but lack of coherent theory and policy in arts *by* older people as well as arts *for* older people. Yet if there can be youth dance in national culture there can be older dance as well. This gap the Centre for Policy on Ageing has shown itself anxious to fill. Its seminars, conferences, discussions and publications[7] in the area of policy and fact-gathering have brought to public notice a little-known area of social action for the elderly. The Centre needs now to go much further to establish itself as a national body to oversee a national strategy of arts by and for older people, including those from ethnic minority backgrounds. The strategy needs to increase access and availability; produce information and manuals of guidance; stimulate the notion of dance and movement festivals for the elderly, including their own choreography; and challenge cultural assumptions that if people are too old to work they are too old also for the arts, too old to dance. This is as much nonsense as it is for disability. As in disability there is here the possibility of another wide extension of dance creativity and public aesthetic education.

Notes and References

1   Attenborough, Sir Richard: Introduction to *Arts and Disabled People* (The Attenborough Report), London, Bedford Square Press, 1985.

2   Carnegie United Kingdom Trust: *After Attenborough: A Carnegie Council Review*, Bedford Square Press, London, 1988.

3   Hospital Arts: *Annual Report 1988–89*. The work of Hospital Arts has done much to transform attitudes to hospital building and decoration. DHSS Building Note 1 1986 states that 'works of art enchance the interiors of hospital buildings'. It goes on to affirm that arts provision should be part of the architect's brief and each project's budget. Peter Senior himself now directs Arts for Health at Manchester Polytechnic, a national centre giving advice and information to all concerned with using the arts as a fundamental element of health care.

4   Downing, Dick and Jones, Tony: *Special Theatre: The Work of Interplay Community Theatre for People with Severe Learning Difficulties*, London, Calouste Gulbenkian Foundation, 1989.

5   *The Observer*, 20 March, 1988.

6   Jabadao: *Nothing in Our Pockets but Fun*, gathered from the folk at Firthfields Day Centre, summer 1989. Such booklets become important sources of local history as well as works of interest in themselves.

7   Armstrong, J., Midwinter E., and Wynne-Harley, D.: *Retired Leisure: Four Ventures in Post-War Activity*, London, Centre for Policy on Ageing, 1987. Midwinter, Eric: *Creating Chances: Arts by Older People*. London, Centre for Policy on Ageing, 1990.

The European Connection

A national dance culture cannot exist of itself. It needs nourishment through connections with other dance cultures. This is the lesson of all cultural history, but particularly of British dance culture as I have shown throughout this book. Such nourishment has come in the past from natural ties of all kinds with other countries. Today it can be seen in the regular travels of dancers and companies across frontiers;[1] in international festivals, competitions and conferences;[2] in the interchange of teachers[3] and books about dance; and in travel scholarships for dance students to study abroad.[4] Governments, too, make use of their dancers' achievements through sponsored visits in the interest of trade, prestige and international relations.

All these connections are useful though mostly the result of separate, however welcome, initiatives. With the exception of government-sponsored foreign tours they are unguided by any kind of policy to spread the benefits of exchange to all levels of dance. In fact, Britain's formal international dance connections are very fragile. No longer a member of Unesco, we are excluded from whatever is organized there for dance. Our membership of the International Dance Council and the dance section of the International Theatre Institute is generally ineffective nationally and internationally. Nationally the membership comprises mostly individuals with little official support, especially in terms of cash, from any of the larger British dance organizations. Internationally, it makes no sense to have two competing organizations in a world in which big equals power. The ITI, and IDC need to bring together their dance interests jointly to serve the cause of dance world-wide. For the present this fractured situation means only inadequate and haphazard exchange of essential knowledge about injuries, teaching methods, musical sources, post-performance career opportunities, pensions, administrative and international exchange arrangements, study centres and research of all kinds. The voice of dance is faint in the world's counsels, political, social, cultural and economic.

For Britain the need to address these deficiencies is especially urgent. The growth of global culture requires compensating restatement, defence and assertion of local cultures both to ensure a proper balance within global culture and to sustain national and local identities. Hong Kong is one of the smaller units in the world today desperately needing an assertion of local identity. This can be done most effectively through its cultural, especially dance, achievements.[5] Britain's need is hardly less emphatic faced as it is with a crisis of national confidence, post-imperial role problems, and the smothering influence of American values transmitted through a common language.

Second, Britain's national dance culture has no government-supported service institutions such as are found, for example, in the Netherlands with its Dance Institute, Mime Centre and Theatre Institute, each responsible for supporting different aspects of the dance culture, though biased towards theatrical performance.[6] The dance department of the Arts Council of Great Britain is, of course, also a service institution though principally for government subsidy and assessment. Understaffed and underfunded, it has done a remarkable job to perform a wider role during the last twenty years but it cannot match the Dutch institutes. So, too, the drama and dance departments of the equally understaffed and underfunded British Council in developing international dance relations. Neither department, however, even if they survive the current reorganization, will be adequate to support entry into a Europe without internal barriers from 1 January 1993. Thereafter dancers, administrators and educators will need to look more and more beyond their own borders towards a level of international collaboration and artistic exchange quite outside British experience except in occasional projects from individual initiatives. One such project is the Montpellier Dance Network which embraces France, Belgium, the United Kingdom and the Netherlands in occasional exchanges of information, promotion and performance opportunities.

The basis of effective international collaboration is the free flow of information of this kind. Every part of British dance culture, from performance and original choreography to community dance, dance education, folk dance and youth dance, will be stronger for knowing what happens in other countries, and learning from it. Information of this scale of universality, no longer haphazard and piecemeal but properly coordinated to cover all sources, is crucial to the nourishment of Britain's dance culture, to an influential British dance presence in Europe and to a more fruitful British participation in relevant world organizations like the International Society for Education through Art and Dance and the Child International, both Unesco-recognized organizations. So far British participation in such organization has depended on personal energy and sacrifice to overcome official indifference. Personal energy and sacrifice are necessary ingredients of most international collaborations but their frequent elevation to be the *only* element of British participation explains Britain's absence from many international dance counsels and thus the parochialism from which British dance culture has suffered too long. To repair this damage requires two kinds of action of equal importance. First that major British dance institutions adopt a more international, especially European, attitude in their work and policies, particularly as regards the education of dance students of all kinds. Second that this be supported by government measures to acquire and disseminate as a priority the sort of international, especially European, information upon which much of the future character of British dance culture will depend. Indeed, not only dance culture but British culture in general.

There are signs that such support may be demanded soon by the European Commission itself. Late in 1988, for example, the Commission's Council of Ministers reached agreement on the mutual recognition of higher education diplomas in the twelve member states. This applies to all regulated professions for which university-level training of at least three years is required. Thus it must apply to the level of British dance education and training described in chapter 4. Moreover a ruling by the European Court of Justice recognized in 1988 that university studies are vocational and therefore should not require European students to pay additional fees in member states. This could mean an influx of European students to study dance at British state-supported tertiary institutions with consequent imbalances for British tertiary dance education and training in general.

There are other signs that the Commission is placing more emphasis on education and cultural matters even though the Treaty of Rome places responsibility on the Community only for economic and social affairs. Late in 1988 the Commission mandated a Committee of Cultural Consultants to provide a perspective on the shape and scope of future cultural policy in Europe. It is possible, therefore, that cultural affairs will be added to economic and social affairs in the Commission's policies for the integration of Europe after 1992. The Committee produced an interim report by March 1989 and a final report in November the same year which is yet to be published.

The final report begins with basic considerations about the nature of culture, that it is 'not an abstract concept, but a set of rich and varied practices which manifest themselves in all aspects of everyday life ... As such it is mankind's most crucial and powerful characteristic.' The report argues that the cultural heritage is endangered today by

'the narrowing of education to the mere acquisition of skills, aggressive behaviour in everyday life, hooliganism', the deterioration of human relations and the destruction of the environment. All these cases serve to highlight the priority which, politicians should give to culture ... The fight against the impoverishment of culture is crucial.

In many ways the Committee's[7] approach to cultural matters is in advance of national policies of many member states of the Community, including Britain. It reinforces also the views put forward in this book though the book was written before the report became available privately. It asserts that

'access to culture is a human right ... It is therefore the duty of all governments and institutions concerned to create the social and economic conditions necessary for this right to be enjoyed. This is a fundamental concept which should be reflected in all the Community's legislative and administrative activities. European culture ... is a multi-racial, multi-lingual and multi-religious phenomenon made up of the sum and interaction of all our national regional and even local cultural identities ... Today ... the pressure creates new factors which disrupt long-established patterns ... The time-sequence of the interaction between culture, technology, the economy and political decisions has been profoundly altered ... Legislative and economic convergence with a view to the creation of a genuine internal market must not be allowed to destroy or obstruct the precious existence of European minority languages and sub-cultures.

This seems to underline the significance of the growth of global culture parallel with global economy and the consequent urgency of national policies to elevate the arts as expressions of local and national identity. There are implications for the teaching of dance at all levels — emphasis on, the way national characteristics are revealed and rooted in folk dance and folk music; the role of dance as a resource in historical studies; dance as a major factor in cultural studies; and the formulation of cultural policy and better funding of dance alongside other arts as vivid assertions of nationality and national influence among other European nations.

Views of the Committee converge also with arguments advanced here for the development of British dance culture.

'Above all, the Community must steer clear of an approach to culture which is liable to gain importance in the years to come; using culture as an 'alibi' or as a social 'tranquiliser' or considering culture as a welcome publicity vehicle or even as a form of investment goods. The Community's cultural activities will gain credibility if it distances itself from such thinking ... Furthermore the Community should take full account ... of its peripheral areas ... those regions furthest removed from the centres of cultural life ... the outskirts and suburbs of the big European cities ... Much of the inspiration for both popular and 'serious' culture is drawn from the peripheral areas ... Finally it is important to consider and take account of the growing role of immigrant culture within each country.

Notwithstanding the Committee's broad definition of culture it becomes clear that the arts occupy a dominant place in the thinking which is reflected in its final conclusions. These have important implications for a widespread European aesthetic education.

'Education and culture are inextricably linked ... Providing an introduction to culture, however, does not mean forcing people to admire masterpieces at a respectful distance but helping them to discover their creative potential which is very often hidden ... The role of science within educational process is of crucial cultural significance ... The educational systems of the Community should situate science within its cultural context ie in its proper place within society ... care should be taken to address the problems of those excluded from usual cultural circuits whether they live in poor regions or on the outskirts of the big European cities ... Special attention must be paid to the very young, not only in the context of ... education ... but also in everyday activities, their free time, their relationship with the environment and with the new mass media technologies with which they are confronted'

and

'which seek to industrialise our imagination ... The greatest danger comes from the glaring imbalance between the power of the few major companies controlling the software market and the weak position of the authors. The issue at stake is not simply the disregard of copyright but 'the expropriation of the very essence of European identity'...

Against this background the Committee makes 'proposals, which are of a fairly general nature, as the building blocks for a coherent cultural policy'. These include an emphasis on *'creativity* in all its forms and manifestations ... *information* on the significance of culture and on cultural activities' and 'appropriate means ... to heighten *public awareness* and awareness among *policy makers* in the cultural sphere'. The Committee's conclusions about general needs would affect dance at every point. 'To maximise the effectiveness of the necessarily limited financial and organisational resources, the scope for creating networks between existing institutions should be explored ... rotation of major events might also prove practicable.' There should be a European Artists' Statute' to improve the situation of artists in all creative fields as regards social security' and a range of measures to help young artists in all fields, especially through European grants and fellowships. There should be a cultural exchange programme for teachers and students, seed money for a European television art channel, broadcast by satellite, 'for disseminating all forms of artistic creation'. Other proposals include a network of Community 'cultural institutes' specializing in individual arts on a European scale, an information network to include a data base, a publication network to assist and extend existing national publications, and, above all, a European Cultural Fund modelled on existing Regional and Social Funds.

Specific proposals relate to individual arts including the heritage, training and dissemination for music, opera, drama, visual arts, architecture, design, cinema, dance and mime. Dance appears not to be fully understood in its widest implications. It tends to be conflated with theatre since only its theatrical elements are explored with little attention to its role outside theatre except in education and training. Nevertheless, there is a helpful range of proposals covering necessities, like better information and documentation on a European scale, more imaginative funding including co-production, rethinking taxation, finance and social security systems, the coordination of theatrical equipment and so on. There is also vigorous emphasis on the need to support dance experimentation, youth dance and contemporary/ modern dance in all its forms to balance the 'long period of only highly-stylised forms of expression ... In almost all European countries ... dance is, to say the least, underfunded ... For all these reasons an international approach to modern dance is essential.'

Clearly, the Committe's view of dance is much too narrow. It needs to embrace classical ballet as well as modern dance on the one hand, especially its dissemination to peripheral areas and young audience, and community dance on the other hand. If this can be done proposals for increased support to existing 'exchanges between dance artists, workshops, courses, summer schools, collaboration and co-productions' make a lot of sense. It acknowledges what is being done already in these fields, especially in dance festivals, but acknowledges that these depend often 'on meagre finances'. The Committee's policy would assist exchanges and contacts between choreographers and, under its notion of a European Summer Workshop for Professionals in the performing arts, would presumably involve the British annual International Dance Course for Professional Choreographers and Composers. At one time funded by the European Commission and now in its fifteenth year, this British course has enjoyed European representation for some time so would take its place alongside the Berlin Workshop Programme, the Werkstatt Dans and other workshops cited by the Committe. In other respects the UK does not yet possess the institutions to take advantage of other proposals for collaboration. A European Dance Centre, for example, might emerge 'out of existing collaboration between organisations such as ... the Dutch Institute for Dance, Theatre Contemporain de la Dance, the Flemish Theatre Institute. etc.' One might add now other institutes in eastern Europe. Britain has no such institute[8] because a degree of government support is needed which is not forthcoming.

Finally,

> 'with the 1992 landmark looming ahead — with all its institutional, but also its symbolic implications — the inclusion of a 'cultural clause' in a future amendment of the Treaty of Rome should be considered an absolute priority.[9] Such an amendment should at the very least state explicitly the responsibility of the Community to affirm and promote Europe's cultural identity, including the recognition and promotion of the diversity of national, regional and local forms of cultural expression.'

The Committee emphasizes the 'rationale behind the Community's cultural activities should consist in encouraging the arts, not in interfering or seeking to control them'. It follows that Britain's national dance culture — and the whole aesthetic dimension of British living — would benefit from the implementation of a European cultural policy, but that there is much to be done in Britain towards such a possibility. A more consciously European attitude among our major dance institutions is only a first step. An examination of implications by our researchers would help to define options and opportunities. The major need is a more positive attitude by the British Government to support with adequate funding and institutions British participation in a European cultural programme. Within this the British dance community would need to act with unity and a determination not shown thus far to realize for its young dancers today the opportunities awaiting them tomorrow.

Notes and References

1   The visit, for example, of Cuembre Flamenca to Sadler's Wells Theatre in June 1990, a marvellous presentation of Flamenco dancing from Spain's Andalusia, excellently introduced in the programme by the late Fernau Hall.
2   For example, the fifth Hong Kong International Dance conference in July 1990.
3   The founding of London Contemporary Dance Theatre and School was built on the exchange of teachers between London and, mostly, New York.
4   The Bonnie Bird Choreography Awards in Britain, France and America encourage travel abroad and require choreographers to create work for the Laban Centre's Student Dance Company, Transitions, thus infusing choreography from abroad into the British company's repertory, which then tours in Britain and abroad.
5   Brinson, Peter: *Dance and the Arts in Hong Kong*, Hong Kong Government, 1990.
6   See *Made in Holland*, a promotion magazine about dance in the Netherlands, especially the preface by Bert Janmaat, director of the Netherlands Dance Institute. Published by the Institute, Amsterdam, 1990.
7   Committee of Cultural Consultants,: *Culture and the European Citizen in the Year 2000*. Final Report, Brussels, European Community.
8   Something along the lines of the British Film Institute is much needed able to embrace the interests of all forms of dance to advance national dance culture as a whole.
9   To establish such a priority implies a bigger change of attitudes at all levels than may seem apparent. Governments by no means are agreed. A recent authoritative book — *The Government and Politics of the European Community* by Neill Nugent, London, Macmillan, 1989 — does not mention the cultural issue, no doubt because the issue does not figure largely in Community politics at present, notwithstanding the Consultative Cultural Committee. The Council of Europe always has been more vigorous in promoting a European cultural policy than the European Commission.

List of Organizations

The following list includes the names and addresses of organizations mentioned in the text.

Academic Institutions

Bedford College of Higher Education
37 Lansdowne Road
Bedford MK40 2BZ

College of the Royal Academy of Dancing
48 Vicarage Crescent
London SW4 3LT

Council for National Academic Awards
344–354 Gray's Inn Road
London WC1X 8BP

Dartington College of Arts
Totnes
Devon TQ9 6EJ

Goldsmiths' College
University of London
New Cross, London SE14 6NH

Laban Centre for Movement and Dance
Laurie Grove
New Cross, London SE14 6NH

Leicester Polytechnic
Department of Performing Arts
Scraptoft Campus
Leicester LE7 9SU

London College of Dance
10 Linden Road
Bedford MK40 2DA

London Contemporary Dance School
The Place
17 Duke's Road
London WC1H 9AB

Middlesex Polytechnic
Queensway
Enfield, Middlesex EN3 4SF

Morley College
61 Westminster Bridge Road
London SE1

Northern School of Contemporary Dance
98 Chapeltown Road
Leeds LS7 4BH

Roehampton Institute of Higher Education
Roehampton Lane
London SW15 5PJ

Royal Ballet School
155 Talgarth Road
London W14 9DE

South-East London College
Dance Foundation Course
Lewisham Way
London SE4 1UT

University of Manchester
Department of Physical Education
Manchester M13 9PL

University of Surrey
Division of Dance Studies
Guildford, Surrey GU2 5XH

Weekend Arts College
Interchange Studios
15 Wilkin Street
London NW5 3NG

West Sussex Institute of Higher Education
Bishop Otter College
College Lane
Chichester, West Sussex PO19 4PE

British, European and Other Organizations

Calouste Gulbenkian Foundation
UK Branch
98 Portland Place
London W1N 4ET

Commission of the European Communities
European Commission — EC
200 rue de la Loi
B-1049 Brussels
Belgium
    UK address: Jean Monnet House
                8 Storey's Gate
                London SW1P 3AT

Community Development Foundation
60 Highbury Grove
London N5 2AG
This is the London headquarters of the National Inquiry into Arts and
the Community due to be completed late 1991.

Department of Education and Science
Elizabeth House
York Road
London SE1 7PH

Digital Dance Awards
c/o National Organization for Dance and Mime
9 Rossdale Road
London SW15 1AD

Euro-Citizen-Action-Service (ECAS)
98 rue du Trône Bte 8
B-1050 Brussels
Belgium

International Dance Council
Unesco
1 rue Miollis
75752 Paris Cedex 15
France

International Theatre Institute
British Centre Dance Committee
49 Springcroft Avenue
London N2 9JH

National Campaign for the Arts
Francis House
Francis Street
London SW1P 1DE

National Curriculum Council
15–17 New Street
York YO1 2RA

National Foundation for Arts Education
Department of Arts Education
University of Warwick
Coventry CV4 7AL

Netherlands Dance Institute
Herengracht 174
1016 BP Amsterdam
Netherlands

Netherlands Mime Centre
Herengracht 172
19116 BP Amsterdam
Netherlands

Netherlands Theatre Institute
Herengracht 168
1016 BP Amsterdam
Netherlands

Policy Studies Institute
100 Park Village East
London NW1 3SR

Community Dance Companies/Projects

Academy of Indian Dance
16 Flaxman Terrace
London WC1H 9AB

Cardiff Community Dance Project
Rubicon
56 Ruby Street
Adamstown, Cardiff CF2 1LN

Cheshire Dance Workshop
Winsford Library
High Street
Winsford, Cheshire CW7 2AS

Chisenhale Dance Space
64 Chisenhale Road
London E3 5QY

Clwyd Dance Project
Theatre Clwyd
Mold, Clwyd CH7 1YA

Common Ground Dance Theatre
Hanwell Community Centre
Westcott Crescent
London W7 1PD

Green Candle
Oxford House
Derbyshire Street
London E2 6HG

Great Georges Community and Cultural Project
'The Blackie'
Great George Street
Liverpool 1

Jabadao
29 Queens Road
Bradford, West Yorkshire BD8 7BS

Powys Dance Centre
Arlais Road
Llandrindod Wells, Powys LD1 5HE

South Hill Park Arts Centre
Dance Project
Bracknell, Berkshire RG12 4PA

Thamesdown Contemporary Dance Studio
The Town Hall
Swindon, Wiltshire SN1 1QF

Welwyn Hatfield Dance Project (Nexus Dance Company)
Campus West
Welwyn Garden City, Hertfordshire AL8 6BX

Yorkshire Dance Centre
3 St Peters Building
Leeds LS9 8AH

Dance Companies
All have educational units or programmes.

Adventures in Motion Pictures
c/o Sadler's Wells Theatre
Rosebery Avenue
London EC1R 4TN

Adzido Pan African Dance Ensemble
The Trade Centre
202–208 New North Road
London N1 7BL

Alpana Sengupta Dance
102 Myrtle Road
Hounslow, Middlesex TW3 1QD

Arc Dance Company
145a Kensington High Street
London W8 6SW

Ballet Creations of London
Flat 5
55 Longridge Road
London SW5 9SF

Birmingham Royal Ballet
Birmingham Hippodrome
Thorp Street
Birmingham B5 4AU

The Cholmondeleys
The Place Theatre
17 Duke's Road
London WC1H 9AB

David Massingham Dance
c/o County Central Library
The Willows
Morpeth, Northumberland NE61 1TA

Divas
92 Centurion Road
Brighton BN1 3LN

Diversions Dance Company
30 Richmond Road
Cardiff CF2 3AS

DV8 Physical Theatre
The Place Theatre
17 Duke's Road
London WC1H 9AB

English National Ballet
Markova House
39 Jay Mews
London SW7 2ES

Extemporary Dance Company
The Drill Hall
16 Chenies Street
London WC1E 7EX

The Featherstonehaughs
The Place Theatre
17 Duke's Road
London WC1H 9AB

Greg Nash Group
32 Sandport Street
Edinburgh EH6 6EP

Images Dance Company
15a Dombey Street
London WC1N 3PB

Irie
The Albany Empire
Douglas Way
Deptford, London SE8 4AG

Julyen Hamilton
Tweede Atjehst. 26
Amsterdam 1094 LG
The Netherlands

Kokuma
163 Gerrard Street
Lozells, Birmingham B19 2AP

The Kosh
Unit G13A
Belgravia Workshops
157–163 Marlborough Road
London N19 4NF

Laurie Booth
Flat D
160 Marine Parade
Brighton

London City Ballet
London Studio Centre
42–50 York Way
London N1 9AB

London Contemporary Dance Theatre
The Place
17 Duke's Road
London WC1H 9AB

Ludus North-West Dance in Education Company
Ludus Dance Centre
Assembly Rooms
King Street
Lancaster LA1 1RE

MacLennan Dance and Company
Chisenhale Dance Space
64 Chisenhale Road
London E3 5QY

Manchester Contemporary Dance Company
The Dance Centre
34 Whitworth Street
Manchester M1 3HB

Northern Ballet Theatre
11 Zion Crescent
Hulme Walk, Manchester M15 5BY

Phoenix Dance Company
3 St Peter's Buildings
St Peter's Square
Leeds LS9 8AH

Rambert Dance Company
94 Chiswick High Road
London W4 1SH

Rosemary Butcher Dance Company
The Dance Gallery
179 Blythe Road
London W14 OHL

The Royal Ballet
Royal Opera House
Covent Garden, London WC2E 9DD

Scottish Ballet
261 West Princes Street
Glasgow G4 9EE

Second Stride
Towngate Theatre
Paget Mead
Basilond, Essex SS14 1DW

Shobana Jeyasingh Dance Company
Interchange Studios
15 Wilkin Street
London NW5 3NG

Siobhan Davies Company
Riverside Studios
Crisp Road
London W6 9RL

Suraya Hilal and Company
Flat 2
76 Priory Road
London NW6 3NT

Dance Organizations

ADiTi
(National Organization of South Asian Dancers)
Jacob's Well
Bradford, West Yorkshire BD1 5RW

Arts Council of Great Britain
Dance Department
14 Great Peter Street, London SW14 3NQ

Arts Council of Northern Ireland
181a Stranwillis Road
Belfast BT9 5DU

Arts Education for a Multi-Cultural Society
Commonwealth Institute
Kensington High Street
London W8 6NQ

Black Dance Development Trust
Clarence Chambers
4th Floor, Rooms 34–35
39 Corporation Street
Birmingham B4 4LG

British Actors' Equity
8 Harley Street
London W1N 2AB

British Ballet Organization
Woolborough House
39 Lonsdale Road
London SW13 9JP

Cecchetti Society
c/o Imperial Society of Teachers of Dancing
Euston Hall
Birkenhead Street
London WC1H 8BE

Community Dance and Mime Foundation
School of Arts
Leicester Polytechnic
Scraptoft Campus
Leicester LE7 9SU

Council for Dance Education and Training
5 Tavistock Place
London WC1H 9SS

Dance and the Child International
Dance Department, Froebel College
Roehampton Institute
Roehampton Lane
London SW15 5JP

Dance Umbrella
Riverside Studios
Crisp Road
London W6 9RL

Early Dance Circle
101 St Stephens Road
Canterbury, CT2 7JT
Kent

English Folk Dance and Song Society
2 Regent's Park Road
London NW1 7AY

Imperial Society of Teachers of Dancing
Euston Hall
Birkenhead Street
London WC1H 8BE

International Dance Teachers' Association
76 Bennett Road
Brighton BN2 5JL

Leicester International Dance Festival
Department of Performing Arts
Scraptoft Campus
Leicester LE7 9SU

National Association of Teachers in Further and Higher Education
Dance Section
Hamilton House
Mabledon Place
London WC1H 9BH

National Dance Teachers's Association
Dance Department
Bedford College of Higher Education
37 Lansdowne Road
Bedford MK40 2BZ

National Organization for Dance and Mime
9 Rossdale Road
London SW15 1AD

National Resource Centre for Dance
University of Surrey
Guildford, Surrey GU2 5XH

National Youth Dance Company
35 Gloucester Road
Kew
Richmond, Surrey TW9 3BS

Royal Academy of Dancing
48 Vicarage Crescent
London SW11 3LT

Standing Conference on Dance in Higher Education
c/o Department of Dance Studies
University of Surrey
Guildford, Surrey GU2 5XH

Scottish Arts Council
12 Manor Place
Edinburgh EH3 7DD

Bibliography

ABBS, P. (Ed.) (1987), *Living Powers: The Arts in Education*, Basingstoke, Falmer Press.

ABBS, P. (1988), *A is for Aesthetic*, Basingstoke, Falmer Press.

ABBS, P. (1989), *The Symbolic Order: A Contemporary Reader on the Arts Debate*, Basingstoke, Falmer Press.

ADSHEAD, J. (1981), *The Study of Dance*, London, Dance Books.

ALLEN, J. (1979), *Drama in Schools: Theory and Practice*, London, Heinemann.

ANOTHER STANDARD (1986), *Culture and Democracy: The Manifesto*, London, Comedia.

APPIGNANESI, L. (Ed.) (1989) *Post Modernism*, ICI Documents, London, Free Association Books.

ARTS COUNCIL OF GREAT BRITAIN, Annual Reports, especially the 35th onwards

ARTS COUNCIL OF GREAT BRITAIN (1974), *Report of the Community Arts Working Party*, (The Baldry Report), London.

ARTS COUNCIL OF GREAT BRITAIN (1989), *Arts Education for a Multi-cultural Society: Reports, Reviews and Working Papers*, London.

ARTS COUNCIL OF GREAT BRITAIN (1990), *Young People Dancing*, London.

ARTS COUNCIL OF GREAT BRITAIN (1990), *Arts & Disability: A check list*, London.

ARTS EDUCATION FOR A MULTI-CULTURAL SOCIETY (1989), *Reports, Reviews and Working Papers*, Commonwealth Institute, London.

BANES, S. (1980), *Terpsichore in Sneakers*, Post Modern Dance, Boston, Houghton Mifflin.

BEAUMONT, C. (1937), *Complete Book of Ballets*, London, Putnam.

BERGER, J. (1969), *Art and Revolution*, London, Writers and Readers Publishing Cooperative.

BERGER, J. (1972), *Ways of Seeing*, London, Penguin.

BEST, D. (1974), *Expression in Movement and the Arts*, London, Lepus Books.

BEST, D. (1978), *Philosophy and Human Movement*, London, George Allen and Unwin.

BEST, D. (1985), *Feeling and Reason in the Arts*, London, George Allen and Unwin.

BEST, D. (1990), *Arts in Schools: A Critical Time*, Birmingham, Birmingham Institute of Art and Design.

BLACKING, J. (Ed.) (1977), *The Anthropology of the Body*, London, Academic Press.

BLACKING, J. (1987), *A commonsense view of all music!*, Cambridge, Cambridge University Press.

BLAND, A. (1981), *The Royal Ballet: The first 50 years*, London, Threshold Books.

BLAND, A. and PERCIVAL, J. (1984), *Men Dancing*, New York, Macmillan Publishing.

BLOM, L.A. and CHAPLIN, L.T. (1982), *The Intimate Act of Choreography*, Pittsburgh, University of Pittsburgh Press.

BOGGS, C. (1976/80), *Gramsci's Marxism*, London, Pluto Press.

BOTTOMLEY, F. (1979), *Attitudes to the Body in Western Christendom*, London, Lepus Books.

BOTTOMORE, T. (1984), *The Frankfurt School*, London, Tavistock Publications.

BRADEN, S. (1978), *Artists and People*, London, Routledge.

BRINSON, P. and CRISP, C. (1980), *Ballet and Dance. A Guide to the Repertory*, Newton Abbot, David & Charles.

BROHM, J.M. (1978), *Sport: A Prison of Measured Time*, London, Ink Links.

BRUCE, V. (1969), *Awakening the Slower Mind*, Oxford, Pergamon.

BUCKLE, R. (1971), *Nijinski*, London, Weidenfeld & Nicholson.

BUCKLE, R. (1978), *Diaghilev*, London, Weidenfeld & Nicholson.

CARLISLE, B. (1988), *The Concept of Physical Education Revisited*, In Proceedings of Conference on Dance and the Physical Education Curriculum, London, NATFHE.

CARNEGIE UK TRUST (1985), *Arts and Disabled People*, London.

CARNEGIE UK TRUST (1988), *After Attenborough*, London.

CLARKE, M. (1955), *The Sadler's Wells Ballet*, London, A & C Black.

CLARKE, M. (1962), *Dancers of Mercury. The Story of Ballet Rambert*, London, A & C Black.

CLARK, M. and CRISP, C. (1980), *The History of Dance*, London, Orbis Publishing.

COHAN, R. (1986), *The Dance Workshop*, London, Unwin, Hyman.

COHEN S. J. (1982), *Next Week, Swan Lake*, Connecticut, Wesleyan University Press.

COPELAND, R. and COHEN, M. (1983), *What is Dance?*, Oxford, Oxford University Press.

CROCE, A. (1978), *After Images*, London A & C Black.

DAHL, D.(1990), *Residencies in Education*, Sunderland, AN Publications.

DEPARTMENT OF EDUCATION AND SCIENCE (1989), *Curriculum Matters 16. Physical Education 5–16*, London, HMSO.

DEVLIN, G. (1989), *Stepping Forward*, London, Arts Council.

EAGLETON, T. (1976), *Marxism and Literary Criticism*, London, Methuen.

EAGLETON, T. (1983), *Literary Theory*, Oxford, Blackwell.

EAGLETON, T, (1990), *The Ideology of the Aesthetic*, Oxford, Blackwell.

ELIOT, T.S. (1944), *Four Quartets*, London, Faber & Faber.

ELIOT, T.S. (1948/72), *Notes towards the Definition of Culture*, London, Faber & Faber.

FANCHER, G. and MYERS, G. (1981), *Philosophical Essays on Dance*, North Carolina, American Dance Festival.

FOSTER, J. (1977). *The Influences of Rudolf Laban*, London, Lepus Books.

FOSTER, R. (1976), *Knowing in my Bones*, London, A & C Black.

FRANLEIGH, S.M. (1987), *Dance and the lived body*, Pittsburgh, University of Pittsburgh Press.

FRASCINA, F. and HARRISON, C. (1988),*Modern Art and Modernism*. London, Paul Chapman Publishing.

FRITH, S. (1978), *The Sociology of rock*, London, Constable.

GABLIK, S. (1984), *Has Modernism Failed?*, London, Thames & Hudson.

GOMBRICH, E. (1960), *Art and Illusion*, London, Phaidon.

GOODALE, T. and GODBEY, G. (1988), *The Evolution of Leisure*, New York, Venture Publishing Inc.

GUEST, I. (1954), *The Romantic Ballet in England*, London.

GUEST, I. (1962), *The Alhambra Ballet*, New York.

GUEST, I. (1962), *The Empire Ballet*, London.

GUEST, I. (1970), *Fanny Elssler*, London.

GUEST, I. (1984), *Jules Perrot*, London.

GULBENKIAN FOUNDATION (1980), *Dance Education and Training in Britain*, London.

GULBENKIAN FOUNDATION (1982/89), *The Arts in Schools*, London.

GULBENKIAN FOUNDATION (1989), *The Arts in Primary School*, London.

HADJINICOLAOU, N. (1978). *Art, History and Class Struggle*, London, Pluto Press.

HALL, S. (1988), *The Hard Road to Renewal*, London, Verso.

HARGREAVES, D. (1982), *The Challenge of the Comprehensive School*, London, Routledge.

HARGREAVES, J. (1989), *Sport, Power and Culture*, Cambridge, Polity Press.

HATFIELD, S.C. and PHILLIPS, R.W. (1989), *Records of Achievement in Physical Education*, North Western Counties Physical Education Association.

HEBDIGE, D. (1979), *Sub culture: The Meaning of Style*, London, Methuen.

HODGSON, J. and PRESTON-DUNLOP, V. (1990), *Rudolf Laban; an introduction to his work and influence*, Plymouth, Northcote House Publishers.

HOGGART, R. (1957), *The Uses of Literacy*, London, Penguin.

HMSO (1965), *A Policy for the Arts: The first steps*, Cmnd 2601, London.

HOLT, R. (1989), *Sport and the British*, Oxford.

HUMPHREY, DORIS (1959), *The Art of Making Dances*, London, Dance Books.

HUTCHINSON, R. (1982), *The Politics of the Arts Council*, London, Sinclair Browne

JAMESON, F. (1988), *The Ideologies of Theory*, Essays 1971–86, London, Routledge.

JENKINS, C. and SHERMAN, B. (1979), *The Collapse of Work*, London.

JENKINS, C. and SHERMAN, B. (1981), *The Leisure Shock*, London.

JOHNSON, P. (1984), *Marxist Aesthetics* London, Routledge.

JONES, D. (1988), *Stewart Mason: The Art of Education*, London, Lawrence & Wishart.

JOWITT, D.(1988), *Time and the Dancing Image*, New York, William Morrow.

JUNG, C.(1967), *The Spirit in Man, Art and Literature*, London, Routledge.

KAPLAN, A. (Ed.) (1988), *Post Modernism and its Discontents*, London, Verso.

KAPO, R. (1981), *A Savage Culture*, London, Quartet Books.

KARSAVINA, T. (1930), *Theatre Street*, London, Heinemann.

KARSAVINA, T. (1956), *Ballet Technique*, London, A & C Black.

KARSAVINA, T. (1962), *Classical Ballet, the Flow of Movement*, London, A & C Black.

KELLY, O. (1984), *Community, Art and the State*, London, Comedia.

KLINGENDER, F. D. (1968), *Art and the Industrial Revolution*, London, Evelyn, Adams and Mackay.

KOEGLER, H. (1987), *Concise Oxford Dictionary of Ballet*, 2nd Edition, Oxford, Oxford University Press.

LABAN, R. (1948/76), *Modern Educational Dance*, London, Macdonald and Evans.

LABAN, R. (1950/80), *The Mastery of Movement*, London, Macdonald & Evans.

LABAN, R. (1956), *Principles of Dance and Movement Notation*, New York, Dance Horizons.

LABAN, R. (1975), *A Life for Dance*, London, Macdonald and Evans.

LABAN, R. and LAWRENCE, F.C. (1974), *Effort*, London, Macdonald and Evans.

LAING, D. (1978), *The Marxist Theory of Art*, Brighton, Harvester Press.

LANGER, S. (1953), *Feeling & Form*, London, Routledge.

LANGER, S. (1957), *Problems of Arts*, London, Routledge.

LAWSON, J. (1964), *A history of ballet and its makers*, London, Pitman.

LLOYD, M. (1949/1974), *The Borzoi Book of Modern Dance*, New York, Dance Horizons.

LOCKE, J. (1693), *An Essay Concerning Human Understanding*, London, Dent.

LUNN, E. (1982/1985), *Marxism and Modernism*, California, University of California Press and London, Verso.

MARKARD, A. and MARKARD, H. (1985), *Jooss: Ballet-Bühren-Verlag*, Cologne, Rolf Garske.

MAYALL, B (1990), *Parents in Secondary Education*, London, Gulbenkian Foundation.

McANDREW, P. (trans) (1979), Bournonville's *My Theatre Life*, Connecticut, Weslyan University and London, A & C Black.

McGOWAN, M. (1963), *L'Art du Ballet de Cour en France 1581–1643*, Paris, Centre National de la Recherche Scientifique.

MIDWINTER, E. (1990), *Creating Chances: Arts by older people*, London, Centre for Policy on Ageing.

MYERS, C. and FANCHER, G. (Eds) (1981), *Philosophical Essays on Dance*, New York, Dance Horizons.

MYERSCOUGH, J. (1989), *The Economic Importance of the Arts in Britain*, London, PSI.

NATIONAL ASSOCIATION OF TEACHERS IN FURTHER AND HIGHER EDUCATION (1988), *Collected Conference Papers in Dance*, London.

NATIONAL CURRICULUM COUNCIL (1990), *The Arts 5–16*, In three volumes from the Council's Arts in Schools Project.

NELSON, C. and GROSSBERG, L. (1988), *Marxism and the interpretation of culture*, Basingstoke, Macmillan Education.

NEW LEFT BOOKS (1977), *Aesthetics and Politics*, Bloch, Lukács, Brecht, Benjamin, Adorno.

NORTH, M. (1972/1990), *Personality Assessment Through Movement*, Plymouth, Northcote House.

NOWELL SMITH, G. and HOARE, Q. (Eds) (1971), *Antonio Gramsci: Selections from Prison Notebooks*, London, Lawrence & Wishart.

NUGENT, N. (1989), *The Government and Politics of the European Community*, Basingstoke, London MacMillan.

PAYNTER, J. (1982), *Music in the Secondary School Curriculum*, Cambridge, Cambridge University Press.

PERCIVAL, J. (1975), *Nureyev*, London, Faber & Faber.

PRESTON-DUNLOP, V. (1963/77), *Modern Educational Dance*, London, Macdonald & Evans.

PRESTON-DUNLOP, V. (1980), *A Handbook for Dance in Education*, London, Macdonald & Evans.

RALPH, R. (1985), *The Life and Works of John Weaver*, London, Dance Books.

READ, H. (1961), *Education through Art*, London, Faber & Faber.

REDFERN, B.(1982), *Concepts in Modern Educational Dance*, London, Dance Books.

REDFERN, B. (1983), *Dance, Art and Aesthetics*, London, Dance Books.

REID, L.A. (1969), *Meaning in the Arts*, London, Allen & Unwin.

ROBERTSON, A. and HUTERA, D. (1988), *The Dance Handbook*, London, Longman.

ROSS, M. (1975), *Arts and the Adolescent*, Schools Council, London, Evans.

ROSS, M. (1978), *The Creative Arts*, London, Heinemann.

ROSS, M. (1983), *The Arts in Education*, Basingstoke, Falmer Press.

ROSS, M. (1989), *The Arts in the Primary School*, London, Gulbenkian Foundation.

ROSS, M. (1989), *The Claims of Feeling*, Basingstoke, Falmer Press.

ROSS, M. (Ed.) (1982), *The Development of Aesthetic Experience*, Oxford, Pergamon Press.

ROYCE, A.P. (1977/1980), *The Anthropology of Dance*, Indiana, Indiana University Press.

RUSHDIE, S. (1990), *Is nothing sacred?*, Cambridge, Granta.

SACHS, C. (1937), *World History of the Dance*, New York, Norton.

SASSOON, A.S. (1980), *Gramsci's Politics*, London, Croom Helm.

SALTER, B. and TAPPER, T. (1981), *Education, Politics and the State*, London, Grant McIntyre.

SCHØNBERG, B (Ed.) (1989), *World Ballet and Dance 1989–90*,London, Dance Books.

SEABROOK, J. (1988), *The Leisure Society*, Oxford, Blackwell.

SHARP, C. and DUST, K. (1990), *Artists in Schools*, London, Bedford Square Press.

SIEGEL, M.B. (1978), *Days on Earth: The Dance of Doris Humphrey*, Yale, Yale University Press.

SIMON, R. (1982/1985), *Gramsci's Political Thought*, London, Lawrence & Wishart.

SORELL, W. (1969), *Hanya Holm*, Connecticut, Wesleyan University Press.

SPENCER, P. (Ed.) (1985), *Society and the Dance*, Cambridge, Cambridge University Press.

SWIFT, M.G. (1968), *The Art of the Dance in the USSR*, Notre Dame, University of Notre Dame Press.

THOMPSON, E.P. (1979), *The Making of the English Working Class*, London, Penguin.

TYNAN, K. (1961), *Curtains*, London, Longman.

TYNAN, K. (1967), *Tynan Right and Left*, London, Longman.

DE VALOIS, N. (1937/1953), *Invitation to the Ballet*, London, Bodley Head.

DE VALOIS, N. (1957), *Come dance with me*, London, Hamish Hamilton.

DE VALOIS, N. (1977), *Step by Step*, London, W.H. Allen.

VAUGHAN, D. (1977), *Frederick Ashton and his Ballets*, London, A & C Black.

WALVIN, J.(1978), *Leisure and Society 1830–1850*, London, Longman.

WHITING, H.T.A. and MASTERSON, D.W. (Ed.) (1974), *Readings in the Aesthetics of Sport*, London, Lepus Books.

WHITLEY, A. (1990), *Handbook for Choreography*, London, National Organization for Dance and Mime.

WILDING, R. (1989), *Supporting the Arts*, London, Office of Arts and Libraries.

WILLIAMS, J. (1974), *Themes for Educational Gymnastics*, London, Lepus Books.

WILLIAMS, R. (1961), *The Long Revolution*, London, Chatto & Windus.

WILLIAMS, R. (1976), *Key Words*, London, Fontana.

WILLIAMS, R. (1977), *Marxism and Literature*, Oxford, Oxford University Press.

WILLIAMS, R. (1980), *Problems in Materialism and Culture*, London, Verso.

WILLIS, P. (1990), *Common Culture*, Milton Keynes, Open University Press.

WILLIS, P. (1990), *Moving Culture*, London, Gulbenkian Foundation.

WINEARLS, J. (1968), *Modern Dance*, 2nd Edition, London, A & C Black.

WITKIN, R. (1974), *The Intelligence of Feeling*, London, Heinemann.

WOLFF, J. (1981), *The Social Production of Art*, London, MacMillan.

Journals

The Dancing Times, Monthly, London.

Dance and Dancers, Monthly, London.

Dance Theatre Journal, Monthly, London.

Dance Gazette (RAD), Quarterly, London.

Dance (ISTD), Quarterly, London.

The Dancer (BBO), Quarterly, London.

Dance Teacher (IDTA), Monthly, Brighton.

DICE (Community Arts), Quarterly, London.
Dance Magazine, Monthly, New York.
Ballett International, (English and German), Monthly, Cologne.
Dance Research, Thrice yearly, London.
Time Out, Weekly, London.
City Limits, Weekly, London.

Index

by Callum Forsyth